MIGRANTS AND MASCULINITY IN HIGH-RISE NAIROBI

T0373347

MAKING AND REMAKING THE AFRICAN CITY:
STUDIES IN URBAN AFRICA

Series Editors

Taibat Lawanson, Marie Huchzermeyer, Ola Uduku

Series Description

This series is open to submissions that examine urban growth and its delivery and impact on existing and new populations in relation to the key issues of the moment, such as climate control, sustainability and migration. Showcasing cutting-edge research into how the African city and urban environments are being made and remade across the continent, the books in this series will open up debate on Urban Studies as a dynamic social interaction and urban encounter, and bring a fresh perspective to its exploration. Broad-ranging and multidisciplinary, the series will be mainly monographs, but we also welcome edited volumes that enable a continental, multidisciplinary approach. Innovative, and challenging current perspectives, the series will provide an indispensable resource on this key area of African Studies for academics, students, international policy-makers and development practitioners.

Please contact the Series Editors with an outline or download the proposal form at www.jamescurrey.com.

Professor Taibat Lawanson, Professor of Management and Governance, University of Lagos: tlawanson@unilag.edu.ng

Professor Marie Huchzermeyer, School of Architecture and Planning, University of Witwatersrand: Marie.Huchzermeyer@wits.ac.za

Professor Ola Uduku, Head of School, Liverpool School of Architecture: O.Uduku@liverpool.ac.uk

Previously published

1. *Architecture and Politics in Africa: Making, Living and Imagining Identities through Buildings*, edited by Joanne Tomkinson, Daniel Mulugeta and Julia Gallagher

MIGRANTS AND MASCULINITY IN HIGH-RISE NAIROBI

THE PRESSURE OF BEING A MAN IN AN AFRICAN CITY

Mario Schmidt

JAMES CURREY

First published 2024
James Currey

ISBN 978-1-84701-352-1

James Currey is an imprint of Boydell & Brewer Ltd
PO Box 9, Woodbridge, Suffolk IP12 3DF, UK
www.jamescurrey.com
and of Boydell & Brewer Inc.
668 Mt Hope Avenue, Rochester, NY 14620–2731, USA
www.boydellandbrewer.com

A catalogue record for this book is available
from the British Library

The publisher has no responsibility for the continued existence or accuracy
of URLs for external or third-party internet websites referred to in this book,
and does not guarantee that any content on such websites is, or will remain,
accurate or appropriate

This publication is printed on acid-free paper

CONTENTS

ILLUSTRATIONS

MAPS

FIGURES

The author and publisher are grateful to all the institutions and individuals listed for permission to reproduce the materials to which they hold copyright. Every effort has been made to trace the copyright holders; apologies are offered for any omission, and the publisher will be pleased to add any necessary acknowledgement in subsequent editions.

ACKNOWLEDGEMENTS

Before I started writing *Migrants and Masculinity in High-Rise Nairobi: The Pressure of Being a Man in an African City*, I had spent more than five years trying to write a book about the struggles of the inhabitants of Kaleko, a small marketplace in Homa Bay County. Progress was slow and revolved around some half-baked ideas that unconvincingly linked the various articles I had written about food, money, and politics. Had I been involved with the place for too long, I asked myself. Was I just lacking that one idea holding together the hundreds of observations made during my visits between 2009 and 2019? I hope that one day I will fulfil my promise to write a book about life in Kaleko. In the meantime, may this one about Pipeline act as its placeholder.

Without Esao Omolo Mwalo, Josphat Mwalo (late), Atanasio Mwalo Mainga (late), Philister Aoko Mainga, Mikal Judith Mwalo (late), Herrytone Onyango, Hemstone Owaga, Corazon Aquino Otieno, Benson Joe Awere, Marion Akinyi Omollo, Patrick Ouma Achila, Judith Osumba, Kevin Mainga, Bill Mainga, Collins Mainga, Herine Otieno, Osborn Otieno, Donna Mainga, and Rose Atieno Omollo, I could have never established the connections I did with the Luo community in Pipeline, Nairobi. *Erokamano maduong'*.

In Pipeline and Nairobi, I am highly indebted to my research assistants Rodgers Abebe, Jack Misiga, Kenneth Muga, Rogger Miller Otieno, and Winnie Otieno, my colleagues David Bukusi, Alfred Anangwe, Tom Osborn, Patrick Forscher, Daniel Ochieng Orwenjo, Mwangi Mwaura, Prince Guma, Adrian Wilson, Nick Rahier, Moritz Kasper, Luke M. Obala, Fiona Cumberland, Miriam Maina, Baraka Mwau, and Gilbert Francis Odhiambo, as well as the employees of the British Institute in Eastern Africa. I also want to thank, in no particular order, Josephine Syombua, Bernard Ogango Wanyancha, David Ng'ang'a (Kush), Ismael Ochieng, Reinhard Atela, Vincent Omondi Onditi, Bob Apolo, Stephen Ouma Otieno, Ochieng *mrefu*, Fredrick Andayi, Richard Osumo, Susan, Onyango Otieno, Joshua Omondi, Ochieng Ogodo, Godwin Omondi, Ibrahim Agoro, Robinson Nyangacha, Augustine Wekesa Wanyonyi, Mercyline Momanyi Mongina and Bravon, Alex Nyoloka, John Kimani, Francis Guya, Kevin Warenga, Silas Nyanchwani, Geoffrey Okum, Aggrey Mariko, John Okoth, Rolex Odongo, Walter Ajira, Brian Owino,

Vincent Oluoch, Habshi Hassan (Mnati), Polycarp Kakungu, Barack Okello, Ivar, Jacob Aliet, Chomba Njoka, Stella Mwangi and Leyla, Andrew Thiga Nyambura, Richard Oluoko, as well as all the waitresses in Trace Sahara, Black Rhino, Amazon, Spinners, Oblivion, Emirates, Icon, and the other bars and liquor stores in Nairobi and Pipeline. Special thanks to Diana, who always secured a nice spot for *jo-pap*.

Beyond two anonymous reviewers, I am indebted to Parker Shipton, Paul Wenzel Geissler, Hadas Weiss, Kai Koddenbrock, Peter Lockwood, Judith Kibuye, Martin Fotta, my colleagues from the University of Cologne (Christoph Lange, Martin Zillinger, Johannes Schick, Phillip Steinkrüger, Anna Krämer, Ole Reichardt, Phillip Grimberg), as well as Clemens Greiner, Michael Bollig, Thomas Widlok, Uroš Kovač, Detlef Müller-Mahn, Léa Lacan, Joachim Knab, Anna Lisa Ramella, and Gideon Tups all of whom I worked with at the Global South Studies Center (University of Cologne) and the Collaborative Research Centre 'Future Rural Africa' (University of Bonn and University of Cologne). Particular thanks to my colleagues Eric Kioko, Emmanuel Nshakira Rukundo and Christiane Stephan, with whom I worked on the project 'Contending with COVID-19 shock in selected African countries: micro-level evidence from Kenya, Tanzania, Zambia and Namibia'. I am also grateful to my colleagues at the Max Planck Institute for Social Anthropology in Halle (Biao Xiang, Andrew Haxby, Ghassan Hage, Christoph Brumann, Samuel Williams, Iain Walker, Jeremy Rayner, Jing Jing Liu, Wanjing Chen), to the members of the 'Pressure in the city' research group (Catherine Dolan, Jörg Wiegratz, Elizabeth Dessie, Wangui Kimari), and to those friends and colleagues who read the whole or parts of my manuscript (Laura Emmerling, Bettina Ng'weno, Elizabeth Saleh, Marie Huchzermeyer, and Isabella Achieng Oluoko). I would also like to thank Sarah Helen Taylor, who copyedited the manuscript prior to its submission, Robin von Gestern, who drew the maps for this book, Jaqueline Mitchell and Megan Milan from James Currey, and Adam Masava, the artist who painted the cover image. My research was funded by the German Research Foundation and the Max Planck Institute for Social Anthropology, which also paid for the pre-submission edit and publishing of the book under the terms of the open access Creative Commons license CC-BY-NC-ND, with additional support from the German Research Foundation.

Special thanks go to my friends Franziska Fay, Nadine Junge, Johanna Merbach, and Sebastian Schellhaas, to my family, especially to my father Gerd, with whom I lived during the COVID-19 pandemic (though I would have probably not chosen this voluntarily), and to the round-headed boy who spent a lot of time with me during his first six months on earth (though he too would have probably not chosen it voluntarily). Above all, this book is dedicated to my mother, Ulrike, and my aunt Ingrid, who both passed on while I was visiting my family for Christmas in 2019, and my grandmother Anita, who passed on in the spring of 2021.

ABBREVIATIONS

CBD	Central Business District
JKIA	Jomo Kenyatta International Airport
KCSE	Kenya Certificate of Secondary Education
KDF	Kenya Defence Forces
KSh	Kenyan Shillings
NGO	Non-Governmental Organization

INTRODUCTION

Most men don't confide in their wives about their problems and frustrations.
You can't discuss your malaria with a mosquito.

Meme circulating on Kenyan social media

'Have you heard about the soldier who was killed by his wife here in Pipeline?'
Andrew[1] asked after completing a set of biceps curls while Carl and I were
waiting for Isaac to finish his set of bench presses. 'Strong, strong, light
weight, light weight' was how Isaac, a manual labourer who worked in the
nearby industrial area and came to the gym whenever his day- or night-shifts
had ended, 'psyched' himself while finishing the last repetitions of his set:
'Big chest, big chest! Sexy weight, sexy weight!' 'Someone who has been
to Somalia, has survived landmines, grenades, and AK-47s only to be killed
by his wife. He must have been a weakling,' said Andrew, a former soldier
of the Kenya Defence Forces (KDF), shaking his head, probably wondering
how a woman could have killed one of his former comrades. 'Maybe she also
lifts weights like we do here in the No Mercy Gym,' I suggested. Isaac, by
then sitting upright, trying to regain his breath and sweating profusely, joined
the conversation: 'In the Bible, it is not specified how many days or weeks
Adam lived alone in peace. Then Eve came and brought stress. Everything
became complicated. Women....' 'They say she bit him in the shoulder and
chest. Who dies from biting? Maybe she was a vampire', 'Yeah, or a member
of the Illuminati'. While Andrew and Carl, the owner of the No Mercy Gym,
exchanged rumours, I lay down on the bench, stabilized my back, grabbed
the barbell, and began my own set. 'Strong, strong!', 'Light weight, light
weight!', 'Big chest, big chest!'

As soon as I had left the gym, I started to search online for information
about the alleged murder. The first article I found featured on the homepage of
The Star, a Kenyan newspaper (Ombati and Odenyo 2021). The deceased was

---

[1]   Most personal names as well as the names of a few places and organizations,
such as Kaleko, the No Mercy Gym, or the NGO Maendeleo, are in fact pseudonyms.
To further protect various identies, I sometimes rely on composite characters.

indeed a KDF soldier. The incident, however, had not happened in Pipeline, a low-income high-rise tenement settlement in Nairobi's east and the main location of this book. His wife was highly unlikely to be a member of the Illuminati, an organization feared by many Kenyans who believe that its members are involved in satanic activities such as sacrificing human blood for material riches. What, then, had happened? The 37-year-old soldier had discovered that his wife, a former gospel singer who had begun trying her luck in the Kenyan pop music scene, was renting a second apartment on the quiet. Upon finding out, the jealous soldier had left his military base at Gilgil, 100 kilometres northwest of Nairobi, and rushed to the couple's home in Kahawa Wendani. When he arrived, he confronted his wife and an argument broke out. The argument escalated and turned physical. The wife bit her husband with what the Kenyan television channel NTV called her 'jaws of death', after which he collapsed. He was rushed to the hospital, where he subsequently died.

Given its cartoonish absurdity, the 'jaws of death' incident could easily have been created by a Nollywood screenwriter. Even so, the fact that Andrew, Carl and Isaac – three migrants who had come to Nairobi with high expectations of a better life – spoke about it while working out alludes to some of the issues that *Migrants and Masculinity in High-Rise Nairobi: The Pressure of Being a Man in an African City* tries to make sense of: stressed-out men who feel that they have 'lost control' over their wives and girlfriends, rampant misogynism, invocations of brotherhood voiced against the 'threats' of feminism and homosexuality, incommensurate marital expectations, and gender-based violence. In some way or another, these issues speak of a social constellation characterized by increasing mistrust between Kenyan men and women who perceive the reciprocal understanding of male and female perspectives as crumbling due to encompassing economic and social pressures, which were further aggravated by the COVID-19 pandemic and by the urban geography of Pipeline, one of sub-Saharan Africa's most densely populated estates, largely inhabited by blue-collar workers, students, and people active in its vibrant local economy.

This book reveals how heterosexual male migrants between the ages of 25 and 40 dealt with the above-mentioned challenges in Kenya's capital. It describes how migrant men from western Kenya (mostly, but not exclusively, *jo*-Luo (Dholuo, 'people of Luo descent', singular *ja*-Luo)),[2] made sense of the gender relations and the economic situation they encountered in the city

---

[2]   Nairobi is characterized by a multitude of different languages and constant code-switching. Most of my interlocutors spoke and mixed at least three languages: their mother tongue (in this study usually Dholuo), English, and Kenyan Swahili or Sheng, this being 'a variety of Kenyan Swahili closely associated with Nairobi's urban youth'

and how they tried to carve out successful lives for themselves and their rural and urban families. I show how male migrants' understanding and enactment of masculinity changed when they travelled from the village to the city, taking with them high expectations of a better life. For most young men who lived in rural western Kenya, migrating to Nairobi was a crucial step in their ongoing transformation from dependent boys and sons to successful men and fathers. Moving to the capital city promised economic success, sexual adventures, and personal development.

Although some came to Pipeline straight from their rural homes and others had been living elsewhere in Nairobi, the male migrants I met during my fieldwork faced similar economic and romantic challenges and spent time in the same masculine spaces: barbershops, gyms, videogame joints, pool halls, betting shops, and bars named after exotic places such as Sahara, Caribbean, Emirates, or Amazon, as well as mental states such as Oblivion and Amnesia, which point to alcohol's ability to make men forget, if only momentarily, about the pressures they were facing. It was inside these masculine spaces that migrant men planned and enacted their personal and economic visions and discussed their frustrations as they tried to fulfil the expectations they believed Kenyan society in general, and Kenyan women in particular, obliged them to meet, thereby downplaying the extent to which these expectations also circulated and structured relationships between the men themselves.

Men as breadwinners

Most of my male and female interlocutors did not intend to replace the narrative of the male breadwinner and provider with radically different understandings of masculinity. There were only a few male migrants who, often cautiously, tried to change what was considered proper male behaviour by taking over family responsibilities that other men and women marked as female and emasculating, such as changing nappies. Instead, most migrant men I encountered tried to challenge, downplay, or adjust to what they perceived as a female distortion of the prevailing narrative of what it means to be a successful man. The traditional narrative of the male breadwinner has its roots in sometimes violently enforced colonial wage labour (Cooper 2003) and was further intensified through the economic effects of the International Monetary Fund's structural adjustment programs, as well as through what Ngala Chome called 'a wider "Pentecostalization" of Kenyan society, through which Christian religious symbols, imagery, and language were rapidly entering the domain of public

(Githiora 2018: 1). Whenever I mark something as 'Kiswahili', I refer to the Kenyan non-standard variety of Swahili.

life' (2019: 547). This Pentecostalization, which began in the 1990s, further solidified social notions about men as authoritative husbands and fathers who provide dutifully for their families. According to this narrative, the husband and father should be an economically stable, stoic, strong, pious and prudent provider and 'head of the house' (Dholuo, *wuon ot*), whose actions and conduct demand and bring forth 'respect' (Kiswahili, *heshima*, Dholuo, *luor*). This attitude was aptly summarized by a member of the No Mercy Gym, when he mentioned that the first rule in his home was 'My way or the highway'.

The male migrants I worked with characterized what they perceived as the female distortion of this narrative as an extreme and exclusive focus on monetary wealth and the material goods women expected at the very beginning of romantic relationships. Comments posted online in response to the 'jaws of death' article in *The Star*, and to a music video of one of the dead soldier's wife's songs, ironically called 'Gimme Love', which was uploaded to YouTube, allude to the gendered dimension of this distortion:

> Corona has brought a lot of stress. Women are now biting your thing when on their knees if you don't give more money. *Mjichunge*. (Kiswahili, 'Take care of yourself')

> This can't be a wife but *mtu wa kunyonya pesa yako tu aende*! (Kiswahili, 'someone who just sucks away your money and leaves!')

> It's time for men to date and marry Gynoids, aka female robots, aka sexbots! A Gynoid will never drive you nuts or kill you [...]! Dangerous women!

> Men should avoid red flags like single mother, model, social media, long painted nails, funny hairstyles. Men should change or perish.

These comments construe women as materialistic and money-minded sociopaths who could potentially castrate their boyfriends and husbands if they were to withdraw their financial support. 'Auma', a famous song by Musa Juma, also disapproves of the detrimental effects that the equation of love and money had on romantic relations, thereby echoing the sentiments of most of my male interlocutors. Describing the behaviour of an unfaithful woman called Auma, the song blames money for her immaturity: 'Today's love needs money, [...] if you don't have money, you will feel ashamed' (Dholuo, *Hera masani dwaro pesa*, [...] *kionge pesa, iyudo wich kuot*).[3] For

---

[3]   Both *benga* music, which emerged in the 1960s and was further popularized by artists such as Okatch Biggy, Musa Juma, and Johnny Junior in the 1990s and 2000s,

many male migrants, money (Dholuo, *pesa*) was indeed desirable, not only as an end in itself, but also because it brought respect, which was paramount for every social relation. Poor men risked being seen as worthless, for it was difficult to establish sustainable social relations without money.

Equating a 'good man' with one who was rich and generous influenced how male migrants who struggled to make ends meet conducted their daily lives and planned their futures. Under constant economic pressure to succeed, the majority aspired to show off their wealth by inviting friends round and giving their girlfriends or wives expensive gifts. It was thus not only the expectations others had of them, but also their personal understanding of how to ensure a brighter future that shaped and sometimes unsettled male migrants' lives, complicated their practices and plans, and helped to foster dominant narratives about what it meant to be a man. As a consequence of the pressure the economic expectations forced on them, many migrant men emphasized other aspects of the cluster of traits characterizing success without directly challenging the equation of a good man with a rich man. These traits included prudence, physical strength, a natural and religiously vested primacy of the male gender, and the playful mastery of the urban space.

Yet, and this is the main political economic contribution of this book, migrant men's diagnoses of women's distortions of an ideal form of masculinity based on the capability to provide, as well as their own defence of this ideal, reproduced the notion of the man as the breadwinner. This reproduction of the notion of the male breadwinner obviated systemic problems of Nairobi's urban economy, which was characterized by widespread unemployment, underemployment, and precarity. These problems were further exacerbated as a result of 1.7 million Kenyans losing their jobs during the three-month period after the COVID-19 pandemic reached Kenya (April–June 2020) (Omondi 2022). The dire state of Kenya's urban economy made it close to impossible for many families to survive on men's income alone. In addition, migrant men felt that the expectations of rural kin as well as wives and girlfriends

---

and the more recent *ohangla* music by artists such as Freddy Jakadongo, Prince Indah, Emma Jalamo and Musa Jakadala were important reference points for Luo migrants in Nairobi. Titles of popular songs such as *'Dag e ngima miyiero'* (Dholuo, 'Live the life that you choose') or *'Kwach ogolo koke'* (Dholuo, 'The leopard has shown his claws') were used in everyday discussions and printed on T-shirts, which were popular with migrant men. Predominantly performed by men, many of these songs discuss relations between the village and the city, as well as romantic and economic issues, often in the form of praise songs dedicated to specific women (Awuor and Anudo 2016 offer a critical analysis of misogynism in *ohangla* music). *Ohangla* artists also acted as role models in terms of their sartorial style, which was characterized by expensive suits, ties, hats, and shoes.

had actually increased. Rather than receiving sympathy for their hardships, many of them felt even more pressured.

Instead of actively criticizing the problems of Kenya's economy (for instance, through political protest), male migrants employed creative practices that were a result of what I call the social disposition of 'expecting success', thereby taking up Marcel Mauss' observation about the 'importance of the notion of expectation' as 'a form of collective thinking' (1969 [1934]: 117, my translation; see also Bryant and Knight 2019, Ferguson 1999). In Pipeline, most men and women had normative expectations of male success. They subscribed to the notion that men *should* be economically successful. However, many of the men I spoke to engaged in practices, narratives, and discourses that revealed their imbued expectations of success. They thus also believed they *would* be economically successful. By creatively postponing true success, socializing the path toward an economic breakthrough, employing the language and behaviour of successful men and wearing and showcasing signs of success, male migrants in Pipeline reassured themselves and others as to the certainty of their future achievements. In so doing, they lessened the intense pressure that resulted from what they perceived as society's expectation of male success.

Some of these practices resembled those explored in the literature on male youth worldwide, such as 'hustling' (Thieme et al. 2021, Van Stapele 2021a), 'bluffing' (Newell 2012), 'waiting' (Honwana 2012, Masquelier 2019), or 'zigzagging' (Jeffrey and Dyson 2013). Even so, male migrants' practices in Pipeline cannot be reduced to any one of these. The type of practice enacted by my interlocutors, both by those who were formally employed and those who were not, was contingent upon the context and who was involved. Depending on his own expectations – as well as those of his girlfriend, his wife, or his male friends – a young male migrant, for instance, could exaggerate his success in front of his rural kin even though he was making do with minor jobs because of his wife's expectation for him to put food on the table and pay the rent.

What I did not encounter during my fieldwork, however, was a predominant focus on the uncertainty of the present. In as much as my interlocutors struggled to earn enough money to get by, prior expectations and their ongoing desire for a successful future continued to drive them forward. *Migrants and Masculinity in High-Rise Nairobi* should thus be read as an attempt to complement the scholarly interest in understanding how disadvantaged urban men in impoverished informal settlements dealt with existing economic stressors (Thieme 2013). However, transferring concepts such as 'navigating' (Vigh 2009) or 'hustling' to the lifeworld of male migrants in Pipeline risks misunderstanding their perspective on their environment, which was neither characterized by 'anxiety' (Falkof and Van Staden 2020) nor by an atmosphere of mere 'survival' (Simone and Abouhani 2005). In fact, Pipeline struck me as a place of aspiration, whose inhabitants believed they would thrive and prosper (Dawson 2022).

Men and masculinities in Africa

The challenges and conflicts male migrants encounter in Nairobi are not unique to the Kenyan context.[4] As the growing literature on masculinities in sub-Saharan Africa testifies (Lindsay and Miescher 2003, Ouzgane and Morrell 2005), African men are confronted with new and increasingly challenging relations between money and social interactions (Boulton 2021, Mains 2011, Smith 2017). These challenges are further aggravated by changing notions of love, marriage, and sexuality (Cole and Thomas 2009, Spronk 2012); new technologies for negotiating intimacy (Archambault 2017); rural expectations of success, remittances and, ultimately, physical return (Cohen and Odhiambo 1992, Smith 2019: chapter 4); the effects of racial capitalism (Matlon 2022); the economics, politics and aesthetics of male violence and paranoia (Hendriks 2022, Pype 2007); non-heteronormative notions of masculinity (Meiu 2020, Vorhölter 2017); the HIV/AIDS and COVID-19 pandemics (Baral 2021, Van Klinken 2013, Wyrod 2016); the ordeals of modern fatherhood (Richter and Morrell 2006); the so-called 'neglect of the boychild' (Pike 2020); and societal discourses about the proper upbringing of children (Fay 2021). Journalists and scholars sometimes subsume these challenges under the so-called 'crisis of masculinity' (Amuyunzu-Nyamongo and Francis 2006, Perry 2005) that is deemed responsible for outbreaks of violence, war, and protests organized by young men who see themselves as members of sub-Saharan Africa's rising 'surplus population' (Trapido 2021).

Voices from several disciplines have protested this simplification and the colonial stereotypes it perpetuates, such as images of aggressive, impulsive, and instinct-controlled black men who stick to archaic notions of masculinity. Scholars have deployed two main strategies to counter this narrative that deprives African men of agency by assuming that dire circumstances compel them to become violent and delinquent. On one hand, we have witnessed a rise in articles, monographs, and edited volumes exploring non-heteronormative notions of masculinity on the continent (Spronk and Nyeck 2021, Van Klinken 2019). On the other hand, scholarly studies on the roles of men in Africa (and elsewhere) increasingly call for heightened attention to the multiple

---

[4]   Confirming to prevailing notions of masculinity was also perceived as challenging in different historical epochs, as shown by Paul Ocobock's *An Uncertain Age: The Politics of Manhood in Kenya* (2017). (See also Blunt 2020, Callaci 2017, Epstein 1981, Mutongi 2000).

forms in which heteronormative masculinity becomes manifest in different contexts (Gutmann 2021). The authors of the introduction to a themed section of the journal *Gender, Place and Culture: A Journal of Feminist Geography* tellingly entitled 'Masculinities in Africa beyond crisis: complexity, fluidity, and intersectionality' summarize these research trends by stating that their primary goal is 'to counteract the tendency to deny pluralistic representations of masculinities in Africa' (Amman and Staudacher 2021). Among the explorations of other types of masculinity across Africa, we find work on 'post-crisis masculinity' (McLean 2021), 'African-centred masculinities' (Mfecane 2018), 'precarious masculinity' (Kovač 2022), 'aspirational masculinities' (Izugbara and Egesa 2020), and 'divergent masculinities' (Bolt 2010).

As much as this research has produced important insights by highlighting alternative ways in which masculinity is enacted, it also entails some risk. By pluralizing masculinity and focusing on non-heteronormative practices, we could overlook the ongoing influence and 'stickiness' (Berggren 2014) of the ever-prevalent global image of a successful man being an economically capable, physically strong, well-educated, independent, pious, and prudent provider (Crompton 1999, Ehrenreich 1984, Komarovsky 2004 [1940], Koppetsch and Speck 2015). The 'crisis of masculinity' hypothesis not only obscures the existence of diverse forms of masculinity but also makes it difficult to analyze practices perpetuating the narrative of the male breadwinner as being deliberately chosen by both men and women (Mojola 2014). For example, instead of understanding incidents of gender-based violence against women as an effect of male migrants' economic circumstances, it might be more fruitful to interpret them as men's attempts to restore their challenged authority, with the ultimate goal being to reap the 'patriarchal dividend' (Connell 2005 [1995]: 79). As shown by the omnipresence and 'ordinariness' of gender-based violence during my fieldwork, many migrant men in Pipeline, like many men elsewhere in the world, felt their masculinity was becoming increasingly fragile and their traditional privilege under attack (Kimmel 2019). Losing their status as the breadwinner frequently led to scathing criticism, and sometimes outright mockery and derision. Deemed 'useless' by their friends, girlfriends, wives and rural kin intensified their feelings of inadequacy and expendability.

This book explores how the persistent influence of the narrative of the male breadwinner impacted discussions, decisions and practices of male migrants in Pipeline. It illustrates how migrant men both contested and tried to emulate this ideal form of masculinity in their everyday lives. Despite agreeing to the narrative of the male provider in principle, they felt that women had begun to focus exclusively on a man's economic wealth when assessing his value. Men criticized this distortion of the narrative of the male breadwinner by, for example, emphasizing the evil nature of fast and illicit money-making activities or contrasting the sexual prowess of poor yet young and muscular men with the vanishing virility of old and feeble Nairobians known as *wababa*, who had to resort to material favours in order to have sex with young women (see Groes-Green 2009, Silberschmidt 2001). As a consequence of their inability to fulfil what they perceived as the excessive economic expectations of their intimate others, migrant men had begun to lessen this pressure by pretending to be wealthy already or by spending more and more time with other male migrants outside their marital homes. While almost everyone I met in Pipeline agreed that men had to provide and perform, it was far from clear what this exactly entailed.

Some methodological remarks

When I started my fieldwork in June 2019, it was not with the intention of writing a book about how notions of masculinity impacted the lives of migrant men in Pipeline. I had just begun a project on the experimentalization of development aid, analyzing how the paradigm of evidence-based intervention influenced the livelihoods of the inhabitants of Kaleko. My long-term field site, this small western Kenyan market centre in Kabondo-Kasipul constituency is roughly an eight-hour bus ride from Nairobi. Realizing that I needed to interact with non-governmental organizations (NGOs) in Nairobi at least one or two weeks each month, I asked my friend Samuel Onyango, a 28-year-old Luo migrant whom I had met in Chabera (a market centre not far from Kaleko) while he was waiting to start his law studies in Nairobi, if he could help me to find an apartment in Nairobi, preferably one not far from his own. Renting an apartment in Nairobi's less affluent east would not only cost less per month than a few nights in a hotel but would also allow me to combine my stays in the city with visiting and hosting friends. Less than a week later, Samuel informed me that he had found a bedsitter – a single room with a private bathroom – less than a five-minute walk away from his own.

Milele Flats (Kiswahili, 'Eternity Flats', see Figure 1), a massive tenement block painted green, orange and black, had just been finished. Only a few of the more than 100 bedsitters were still vacant. After climbing up to the seventh floor, Samuel and I inspected the bedsitter, a room less than fifteen square metres with a small bathroom and a tiny kitchen area equipped with cupboard, sink and tap. Tiled and freshly painted, it was large enough for one person. I indicated my wish to rent the apartment, and the caretaker gave me the bank account details for the deposit and the first month's rent, after which Samuel and I went to one of the numerous shops offering bank services, paid the rent (6,500 Kenyan Shillings [KSh] for the first month plus the 6,500 KSh deposit, a total of roughly 130 US), and returned to Milele to give the transfer slip to the caretaker to secure the deal.

Figure 1   Milele Flats. Photograph by the author, 2 June 2022.

During the three years I spent in Pipeline, I leaned on networks I had established in western Kenya. Samuel's assistance in finding accommodation helped me find my feet and I mostly hung out with friends I knew from western Kenya as well as friends of theirs. My integration into rural-urban networks intensified when, fed up with nearly two months of no running water, I met up with William Odhiambo, one of Samuel's childhood friends who had gone to secondary school in Chabera but had grown up in Kaleko and whom I had come across a couple of times. William and I decided to move into a one-bedroom apartment that was a five-minute walk from Milele Flats. Shortly thereafter we were joined by Dennis Okech, a mutual friend from Kaleko, who had just left his wife.[5] Over time, we housed relatives and friends from Kaleko, Chabera and other places in Nyanza who were passing through Nairobi.

Pipeline's maze-like layout fascinated me from day one. The estate struck me as unique, yet in terms of the scholarly literature on Nairobi it was all but completely overlooked (Huchzermeyer 2011, Ondieki 2016). Even though huge tenement blocks housing hundreds of people had replaced older housing structures all over Nairobi, the population density of Pipeline was unparalleled, except for some areas along Thika Road (especially in the constituency of Kasarani), and far surpassed the density of informal settlements such as Kibera. Intrigued by the myriad ways of how the estate's inhabitants made ends meet, I decided early on to gather data for one or two articles on Pipeline's history and economy. I spent my days conducting participant observation in the offices of Maendeleo, a research and advisory firm that had the infrastructure to implement behavioral economic experiments, and my evenings, nights, and weekends in Pipeline, where I watched football, went out for drinks, and shared my professional and romantic struggles with friends old and new.

Shortly before I had to leave Kenya due to the COVID-19 pandemic, I realized that my perspective on Pipeline and the lives of its inhabitants was decisively male. I fraternized with male labourers who worked in the nearby industrial area, played endless rounds of pool with men, drank beer with aspiring male politicians and landlords, worked out in a gym whose only regular female visitors were the owner's wife and young daughter, and played checkers and the FIFA videogame with, and surrounded by, teenage boys and young men. When I returned to Pipeline in November 2020, my new research focus was clear: migrant men and their experience of economic and romantic pressure.

Being around men tended to mean not being around women. Even though I can rely on roughly 25 long qualitative interviews with female migrants who lived in Pipeline, I spent far less time with women than men. This imbalance resulted from the 'social invisibility of women in male-dominated contexts' (Smith 2017: 129) as well as the relatively strict separation between the sexes. Most of my male friends would interpret any social encounter with a woman

---

5   I lived in my Milele Flats bedsitter from August to December 2019 and February to March 2020, when I had to leave Kenya because of the COVID-19 pandemic. In November 2020 and from January to March 2021, I shared a one-bedroom apartment with Dennis Okech and William Odhiambo, who moved out in March 2021. I continued to live with Dennis until I returned to Germany in May 2021. After spending the summer in Germany, I returned to the one-bedroom apartment in Pipeline, where I lived on my own from August to December 2021, February to March 2022, and May to September 2022.

as flirtatious, often with sexual undertones, which sometimes led to uncomfortable comments about the woman's physical traits. If she was known to them personally, they would also discuss her virtues and vices. Consequently, most of the women I got to know were female relatives of my male interlocutors. In an effort to correct this imbalance, I chatted with and spent as much time as possible with women I met on a formal, regular basis, such as the owner of a shop where I bought daily necessities or the female security guard in the high-rise block in which I lived. Nonetheless, everything I write about in this book is influenced by a male perspective.

Migrants in high-rise Nairobi

Pipeline's urban geography, architecture, and materiality were saturated with promises and expectations of wealth and modernity, especially from the perspective of rural migrants. It was an aspirational estate where landlords lured migrants with the promise of tiled and clean housing, a free subscription to Premier League football and a supposedly reliable supply of water and electricity. For less than 4,000 KSh per month, for example, you could rent a single room with shared bathrooms. While the estate's fancy bars allowed men to participate in the 'sweet life' of those with money, proudly displayed consumer goods such as flat screens, smartphones and laptops reassured others of a migrant man's upward trajectory. Even so, few of my interlocutors thought of Pipeline as a long-term place to stay. Instead, they viewed the estate as the launching pad for their personal development and professional careers. Preparing their onward migration to greener pastures, some attempted to save a portion of their meagre salaries, while others bought into Kenya's narrative of entrepreneurship and tried their luck by becoming 'self-employed' (see Dolan and Gordon 2019) in Pipeline's thriving local economy, where vendors sold almost everything from pre-cooked food, electronic gadgets, children's toys, and clothes to illegally brewed alcohol (Kiswahili, *chang'aa*), drugs, and sexual services.

Male migrants from western Kenya had to deal with many of the pressures created by the narrative of the male breadwinner in an intensified way. The spatial movement from the rural to the urban entailed leaving behind what many perceived as a life of the past (see map 1). Through talking with migrants who had lived in Nairobi for some time, I realized that they viewed their parents' lifestyle as infected with a burdensome traditionalism and governed by social rules that they perceived as suffocating. Somewhat ironically, when they first arrived in the city, their clothes, bodily and sexual practices, language, and material goods immediately gave away their rural origins. If they did not want to be branded as 'village' or 'farm boys' (Dholuo, *apuodho*, from

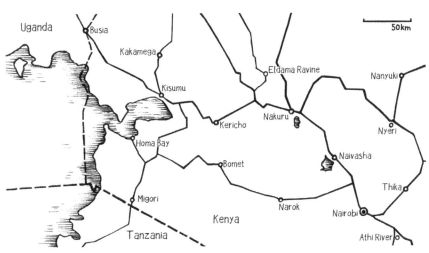

Map 1   Southwestern Kenya. Map drawn by Robin von Gestern.

puodho, 'farm'), male migrants had to adjust to urban dress codes, acquaint themselves with the city's complex public transport network (Mutongi 2017), and learn how to deal with the many perils of urban life such as pickpockets, con artists as well as unexplored sexual practices such as kissing and oral sex.

Upon arriving, they immediately came face to face with these pressures to adapt to urban life as well as the demands from home. Rural kin soon wanted proof of success, and those relatives who had contributed to their secondary education expected remittances and regular updates on their educational or economic progress. However, because of the differing challenges of urban and rural life, expectations of friends in the city and relatives at home did not always match. For many of my male interlocutors, the allure of urban living, such as women, material goods, alcohol, and drugs, which could be enjoyed in the shadow of the city's anonymity,[6] ate up the same meagre monetary resources that relatives were anticipating. The COVID-19 pandemic

---

[6]   During their youth in the village, many of my male friends could not invite a girlfriend to their father's house to 'chew her' (Dholuo, *nyamo nyako*, 'to chew a girl', *nyamo* is exemplarily used for sugar cane, which is chewed and then thrown away), as this would have constituted a ritual transgression. To get round this, Samuel and some of his friends used an abandoned house in Chabera to perform what they called their 'nocturnal surgeries' (see Githinji 2008 on sexist language in Kenya). Other opportunities for sexual exploration arose when young men visited boarding schools or attended funerals, when people engaged in night-long dancing and partying (known as *disco matanga*, or *lawo thum*, Dholuo, 'chasing the music') and young women could be seduced in nearby fields.

brought into even sharper relief the ongoing economic and social relevance of this 'urban-rural connection' (Geschiere and Gugler 1998, see also Ross and Weisner 1977, Weisner 1976). The measures to curb the spread of the virus not only restricted travel between Nairobi and western Kenya, but also led to an economic crisis that made it more and more difficult to send remittances home, which upset carefully negotiated financial arrangements.

To contextualize migrants' lives and economic expectations in Kenya's capital, the next section describes Kaleko, the rural place I know best. A short introduction to life in Kaleko and neighbouring market centres such as Chabera, illustrates the extent of the urban–rural contrast and helps us understand why many male migrants initially, and quite euphorically, conceptualized Nairobi as a launching pad for their careers, and for masculine success more broadly, only to later realize that things would not work out as smoothly as expected.

Male migration as an aspirational practice

'Many schoolchildren had no shoes, there was no electricity, no blackboards, and our desks were placed on bare soil. On top of all that we had to fetch firewood for our teachers, imagine, early in the morning before school.' After we had finished our dinner, Samuel and his close friend Caleb Omondi, who also hailed from Chabera, began to tell stories about life growing up in rural western Kenya. Maybe trying to impress Jane, a friend who had grown up in a village close to Nairobi, Samuel and Caleb engaged in a practice I had observed among other male migrants. By portraying western Kenya as backward and underdeveloped (Morrison 2007), migrant men painted a picture of their journey as 'a rite of passage in which the migrant must confront risk and the unfamiliar to ensure his social becoming' (Kleinman 2019: 13) and of themselves as pioneers who had transformed from boys walking barefoot and dressed in torn clothes to men wearing suits and designer shoes. Irrespective of their absolute wealth, many male migrants from western Kenya (see map 2), a region viewed by most as politically and historically neglected, arrived in Nairobi with a feeling of superiority vis-à-vis poor urban residents or migrants from places closer to Nairobi. Puzzled by the difference between her school days and those of Samuel and Caleb, Jane told us that those stories reminded her of how her mother had described going to school when she was young. In coming to Nairobi, it seemed, Caleb and Samuel had not only travelled in space but also forwards in time.

Urban Kenyans considered places such as Kaleko and Chabera not only far away geographically but also as temporally distant and backward. Rural villages did indeed offer few economic opportunities for young men. In 2009,

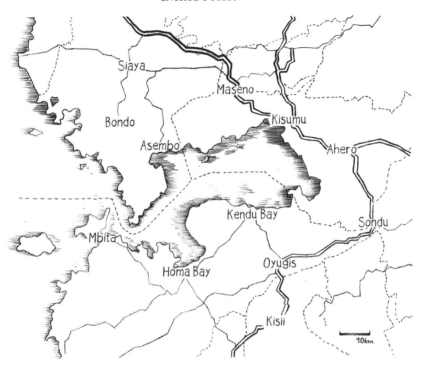

Map 2   Piny Luo (Dholuo, 'Luo land'). Map drawn by Robin von Gestern.

when I visited Kaleko for the first time, I felt as if I was being transported back in time. Donkey carts transported bricks that local youths had made by hand, and women in colourful traditional clothes carried sacks of maize on their heads to the local market. Passing through the maize fields that surrounded polygamous homesteads (Dholuo, *dala*, see figure 2), which were organized according to patrilocal and patrilineal principles that were more than a century old, I quickly realized that social and political relations were still influenced by the clan and lineage structures referenced by E.E. Evans-Pritchard (1949). Few houses had electricity and there was no running water or a basic sewage system. It was not surprising that many young people perceived Kaleko as a place stuck in the past. Other than farming and selling the produce at the local markets, working in the local informal economy, or becoming a teacher or nurse, job opportunities were limited. When asked why so many men migrate to Nairobi, one male migrant from Homa Bay County stated that 'if money could be found in the village, we would not be in Nairobi'. Most young men, in other words, did not see a future in Kaleko (Schmidt 2017a).

The narratives of entrepreneurial and professional success in the capital and signs of urban modernity, such as the newest technological gadgets, sparked

Figure 2   Patrilocal homestead in Kaleko. Photograph by the author, 20 April 2015.

and catalyzed the migratory dreams of young men from Kaleko and other places in rural western Kenya throughout the twentieth century and into the twenty first (Cohen and Odhiambo 1989). During my fieldwork, many men still considered migration the most promising way to explore new worlds and make money, and then return home later in life. Due to a high population density and an increasing shortage of land around Kaleko, many young men were well aware that they would not necessarily be able to build homesteads adjacent to those of their fathers' or uncles', as had long been traditional cultural practice (see Geissler and Prince 2010: chapter 4). The majority would either have to buy land elsewhere or be content with tiny plots that would barely allow any form of subsistence agriculture. This impending scarcity of land in western Kenya further intensified the pressure on young men to migrate to the capital to make enough money to be able to retire in their natal village.

A successful migration would fulfil the promises of a narrative of migrant modernity, one to which many Kenyans still adhere. Focusing on excelling in the domains of 'schooling, formal employment, and households' (Smith 2008: 114), these expectations of migratory success have historical roots in western Kenya's colonial history as a labour pool and have also been perpetuated by stereotypes of *jo*-Luo as excellent academics, lawyers, and politicians. Such expectations were further reinforced through the narratives of success shared by elder migrants. However, the structural adjustment reforms of the 1980s and 1990s, coupled with an explosion in the number of college and university degree-holders, made it difficult for migrants to achieve economic success in Kenya's capital. Three decades later, the economic recession and inflation caused by the COVID-19 pandemic and the war in Ukraine further impeded migrants' attempts to meet their rural families' expectations, never mind their own. Caleb, whose salary was cut by 50 per cent during the first months of the pandemic and who shared his Nairobi apartment with his girlfriend and three relatives, summarized this predicament as follows:

> Due to the economic pressure, you know, maybe what you were offering before might be different from what you are offering now. […] Like right now there are priorities, right? And maybe your cousin or somebody tells you like, 'I need this amount of money', and you don't have that money right now, because you know with them, the expectation is still intact, they have the mentality that you are working, and that you are in Nairobi, the mentality they have is that you have money.

Relations between the village (Dholuo, *gweng*, Sheng, *ushago*, *shags*) and the city (Dholuo, *boma*) were complex, and both places figured in the minds and plans of migrants as more than geographic locations. While the virtual presence of money and urban commodities influenced the dreams and visions of male migrants long before they left for the city, behavioural traits that were associated with rurality and backwardness, such as speaking with an odd accent or refusing to eat unknown food, shaped how migrants were seen during their first few months after they arrived. For many migrant men the city was simply a place to make money, experiment with new lifestyles, and make a family of their own before returning to their ancestral homes. However, as this book will show, these goals tended to obstruct one another.

Organization of the chapters

This book has two parts, each consisting of three chapters. The first part – *Experiencing Pressure* – introduces Pipeline and discusses the romantic and economic challenges men encountered after migrating to Nairobi. It describes how their own expectations and those of their rural kin, wives, girlfriends, and male friends structured, influenced, and disrupted their attempts to find success. *Experiencing Pressure* thus outlines the social and economic consequences of the ongoing relevance of the narrative of the male provider and explores some of the frustrations male migrants experienced. The second part – *Evading Pressure* – focuses on three homosocial spaces in which men tried to evade or overcome the experience of pressure: an ethnically homogenous investment group of Dholuo-speaking Kenyans who socialized with one another in the bars and pubs of Pipeline, the interethnic No Mercy Gym, and the sphere of self-help culture embodied by those I call 'masculinity consultants', such as pastors, authors and motivational speakers who tried to capitalize on male migrants' experiences of pressure by giving advice on how to become an economically and spiritually successful man, husband, and father.[7] Going to bars and clubs, working out, or reading self-help literature allowed periods of release, renewing the energy male migrants required to sustain their efforts to provide for their urban and rural relatives. Ultimately, though, these practices failed as lasting solutions for their economic and social frustrations. The most socially validated form of masculinity – economic success – remained both a sought-after 'privilege and a source of lived insecurity' (Hendriks 2022: 144) for most male migrants in Pipeline.

Chapter 1 offers an introduction to Pipeline's materiality, history, and geography. It shows that the emergence of the estate must be understood against the background of Nairobi's colonial and postcolonial history and housing policies characterized by racial segregation, political corruption, and illegal land grabbing. The chapter closes a research gap in the scholarly literature on Nairobi that has predominantly focused on informal settlements, such as Kibera or Korogocho, by portraying some of the challenges and forms of exclusion caused by Pipeline's urban architecture, the state's neglect of the significant increase in tenement housing that began in the early 2000s, as well as the residents' rather instrumental approach to living in the estate's high-rise accommodation. I conclude by suggesting that in being ignored by the state yet catalyzing the aspirational dreams of migrant men and landlords alike,

---

[7]   I focus on these places because they differ from other masculine spaces such as barber shops, open-air pool halls and videogame joints in one major respect. Male migrants who wrote or read self-help books, participated in investment groups, or worked out in gyms tried to change their futures actively. These spaces seemed better suited to gaining an understanding of the influence of the expectation of success. Although men also frequented betting shops to change their futures actively, I decided not to include them as a case study in this book. It is nevertheless important to mention that betting shops were one of the social spaces that migrant men visited after work to avoid spending time with their families. Aware of the economic and social pressures men faced, the owners of betting shops allowed potential customers to hang around and watch the evening news or chat with friends even if they did not have money to bet. Furthermore, engaging in systematic betting, which not only demanded a detailed analysis of the strength of players and teams but also fiscal prudence, allowed unemployed men to experience the dignity of having something comparable to a business or job (Schmidt 2019).

Pipeline is best understood as a place everyone expected a lot from while no one was really willing to emotionally invest in it.

Chapter 2 describes Pipeline's economy and the strategies male migrants employed to navigate both 'landscapes of debt' and 'horizons of expectation' (Cole 2014). It distinguishes the experience of pressure from the experience of stress by defining the first as a negative somatic reaction resulting from an actor's assessment of expectations as reasonable in kind but not in degree, that is to say, qualitatively justified but quantitatively excessive. This conceptualization of pressure has several benefits. Apart from explaining why migrant men's experience of pressure was often accompanied by quantitative qualifiers, such as 'not yet, but soon I will be one of those successful men', or 'you are right, but you ask for too much', it also allows us to grasp the intimate and culturally as well as socially inflected nature of the relation between the cause of pressure and the person who experiences it (see Jackson 2013 on the history of stress as a diagnosis and metaphor in the twentieth century). Male migrants were intimately attached and emotionally committed to what they perceived as the causes of their pressure, such as the narrative of the male breadwinner, urban life, or the expectations of their wives, girlfriends, and rural kin. Finally, understanding migrant men's pressure as caused by expectations that they considered qualitatively justified helps to explain why they rarely engaged in more radical political critiques of Kenya's highly unjust capitalist system. Male migrants did not want to change the rules of the game. They just wanted to win it.

Chapter 3 focuses on how migrant men's experience of pressure destabilized their romantic relations. After illustrating how men classified women according to various categories that were constantly threatening to merge, I discuss how migrant men and women employed practices that aimed at stabilizing the marital house as a social unit. As these practices derived their alleged efficacy from the economically unsustainable idea of the man as the main breadwinner, they further complicated the already intricate relations between money, sexuality, and love. The resulting mistrust and the anxiety of being unable to perform traditional gender roles intensified public negotiations of sexual performances, economic responsibilities, and romantic requests. These public negotiations took place through new forms of smartphone-based communication such as WhatsApp. The chapter ends by extending the discussion of mistrust and secrecy to the issue of urban–rural kin relations. In an environment where many couples lived together in interethnic relationships, husbands and wives often did not know each other's in-laws or mother tongue, which led to further misunderstandings.

Chapter 4 focuses on a welfare group called HoMiSiKi, which consisted entirely of Luo migrants and was named after the first syllables of the four western Kenyan counties predominantly inhabited by *jo*-Luo: Homa Bay, Migori, Siaya, and Kisumu. The group's main goal was to support members in case of sickness or funerals and to save enough money to invest. The chapter illustrates how its official structure and ambitious aims provided a justification for married men to leave their apartments and spend time with other men in their 'playing field' (Dholuo, *pap,* traditionally denoting a field where people danced, initiated sexual relations, organized wrestling matches and other social activities). As *jo-pap* (Dholuo, 'people of the playing field', singular *ja-pap),* they engaged in practices of wasteful masculinity, such as extramarital sexual relationships, physical violence and an excessive consumption of alcohol. The chapter concludes with a description of how the COVID-19 pandemic negatively affected HoMiSiKi's economic plans but intensified celebrations of wasteful masculinity among individual *jo-pap,* which ultimately led to the collapse of the investment group.

Chapter 5 outlines the history of recreational weightlifting in Pipeline by narrating how Carl, one of the estate's gym pioneers and the owner of the No Mercy Gym, started his career as a gym instructor twenty years ago. Following an introduction to Pipeline's gym scene, I delve into the experiences of five members of the No Mercy Gym who trained together almost daily, demonstrating how small interactions (looks, comments, or instructions, for example) and institutionalized practices, such as contributing to funeral costs or participating in post-workout meals and drinks, defined the gym as a masculine space and fostered a strong sense of belonging among its members. The chapter goes on to argue that the recreational weightlifting at the No Mercy Gym represents a paradigmatic form of coping with the experience of pressure produced by a situation in which the causes and effects of economic success appeared to have been disentangled. Lifting weights provided meaning to migrant men by giving them a sense of self-efficacy that they could not find in Kenya's ruthless capitalist economy.

The final chapter explores how masculinity consultants offered guidance to Kenyan men who were seeking ways to alleviate economic and romantic pressures. While Philemon Otieno, a migrant and motivational speaker from western Kenya, suggested combining practices and narratives of charismatic Christianity with those of US-American self-help culture to achieve economic success (see Boyd 2018, Fay 2022), other masculinity consultants such as Amerix, who rose to nationwide fame by giving Kenyan men advice on social media, as well as self-published authors Silas Nyanchwani (2021a, 2022) and Jacob Aliet (2022a), recommended that male migrants reject feminist values and adopt practices focused on re-establishing the patriarchal norms that they believed would transform them into strong and self-sufficient men. These recommendations were strongly influenced by ideas found in the digital 'manosphere', this being a conglomeration of websites, blogs, chat groups, and online forums centred around an anti-feminist redefinition of masculinity (Ging 2019, Kaiser 2022, Van Valkenburg 2021). Widening the book's perspective by focusing on how Kenyan men appropriated, disseminated, and contextualized such masculinizing strategies links the experiences of male migrants in Pipeline with nationwide discussions about the dire state of gender relations, which were further fuelled by men's growing fear of becoming expendable (see Schmidt 2022a).

The conclusion draws out the structural similarities of the three case studies and summarizes the book's findings against the background of the concepts of the experience of pressure and the expectation of success. It recapitulates how discussing and trying to overcome male frustrations and failures has become an integral part of constructing man-, father-, husband- and brotherhood in contemporary Nairobi, where migrants coped with economic and social pressures exacerbated by the narrative of men as providers by creating and frequenting masculine spaces where a feeling of manhood and brotherhood was created, maintained and celebrated (see Fuh 2012). However, this celebration of brotherhood did not entail a critique of but merely allowed migrant men to momentarily evade Kenya's increasing capitalist focus on economic actors' entrepreneurial work ethic. In Pipeline, male validation continued to be characterized by trying, and often failing, to be the breadwinner. Masculinity, in other words, was not only defined by meeting the normative expectations of others but also by genuine efforts to meet them. Trying one's best or simulating success often had to suffice. Being a man in Pipeline was thus a balancing act of trying, pretending, and failing to meet self-expectations and those of others.

Migrants and Masculinity in High-Rise Nairobi portrays what Philippe Bourgois has called 'the individual experience of social structural oppression' (2003 [1996]: 15). It shows how, amidst economic crises and the Kenyan state's failure to offer affordable healthcare and education, migrant men remain under continuous pressure to provide for their loved ones. The book thereby complements the burgeoning literature on how social units such as families (Cooper 2019) or NGOs (Muehlebach 2012) are compelled to or willingly take over responsibilities from a neoliberal state that neglects its citizens. Instead of criticizing the state's negligence and demanding their rights, men and women in high-rise Nairobi remain entangled in a blame game that continues to escalate their economic and romantic pressures. The alleged crisis of masculinity is not primarily a problem of gender relations, but more a result of Kenya's capitalist economy, which relies on the production and exploitation of migrant men's pressured bodies and minds and pits their interests against those of women (see Ntarangwi 1998). Rather than looking to support from the state, men and women in Pipeline expected everything and nothing from each other, a situation that led to misunderstandings, mistrust, violence, and even death.

PART 1

EXPERIENCING PRESSURE

1

The History and Infrastructure
of an Aspirational Estate

You don't need to break down a Riemann Hypothesis to know where
newbies in the city will head to, especially when they are looking for jobs.
Journalist Irvin Jalango (2016) about Pipeline

In November 2018, when I went to Pipeline for the first time, Samuel picked
me up from my hotel in Nairobi's central business district (CBD). When we
got off at one of Pipeline's *matatu* (Kiswahili, 'bus used for public transport')
ranks after being stuck in Nairobi's notorious traffic for over an hour, I found
myself jumping over foul-smelling sewers and crossing railway tracks on
and around which people sold, among other things, clothes, shoes, fruits,
chapos (Kiswahili, *chapati*, 'fried flatbread'), vegetables, kitchen utensils,
mturaa (Sheng, 'Nairobi sausage', minced meat sausages with spices), gas
cylinders, mattresses, traditional medicine, fried, fresh and dried fish, and
githeri (Kiswahili, 'boiled beans with maize'). Navigating this open-air market
was an endless mass of people trying to make their way home. *Boda-boda*
(Kiswahili, 'moto-taxis') and hooting lorries used any space available to move
a few centimetres forward. I followed Samuel through a maze of small roads
and high-rise buildings. Due to the estate's density, we had to pass through
the ground floors of some tenement blocks, making use of what were locally
known as 'bypasses' connecting Pipeline's main roads (see figure 3). I soon
lost all sense of direction, partly because I was trying to avoid stepping into
muddy areas filled with sewage and garbage but also because I was fascinated
by what was happening around me. When we arrived at Samuel's apartment,
a mere ten minutes later, I confessed that I would never find my way back
to the *matatu* rank. Samuel laughed and told me that if I lived in Pipeline, I
would know my way around it in less than a week.

When I mentioned my plans to move to Pipeline, many of my Kenyan
middle-class friends were shocked. Their reaction echoed the journalistic
coverage of the estate. Alternatively called 'disaster zone' (Otieno 2017),
'concrete tenement jungle' (Mwau 2019), or the 'laughing stock of Nairobi'
(Ambani 2021), journalists portrayed Pipeline as an urban failure. Media

Figure 3   One of Pipeline's many bypasses connecting the estate's main streets and ensuring that high-rise blocks can be constructed next to each other without wasting space. Photograph by the author, 18 August 2022.

stories include a young child who came home to find her mother stabbed to death by her father, who then committed suicide (Njagi 2012, see also Muiruri 2021); tiny apartments being used as makeshift abortion clinics or overcrowded child day-care centres where toddlers spent their days like lab mice (Ambani 2021) without getting enough sunshine to prevent diseases such as rickets

(Njanja 2020); and dead embryos placed in sewers by Pipeline's sex workers who offer their services for less than 100 KSh (Wanzala 2018).

Leaving aside this homogenous journalistic coverage imbued with middle-class anxieties about a place where 'children of a lesser God' (Ambani 2022) live, locally circulating rumours were equally imaginative. They ranged from accounts about kidnapping syndicates who sold children to rich and infertile businessmen, to gossip about a sinister group that abducted obese women and sold their flesh or made soup with their fat. Although understudied (exceptions include Huchzermeyer 2011, Maina and Mwau 2018, Mwau 2020, Ndegwa 2016, Obala 2011, Obala and Mattingly 2014, Ondieki 2016, Smith 2020, 2023), Pipeline and other high-rise tenement conglomerations in Nairobi were subject to excessive fantasies. Two key reasons for the extent to which high-rise settlements such as Pipeline triggered the imaginations of Nairobians were their distinctiveness and novelty. While this type of densely populated settlement is a common sight elsewhere in the world (see Jansen 2015, Mathews 2011, Schwenkel 2020), cities in sub-Saharan Africa tended to expand horizontally, not vertically, during the twentieth century, resulting in relatively low levels of population density.

Recent research (Agyemang et al. 2018, Gastrow 2020a, Goodman 2020, Smith and Woodcraft 2020), however, suggests that portrayals of African cities as mostly consisting of horizontally sprawling informal settlements are one-sided and risk constraining political initiatives to improve urban living conditions. In fact, the trend toward vertical housing in Nairobi has turned Marie Huchzermeyer's prediction that verticalization would take over the housing sector in Kenya's capital into reality (2011: chapter 9). During my fieldwork, tenement housing blocks were no longer the future of Nairobi but the everyday urban environment, especially for most migrants who had come to Kenya's capital to carve out a better life for themselves and their rural families. Scholars and politicians who have ignored the verticalization of Nairobi's housing sector should therefore better their understanding of how tenants live in dense and congested places like Pipeline sooner rather than later.[1]

---

[1]   Focusing on the lives of migrant men in Pipeline complements the scholarly literature on Nairobi. In the last decades, urban geographers, anthropologists, and other social scientists have published works on diverse areas of Nairobi, for example, the city's western, more affluent parts (Spronk 2012), informal settlements such as Kibera, Korogocho and Mathare (see, for instance, Guma 2020, Kimari 2017, Neumark 2017, Thieme 2013), as well as Eastleigh (Carrier 2016) and Kaloleni (Smith 2019), thereby allowing us to grasp Nairobi's fragmented and multiple nature (see Charton-Bigot and Rodrigues-Torres 2010).

The estate's controversial image might also partly result from the politically, economically, and architecturally dubious ways in which it came into
existence. In the wake of the 1980s structural adjustment reforms (Rono 2002),
politicians tolerated, or even encouraged, the destruction of informal settlements in the name of 'slum upgrading' (Huchzermeyer 2008, see also De
Feyter 2015), indicating that they had no proper plan for dealing with the
country's ongoing urbanization and growing need for housing. Scrupulous and
wealthy private investors, however, quickly saw the lack of accommodation as
a business opportunity and started, sometimes illegally and sometimes legally,
to acquire land on which to construct high-rise blocks. As of the early 2000s,
and relying upon what Constance Smith has called 'a semi-licit assemblage
of circumvented planning laws, pliable oversight, off-the-books negotiations',
and 'opaque documentation', these businessmen collaborated with 'an opportunistic construction industry using poor-quality materials' (Smith 2020: 15)
to radically reshape Nairobi's housing sector. How male migrants carved out
their economic and social lives in the material and architectural results of this
'gray development' (ibid.) – endless rows of vertical housing blocks that are
too quickly equated with total anonymity or even social anomie – is the key
interest of this book.

The geography and demography of Pipeline

What many Nairobians call Pipeline is an area that covers two square kilometres
and comprises two electoral wards within Embakasi South constituency:
Pipeline and Kware (see map 3).[2] Though divided by a street, these wards
form a coherent complex of hundreds of high-rise blocks residents call 'plots'.[3]
The estate is bounded by Outer Ring Road to the east and Airport North Road
to the south. Pipeline merges into the informal settlement of Mukuru Kwa
Njenga and the Imara Daima estate toward its west. Its northern border is
marked by a large water-filled quarry that gave Kware its name. Mombasa
and Jogoo Road connect the estate with Nairobi's CBD, colloquially known
as 'town'. While an overcrowded passenger train transports people from the
estate to the CBD in the early morning and back in the late afternoon (40

---

[2]   I use the term 'Pipeline' to refer to the agglomeration of high-rise tenement blocks
in Kware and Pipeline ward. Whenever I use 'Kware', I refer to Kware ward. Where
I need to emphasise that I am talking about Pipeline ward, I use 'Pipeline ward'.
[3]   The use of the term 'plot', which usually refers to a piece of land smaller than an
acre (for instance, 50 x 100 feet), is revealing. As most high-rise buildings in Pipeline
fully occupy the small piece of land that the owner bought, buildings had become
synonymous with the pieces of land on which they were built.

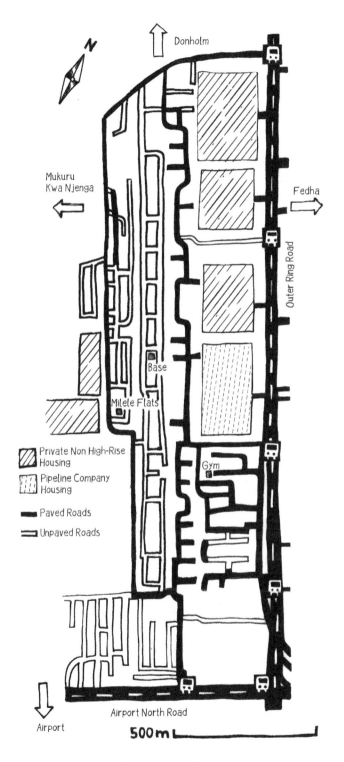

Map 3 Pipeline. Map drawn by Robin von Gestern.

KSh), minibuses drive to town throughout the day (between 40 KSh and 100 KSh depending on the time of travel).

According to Kenya's Independent Electoral and Boundaries Commission, Pipeline and Kware wards together had roughly 70,000 registered voters in 2022 (IEBC 2022). Considering that 'a significant number of tenants are not registered as voters in the city' (Maina and Mwau 2018: 221) and that Kenyans under the age of eighteen cannot register as voters, I initially estimated Pipeline's population to be around 170,000. However, a survey of a two-hectare area around the plot I lived in revealed slightly over 3,000 housing units, 41 general shops, 31 beauty salons, fifteen liquor stores, nine butcheries, three private clinics, and a mere two private schools. As my interviews with inhabitants revealed an average of 3.5 household members, we can tentatively assume a population density of around 5,000 people per hectare. This suggests that Pipeline's population could well be over 250,000, making it one of the most densely populated estates worldwide.

During my fieldwork, most of Pipeline's inhabitants were migrants under 40 who were either unmarried, single parents, or part of a family with a few young children. While many of my interlocutors suggested that the majority of Pipeline's inhabitants ethnically identified as Kamba, Pipeline was not segregated into areas exclusively or predominantly inhabited by people from the same ethnic group. I cannot rule out the possibility that some landlords preferred tenants of their ethnic background, but in the plots where I lived or spent most of my time the tenants hailed from all over Kenya. Many of my interlocutors from *piny Luo* (Dholuo, 'Luo land') preferred to mingle with other *jo*-Luo for cultural and linguistic reasons, and some barber shops, gyms, pool halls and bars attracted people from the same ethnic group (see Parkin 1978: 36–7). In the end, though, Pipeline's promises of modernity and its proximity to Jomo Kenyatta International Airport (JKIA) and Nairobi's industrial area made it an attractive estate for male migrants from all over Kenya who were looking for casual work or formal employment. While some migrants found work in factories, hotels, or restaurants, others tried their luck in the estate's vibrant local economy or were engaged in Kenya's emerging gig economy as Uber drivers (Iazzolino 2023) or students writing essays for US-American, Chinese or British students (Kingori 2021).

Pipeline belongs to Nairobi's economically and politically marginalized eastern part (see map 4). While almost all governmental, parastatal, and inter-national organizations have their offices either in the CBD or in Nairobi's lush and green western parts, most of the city's manual workers and their families live in the cramped single rooms of high-rise tenements, or in the *mabati* (Kiswahili, 'iron sheets') shacks of informal settlements such as Mathare and Mukuru Kwa Njenga in Nairobi's east. The inhabitants of eastern Nairobi,

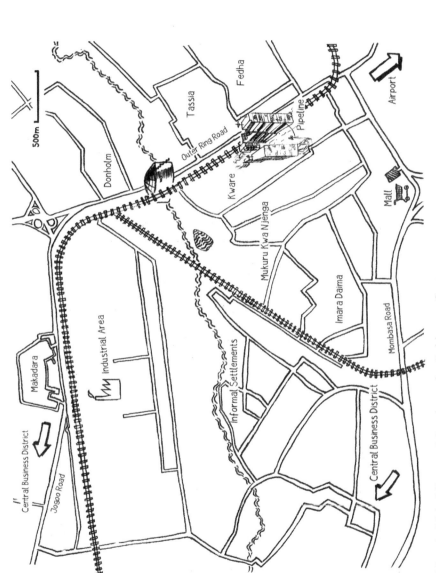

Map 4   Nairobi's east. Map drawn by Robin von Gestern.

who include Uber drivers, industrial labourers, low-paid white-collar workers, housemaids, sex workers, and *matatu* conductors, keep the city running by maintaining the town's water and electricity infrastructure, driving expats from appointment to appointment, or assuring that passengers and cargo leave the international airport on time. This bifurcation of Kenya's capital into a rich western and a marginalized eastern part has its roots in colonial times, when the CBD and the western parts housed the colony's white elite and black Kenyans occupied the city's eastern fringes.

Nairobi's east is also geologically marginalized due to the black cotton soil dominating its surface. In contrast to the red soil found in Nairobi's west, black cotton soil is a highly compressible soil type found in the city's low-lying areas. Due to its lesser ability to absorb water, unpaved roads in Pipeline become extremely muddy during the rainy season (see figure 4), and the construction of houses requires deep foundations. It is thus no mere coincidence that the colonial elite favoured Nairobi's western areas. The inherent problems of black cotton soil led the urban planners who drafted the Nairobi Metropolitan Growth Strategy in 1973 (Nairobi Urban Study Group 1973: paragraph 60) to advise that the city should expand to the north-east, in the direction of Thika, and not to the east. Comparable to other parts of the 1973 master plan that emphasized the need to decentralize Nairobi and upgrade its transport infrastructure, this advice, which would have prevented Pipeline from becoming the 'concrete tenement jungle' (Mwau 2019) of today, was never taken seriously. History took a different path, but the authors of the 1973 strategy proved correct in their prediction that the Kenyan government would not be able to supply the amount of housing demanded by Nairobi's steadily increasing population (Nairobi Urban Study Group 1973: paragraphs 29–30).

Pipeline's spectacular rise

In February 2021, Kenyan television channels, radios, and newspapers broadcast news about the death of Njenga Mwenda Kariuki. Njenga was among the first migrants to come to the area surrounding Pipeline in the 1950s and gave the informal settlement Mukuru Kwa Njenga (Gĩkũyũ, 'Valley of Njenga') its name. After the colonial government had forcefully removed him from his ancestral lands near Limuru (Ondieki 2021), Njenga tried his luck on the outskirts of Nairobi. Aware of opportunities for menial labour close to a stone quarry, he settled along the Ngong river and opened a bar, where he sold food and *chang'aa* (Kiswahili, 'illegally brewed liquor') to quarry workers (Odenyo and Njoroge 2021). Over the next decades, the settlement attracted more and more migrant labourers seeking work in one of the quarries or the growing informal economy that served the workers. These migrants

Figure 4   Muddy road in Kware ward. Photograph by the author, 2 June 2022.

constructed the shacks that would later form the informal settlements of Mukuru Kwa Njenga and Kware, where Patrick Ouko, one of the founding members of the investment group HoMiSiKi, lived with his parents and his grandparents in the 1990s.

Patrick's family hailed from the area around Sondu, a market centre less than 30 minutes from Kaleko. Although he spent most of his childhood and adult life in Pipeline, Patrick had been schooled in the village for his last primary and first secondary school years, a common practice among migrants aimed at helping children to get to know their ancestral homes and rural relatives. When we met for the first time in August 2019, Patrick was a 29-year-old father of two young children. Working for a dairy company's

Figure 5 Kenya Pipeline Company housing estate next to Outer Ring Road, established at the end of the twentieth century. Photograph by the author, 2 July 2022.

logistics section, he also owned a barber shop, a regular meeting point for migrants from western Kenya situated on the first floor of one of Pipeline's plots opposite the plot I would move into in November 2020. Patrick agreed to take me through Pipeline and tell me about the estate's history:

> When I was young, we walked through high grass to get to our school in Imara Daima. There were no high-rise buildings, just *mabati* houses everywhere. This was just a slum built on a swamp, and most of the people who lived here were Kamba. It is close to their home in Machakos. People now call this whole area Pipeline. Some don't even know that they are living in Kware ward. Others think that when they call the place Pipeline, people will forget about the slum Kware.

During our walk, Patrick greeted people at every corner and I wondered how the estate could have developed from a sparsely populated informal settlement into Nairobi's most densely populated high-rise estate in less than twenty years. Having lived in the area for so long, Patrick navigated the bypasses with ease and directed my attention to important landmarks, such as the Kenya Pipeline Company housing estate situated along Outer Ring Road that had been built at the end of the twentieth century (see figure 5). When I asked him

Figure 6   Spared *mabati* structure. Photograph by the author, 19 February 2022.

about a *mabati* structure where *fundi* (Kiswahili, 'craftsmen') repaired beds and socialized, Patrick began to narrate the story of how Pipeline became the high-rise estate of today. It was a story of loss and violence.

Ten years prior, Patrick and his grandmother were among thousands of residents in the informal settlement who were informed that their homes would be demolished unless they purchased the land on which they stood. Patrick and his grandmother were unable to raise the funds needed to buy the plot and so bulldozers destroyed their house a few weeks later. As a result, they were forced to relocate to Tassia, on the other side of Outer Ring Road. The *mabati* structure where *fundi* socialized was spared only because the bulldozer had broken down right in front of it, leading to rumours of witchcraft. Thereafter, nobody dared to continue with the destruction (see figure 6).

Patrick and Njenga's life stories exemplify the extent to which Pipeline has transformed over the last 75 years. In the 1950s, on what was once bare and uninhabited land where lions and hyenas roamed, migrants who had been forcefully evicted from their agriculturally fertile ancestral homes in Kenya's central highlands constructed their shacks and thereby laid the ground for the informal settlements that came to be known as Kware, Mukuru Kwa Njenga, and Viwandani. These informal settlements grew through the constant influx of migrants from nearby Ukambani and elsewhere until, from the early 2000s, private investors started to transform them into the high-rise settlements of today, aided by youth groups ready to defend the land using violence, and by politicians who turned a blind eye to illegal land grabbing (chapter 4, see also Obala 2011).

When I first came to Pipeline, there were few empty plots and the remaining *mabati* structures were being replaced high-rise blocks. Since then, investors have started to build high-rise buildings at the edge of Mukuru Kwa Njenga, where over 13,000 homes were destroyed at the end of 2021 (Ashly 2022, see also Macharia 1992). The forceful demolition of parts of Mukuru Kwa Njenga in 2021, and of Kware in 2009, which was home to over 5,000 residents at that time (Metcalfe and Pavanello 2011), illustrates that the ongoing transformation of Nairobi's slums into privately owned high-rise tenement settlements cannot be understood without considering the city's violent colonial and postcolonial history, one characterized by repetitions of structurally similar and ultimately ineffective attempts to solve the city's housing crisis.

A short history of housing in Nairobi

Nairobi came into existence as a railway depot at the end of the nineteenth century, when the construction of the Uganda Railway connecting Mombasa with the interior parts of present-day Uganda reached the area around what would later be called the Nairobi River (Ogot and Ogot 2020). The new railway depot attracted labourers, traders, and sex workers from different ethnic backgrounds who were united by the feeling that migrating to Nairobi would allow them to make money to pay the taxes demanded by the colonial government, support their rural kin, and progress with personal goals (White 1990). So-called 'African villages' soon cropped up in the surroundings of the railway headquarters, the government buildings, and the Indian Bazaar, perpetuating the city's emerging racial divide. Many of the houses in these villages were built by private investors who rented out small rooms to mostly male migrants who were not allowed to roam freely in the city and were legally obliged to return home to their wives and families once their contracts had expired (Anderson 2000). While Nairobi has been racially divided since its inception, 'the colony as a whole [became] segregated by gender' (Spronk 2012: 50) as men migrated to Nairobi and left their wives in the rural villages. The labour migration of men thereby also played a significant role in fostering the narrative of the male breadwinner.

To control the African population, the colonial government demolished the 'African villages' in the name of hygiene, sanitation, and health standards (Simpson 1915). In the 1920s, it founded Pumwani as the first officially sanctioned settlement for Africans (Ese and Ese 2020: chapter 3). There, black Kenyans could rent plots for an annual fee and build their own houses. Entrepreneurial Kenyans with enough capital seized this opportunity and began to rent out rooms to migrant workers. In the following decades, the 'site and service concept' of Pumwani, which provided rooms for migrants who were not allowed to become permanent residents of the city, gave way to the idea of municipal housing. This shift in the colonial housing policy tried to account for the fact that Nairobi had become home to a significant number of African men, women, and families (Huchzermeyer 2011: 127).

The 'Nairobi Master Plan for a Colonial Capital' (White et al. 1948) outlined the principles of this new municipal housing strategy. Its authors believed that changing Nairobi's housing conditions could transform the 'African' into 'a tinged copy of the urban Englishman' (Slaughter 2004: 39). The spatial rearrangement that the master plan had in mind was based on the 'neighbourhood unit'. These units were conceptualized as 'small enough to facilitate acquaintance' but 'large enough to provide a full range of local social, recreational and educational facilities' (White et al. 1948: 46). The spatial arrangement of the units would allow inhabitants to reach their work places quickly, and each unit was supposed to include all amenities necessary for a healthy and good life, such as hospitals, schools, churches, open-air spaces, and community centres.

Despite these rather progressive intentions, the plan had little impact on the lives of most Nairobians. The 1950s and 1960s were characterized by an increasing demand for housing that could no longer be satisfied by the emerging municipal housing estates organized according to the principle of the 'neighbourhood unit'. The master plan's projection of around 270,000 inhabitants by 1975 (White et al. 1948: 42) was reached as early as 1960. As a result, rather than living in municipal housing estates such as Makadara or Jericho, most Nairobians lived in sprawling informal settlements. Instead of expanding according to a clear concept, the city developed in an 'ad hoc manner' (Huchzermeyer 2011: 163), aggravating the problematic housing situation and leading to overcrowding, high rents, crime, and illegal subletting, issues that continued to trouble the housing situation of Nairobi well after Kenya became independent in 1963.

While fears of racial mixture, crime, a chaotic transport sector, and problematic hygienic conditions were the leading drivers of colonial government interventions, the widening potential to siphon off national and international funds became one of the main objectives during Daniel arap Moi's presidency (1978–2002). The structural adjustment reforms imposed on Kenya in the 1980s and 1990s gave politicians and bureaucrats further justification to neglect the housing sector and turn a blind eye to land-grabbing and the illegal construction of houses. It was against the background of the government's unwillingness and inability to develop a feasible housing strategy that high-rise tenement estates started to emerge in the late 1980s and, increasingly, have taken over Nairobi's urban landscape since 2000. By demolishing informal settlements like Kware, the Kenyan government handed over urban space to the speculative interests of Nairobians with the political connections and financial means to invest capital in the housing sector. Whilst the academic and political world discussed the improvement of informal settlements under the banner of 'slum upgrading' (Huchzermeyer 2008), a form of urban 'incrementalism' from above emerged (Silver 2014). Wealthy and well-connected Nairobians successively purchased or grabbed every available piece of land to construct one identical-looking high-rise block after the other, setting off the spectacular transformation of Nairobi's housing sector that a friend of mine once succinctly described by saying that 'when money speaks, even stones listen'.

The suspicious wealth of landlords and the absence of the state

One evening in March 2021, five of us were sitting in Patrick's *kinyozi* (Kiswahili, 'barber shop'), which was one of the main meeting points of a group of male Luo migrants informally known as *jo-pap* (Dholuo, 'people of the playing field', see chapter 4). After a *ja-pap* named Paul had bragged about the size of his girlfriend's buttocks and teased me by saying that he would have brought her along had he felt sure that she would not elope with me, he stood up and made a clicking sound:

> Clack, clack, clack. Have you ever woken up because you hear coins being dropped on the ground? Those are landlords trying to make more money. The sound is heard throughout the plot. Then there was this dead boy they found in front of a plot. His skull was cracked open, but no blood, there was no blood. So, let me ask you, how come that in that plot, you are not allowed to slaughter a chicken?

I had brought a bottle of rum with me, and the alcohol eased the conversation. While we debated whether Paul's stories about coins used in money making rituals and dead bodies without blood were true, Patrick, who was shaving a customer, smiled at me as if to tell me not to worry about witchcraft, Satanism, and sorcery, and expressed his scepticism: 'How can someone living on the first floor hear the sound of a coin being dropped on the sixth or seventh floor? Those are just stories, my friend.' Intrigued by Paul's remarks, however, I asked him who he thought was responsible for these strange practices and who might have consumed the dead boy's blood, to which he replied: 'Witchdoctors sacrificing blood. Let me ask you, how can a man younger than me possess five plots here in Pipeline?'

Scholars have observed rumours juxtaposing witchcraft and the economy in rural and urban areas across sub-Saharan Africa (De Boeck and Plissart 2014 [2004], Geschiere 1997, Sanders, 1999, Simone 2002) and Kenya (Schmidt 2022b, Smith 2008, White 2000: chapter 5). In Pipeline, interpreting economic success as resulting from witchcraft or satanic practices often involved a critique of forms of capital accumulation based on individualistic behaviour, an unwillingness to redistribute wealth, or fast and easy ways of making money (see Elliott 2022), which were contrasted with honest and 'hard work' (Dholuo, *tich matek*) that involved sweat but would not lead to wealth overnight. As most of my male acquaintances and friends were students or employed in Nairobi's formal economy and earning less than 20,000 KSh per month despite working often more than eight hours a day, it was not surprising that rumours about blood-sacrificing landlords gained traction.

Peter Kipsang, a migrant in his 40s from around Kericho, was one of those landlords who had decided to try to make a fortune in Pipeline's booming real estate sector. A friend had introduced us when I had expressed my wish to talk to a landlord. After I had seen and greeted him a few times in one of Pipeline's bars or *nyama choma* places (Kiswahili, 'roasted meat'), Peter invited me to his spacious three-bedroom house in one of the gated non-high-rise estates in Imara Daima, which was within walking distance of Pipeline. Peter had recently moved out of one of Pipeline's rare three-bedroom apartments. With four children and enough money – the monthly profit of his plots was over 500,000 KSh – he had concluded that Pipeline, which he jokingly called a 'manufactory of children', was not the right place to raise his family. They deserved better.

After eating *pilau*, a popular rice dish from the Kenyan coast often served at weddings and funerals, Peter began to narrate how he, a mere employee of a real estate company, had decided to invest in a plot in Pipeline with a friend over twenty years ago: 'Back then, it was still a lot of *mabati* houses, but I saw how my company was making money, and I decided to try my luck. It is good to invest in things that you know.' He bought land not far from the Kenya Pipeline Company housing estate and constructed one of the first plots in Pipeline around the year 2000. Since then, he had managed to construct another plot and was in the process of acquiring land for a third in Mukuru Kwa Njenga ward. When I asked Peter about the paved roads that had replaced most dirt roads in Pipeline ward some years ago, he told me with pride that the landlords had organized this upgrade and that they were also responsible for the connection of the sewage lines, the water supply, and the rubbish disposal. Instead of connecting their plots to the city's water distribution network, most landlords dug a borehole or rented one nearby. The estate's few public dumping sites were notoriously overflowing, and without the private rubbish collection, the estate would otherwise be inundated with waste. The state's near total absence in the area was also demonstrated by the fact that, despite having over 200,000 inhabitants, Pipeline neither had a public school nor a public hospital during the time of my fieldwork. This governmental neglect opened further money making opportunities for private investors such as Peter, who summed up the situation as follows: 'In Kenya, the state doesn't care, you need to take care of everything.'

Peter did not at all strike me as a cold-blooded capitalist. He was welcoming and I felt that he cared about the well-being of this tenants. However, it would be a mistake to romanticize Pipeline's landlords, some of whom owned more than ten plots, and consider them benevolent philanthropists serving the public. Politicians and businessmen, and high-ranking civil servants such as a former commissioner of the Kenyan police, had invested in Pipeline for personal profit. Many of the private clinics and schools were run by people who lacked the necessary qualifications. Nor were landlords and scrupulous quacks specializing in illegal abortions the only actors who viewed Pipeline as a space offering money making opportunities. Police officers took bribes from illegal open-air pool halls and bars, and sex workers from neighbouring estates capitalized on Pipeline's pressured men. Rich Kenyans opened bars and restaurants along Airport North Road that attracted wealthy Kenyans from nearby Kitengela wishing to initiate sexual encounters with newly arrived young female migrants. While the goals of landlords and tenants, police officers and businessmen, as well as sex workers and clients, often clashed, these individuals were equally pragmatic and considered the estate a catalyst for their personal and professional urban plans and careers.

Pipeline as a place of aspiration

When I asked Samuel about estates built according to the guidelines of 'neighbourhood units', he suggested we visit his aunt Marceline in Makadara, an estate 'developed from 1954 onwards as an area where individuals, landlords or employers could build at their own expense along prescribed lines' (Hake 1977: 64). Not far from Pipeline, Makadara is located alongside Nairobi's Jogoo Road, and we arrived after a short ride in a *matatu*. On our way to Marceline's house, we passed dozens of identical one-story buildings. In stark contrast to Pipeline's maze-like architecture, there was ample communal space in front of and next to each house. I was surprised that Samuel greeted and exchanged news with neighbours who were sitting in front of their houses enjoying the cool breeze or washing clothes, a form of neighbourly closeness and warmth that was hard to come by in Pipeline, where such relations were more fleeting and pragmatic, or could even turn hostile if, for instance, an item was stolen. 'You can clearly see that people had a plan here, not like in Pipeline,' Samuel lamented before we were greeted by his aunt, who had taken him in when he arrived in Nairobi. By living in his aunt's house, which his grandfather had also inhabited, Samuel followed in the footsteps of many other urban migrants who expected help from family members when they first came to Nairobi.

Although Samuel had appreciated the neighbourly atmosphere of Makadara, he left his aunt's tidy, spacious, and comfortable house in search of independence and distance from his relative. He took his first step toward independence by sharing a university hostel room with Arthur Omondi, a childhood friend who had come to Nairobi to study for a bachelor's degree in digital marketing. After they had to vacate the university hostels, they pooled resources and moved to a house in Jericho, an estate close to Makadara. In Jericho, which had also been built in the 1950s and radiated the same atmosphere of neigh-bourliness as Makadara, a house-owner sublet one room to Samuel and Arthur for more than 200 per cent of what he had paid for the house, a common exploitative practice in municipal estates where rents had remained relatively cheap. To complicate matters further, most tenancy agreements were given over to relatives, making it almost impossible for migrants to find empty houses. Uncomfortable with the lack of privacy in Jericho, Arthur and Samuel finally decided to move to Pipeline in September 2017. They hired a *mkokoteni* guy (Kiswahili, 'handcart') to help them to transport their few belongings, including a mattress, household utensils, and clothes. Eric, a student friend of Arthur's who had migrated from Nakuru County, had recommended Pipeline as an estate where they could find affordable modern rooms and plenty of cheap food. Unlike Makadara and Jericho, which had problems with violent youth gangs and theft, Pipeline was also known for being one of the safest estates in Nairobi because many of its inhabitants went to and came back from work throughout the night.

When I asked him about his first months in Nairobi, Samuel, whose ancestral home is in Seme but who grew up in Chabera, where his father had been a teacher, laughed while he told me that he had arrived much like any other typical village boy full of high expectations that quickly clashed with reality:

> When I came to Nairobi, I didn't even have a suitcase or backpack. All my stuff was in a *gunia* (Kiswahili, 'large sack normally used for trans-porting food such as maize or potatoes'). Before I arrived, I had thought that in Nairobi, jobs would chase me and not the other way around. I did many odd jobs in the beginning: washing the blood-stained clothes of butchers, *mjengo* (Sheng, 'job on a construction site') and others. But now I am living in Pipeline. That's progress, like in a movie.

Samuel, who had come to Nairobi to study law but had to battle for a while until his family had pooled the resources to allow him to start his course, did not share the middle-class sentiments of Pipeline as a nightmarish place. His opinion was more ambivalent. While aware of some of its problems, Samuel, like most male migrants in Pipeline, viewed the estate as a launching pad for his professional career and as a place where he could satisfy his longing for consumerist commodities, independence, money, and sexual adventures in a relatively anonymous way. Despite this comparatively positive view, Samuel strongly held onto the idea of moving to an estate like Nairobi's Karen, home to famous politicians, well-off Kenyans and rich expatriates, or back to his rural home after completing his studies and establishing himself as a prominent lawyer. For him, like most male migrants I met, Pipeline was a place of transit to a better life.

Imitating the middle-class

The pressure always mounts from the twelfth, the agent appears by the twelfth, we promise to pay by the fifteenth, when the fifteenth comes and you don't have the cash, you go into the dark.

Mark Odhiambo, migrant and ja-pap *from western Kenya*

The most common types of apartments (which many locals often called 'houses') available for rent in Pipeline were single rooms (from roughly 3,500 KSh to 5,000 KSh per month), bedsitters (6,000 to 8,500 KSh), and one-bedroom apartments (9,000 to 15,000 KSh). The number of units per high-rise block varied according to the size of the plot and the type of apartments offered. While Milele Flats, for instance, had slightly over 100 bedsitters, the plot where Samuel and Arthur lived had over 300 single rooms. Both the bedsitters in Milele Flats and the single rooms in the plot where Arthur and Samuel resided were roughly sixteen square metres in size, the standard for most apartments across Pipeline. Despite their similar external appearance, the quality of housing plots offered differed greatly. Recently built plots generally had tiled rooms and steel doors, while many older ones had wooden doors, concrete floors, and poorly maintained latrines. Some older plots had additional problems such as insect and rat infestation, mould, or peeling paint. Water was rationed in most plots and was either available every other day, twice a week, or less. A few remaining *mabati* structures were also still used for housing. At the opposite end of the spectrum, some plots in Fedha – the estate across Outer Ring Road – had lifts, CCTV surveillance and biometric access.

While bedsitters offered the convenience of a private bathroom, their living area was smaller than that of single rooms, whose inhabitants shared bathrooms with the other tenants residing on the same floor. As a result, bedsitters were typically occupied by financially better-off single men and women, or by single parents. Most families without the financial means to rent a one-bedroom apartment tended to occupy single rooms, dividing the space into an eating and living area and an area for sleeping (Mwau 2019). By placing a curtain or a length of cloth across the middle of the room, tenants created a private and a public section, thereby copying the arrangement of domestic space common in rural homes. Since many migrants housed nephews, nieces, cousins, or siblings who had recently migrated to the city to study, look for work, babysit, or assist in the house, the eating and living area was sometimes turned into a second sleeping area during the nights.

When furnishing and decorating their apartments, migrants included as many signs of urban success as possible. Because of the thirst for material goods, their rooms resembled cramped or scaled-down versions of middle-class apartments. In contrast to the inhabitants of houses in Makadara, whose owners tried to make 'a home amid urban decay' (Smith 2019: 9), the inhabitants of Pipeline were not interested in transforming their apartments into permanent homes. They confined themselves to collecting what could be called 'immutable mobiles' (Latour 1986) highlighting different degrees of urban middle-class success: flat-screen televisions, empty bottles of expensive alcohol, ceramic cups and plates, beautiful glasses, fridges, carpets, sofas, tables, chairs, and drinking water dispensers. By occupying specific positions in a hierarchy of commodities finely ranked from cheap soap bars to expensive liquid soaps, from wooden tables with a village flair to modern glass ones, or from small analogue to large digital televisions, these consumer goods, like written rental agreements, employment contracts, and other indexes of formality and order (see Gastrow 2020b), signalled a migrant's position on the ladder of modernity.

Nevertheless, living conditions in Pipeline were far from convenient. Apart from frequent electricity blackouts and water shortages that forced residents to buy water from vendors who illegally tapped into the municipal water supply (Kimari 2021), the relations between tenants and landlords were strained. As most landlords were not interested in being known to their tenants, they delegated the collection of rent and the maintenance of their plots to agencies that employed caretakers and watchmen. This made it hard for tenants to voice complaints directly to the agencies or their landlords, a stark contrast to many other estates in Nairobi where landlords and tenants sometimes lived in the same house or close to one another. The absence of landlords turned caretakers into middlemen who absorbed the complaints of tenants, only to put forward the excuse that their hands were tied by the landlord's decisions.

As the demand for housing was constantly high, tenants who had difficulties finding money to pay the rent could not expect to be treated with leniency.

Electricity could be cut off a few days after the beginning of the month, and after a week or two, tenants might come home from work and find their rooms padlocked, forcing them to seek shelter at a friend's place.[4] If a tenant continued to default, the agency could force open the apartment and remove the tenant's belongings to keep as collateral until the arrears were paid in full (see Huchzermeyer 2011: 215–16). Tenants also had to deal with a range of other issues. For example, due to the density of Pipeline's architecture, apartments on the lower floors received almost no natural light (Njanja 2020); the mobile network was at best unstable; and the lack of ventilation made rooms very hot and humid. Having to leave one's room to get some fresh air or to make a phone call helped to create a rudimentary form of neighbourliness that was often organized along ethnic lines but it seldomly lasted beyond the period during which people lived in the same building. The balconies and corridors became social spaces where women plaited each other's hair, washed clothes and chatted with one another, thereby familiarizing themselves with the newest fashions and hairstyles, rumours, and other useful information. It was along these corridors and on the rooftops that children played football or other games, and tenants engaged in side businesses such as small-scale tailoring. Though social interactions occurred throughout the building, balconies and corridors were almost exclusively the domain of women and children (see also Huchzermeyer 2011: 208–9). This is unsurprising as balconies were not only situated near the archetypical female place – the house – but were also understood as breeding grounds for rumours and gossip, practices that both men and women characterized as female.

The absence of public spaces for unsuccessful men

'Why are you dressed that smart?' I blurted out when I found Samuel sitting on his bed and staring at the wall, wearing a freshly ironed shirt and the trousers of a tailor-made suit. He had quit an internship at a law firm in town a few days before because they had only been paying him 8,000 KSh per month, and his boss had not allowed him to take a day off to take care of his pregnant wife, Immaculate Chepkemei, a migrant from Kericho County who worked as a sales agent for a travel company. Not taking his gaze off the wall, Samuel responded: 'I want to build the impression that I am working.' 'For whom do you intend to build that impression?' I asked, to which Samuel, who had

---

[4]   Though almost all apartments had prepaid electricity meters, most were installed on the ground floors and controlled by the caretakers. Tenants paid for electricity through a gadget plugged into a socket in their apartments, but the meter could be switched off at any time, even if the tenants had purchased electricity in advance.

confessed to me in the weeks before that he felt 'down' and without energy, answered solemnly: 'For myself alone.'

When I first moved to Pipeline, I was fascinated by the speed with which people conducted their business. Everyone appeared to be always on the move. In contrast to many other estates in Nairobi, Pipeline had the atmosphere of a proper urban space. It was loud, chaotic, dense, anonymous, fast, and overcrowded. The streets acted as arteries transporting goods and people from one place to another, and anyone who stood around on the estate's main thoroughfares risked blocking the flow of cars, lorries, moto-taxis, commodities, and people. It took me a while to realize that quite a few unemployed men just roamed around the estate aimlessly, hung out with friends who owned a shop, spent their days indoors watching television, or simply sat around doing nothing, sometimes dressed in their nicest clothes.

In sharp contrast, employed men joined the masses in the early morning to walk to the industrial area or to commute to their places of work in town, only to return late in the evening. Going to and coming home from work was a means to an end during which men engaged in what Erving Goffman called 'civil inattention' (1963: 83–8). They registered the actions of, yet rarely interacted with, a multitude of strangers. When Samuel had landed another internship with a law firm in Nairobi's west, for instance, he left his apartment before seven a.m. and returned at around eight or nine p.m. The only public male social space that Samuel frequented on his way to work was a carriage of the morning train in which a group of male Luo migrants met and shared stories until they arrived in town 30 minutes later, thereby turning their journey to work into a period of entertaining male braggadocio.

Men without work or regular business activities had limited options for socializing in Pipeline, as public spaces that were free for men to use were almost entirely unavailable. While women could socialize on balconies, men either had to stay in the house or spend their dwindling savings to visit a bar, a videogame joint, a pool hall, or a gym (see chapter 5). Due to a lack of financial resources, these options were not available to everyone, and some migrants simply did not have the social network to enjoy such places. When I found Samuel idling in his apartment, for instance, he did not have the money to visit a gym on a regular basis or go to a bar.[5] Pipeline's urban geography

---

5   An alternative I explore in chapter 4 was to reclaim the urban space as a 'playing field' (Dholuo, *pap)*. Behaving as a *ja-pap* turned the vice of failing to embody economic value into a virtue by repudiating the expectation to become economically successful. Such appreciations of wasteful masculinity were probably also responsible for portrayals of Pipeline as a perfect place for single men with enough money to enjoy the estate's bars and engage in sexual adventures. While offering an opportunity

and architecture, as well as the inhabitants' shared aspirations, in other words, excluded unemployed men from public space. To keep their own and others' expectations alive, men without a job or business were pushed to look for money elsewhere if they did not want to remain stuck inside their rooms, hiding their economic failure but risking slowly sinking into depression or being ridiculed as useless by their wives and girlfriends.

Pipeline was not built according to a specific plan. Rather, its genesis depended on investors copying each other, trying to profit from Kenya's ongoing housing crisis. For those landlords who turned Pipeline into one of the world's most densely populated places, the estate thus had mere 'exchange value' (Lefebvre 1996 [1968]: 67–8). Migrants who came to Pipeline were also not interested in transforming the estate into a more humane place. It neither had social spaces open to everyone nor community projects that aimed at improving the living conditions of its inhabitants. Pipeline was a hypercapi-talist place where everyone depended on the capitalist aspirations of someone else. Migrants looked for jobs to make money, landlords wanted to invest their capital, and Kenya's business elite and entrepreneurs needed men who were willing to work in the industrial area or at the airport. This shared understanding of Pipeline as place into which people invested economically but not emotionally made it hard for migrant men and women to feel at home and posed a challenge for politicians who wanted to gain traction with Pipeline's population.

Urban exclusion and the lack of collective action

While working out in the No Mercy Gym on a sunny afternoon, I received a text message from Benson Ouma inviting me for a beer in one of Pipeline's bars. I quickly finished my last set of reps and went straight to the bar, which was less than 25 metres from the gym. Benson, a 31-year-old bank clerk who grew up in a small village close to Maseno in Kisumu County, was already waiting and sipping a Guinness. Enjoying the view into one of Pipeline's urban high-rise canyons and waiting for my cold lager, I started talking about some of the challenges I faced, such as noise, lack of water, fear of collapsing buildings, and electricity black outs. Benson, who was preparing to contest the seat of the Member of the County Assembly of Nairobi representing Kware ward in Kenya's general election in 2022, agreed that these matters were obstacles that justified calling Pipeline a slum, just like Kibera or Mathare, and tried to convince me to cooperate with him on some business projects

---

to enjoy male camaraderie, hanging out in *pap* was frequently described as a waste of time by male friends, girlfriends, and wives.

that would improve the livelihoods of the estate's inhabitants: 'Kibera is not the only slum of Nairobi. That's why I wanted to talk to you. We can start some projects here in Pipeline. We don't have NGOs here.'

Benson's portrayal of Pipeline as a slum without NGOs reminded me of the fact that hundreds of NGOs had tried to improve the livelihoods of the inhabitants of Kibera, one of Nairobi's best-known informal settlements. In contrast, and as a result of 'donor agencies' focus on the global "slum" problem' (Huchzermeyer 2011: 224), Nairobi's emerging high-rise settlements received no attention from the development aid sector. Though I had seen one NGO in Pipeline, I later found out that it was dominated by members of the officially banned but still well-organized *Mungiki* youth gang, who used it as a cover for illegal activities such as extorting protection money from migrants active in the informal economies in Pipeline and Mukuru Kwa Njenga.

After I expressed my agreement with his diagnosis that Pipeline lacked political grassroots organizations, Benson told me about his attempts to raise political awareness among Pipeline's population and tenants interested in political change and improvements to their living conditions. Benson was not only an aspiring politician and the chairman of the ethnically based investment group HoMiSiKi (see chapter 4) but he had also founded two WhatsApp groups: one in which members discussed general political issues and one for tenants living in plots owned by the landlord who owned the plot where Benson lived. In these rather dormant chat groups, he tried to instil a feeling of community by, for instance, addressing group members as 'people of Embakasi South'. He urged members to voice their frustrations, thereby trying to ignite their interest in political change. At the same time, Benson was striving to involve people from the corporate sector in his political aspirations by convincing them to donate money. With that money, Benson could start some projects aimed at improving the livelihood of Pipeline's inhabitants, of which a community hospital was the most ambitious idea. Keeping in mind his voter base, he also planned to direct some of these funds to the members of HoMiSiKi, for whom he wanted to purchase water tanks so that some younger members could start a car wash business.

A quiet and reserved man, Benson did not strike me as a typical Kenyan politician. Though he regularly handed out small sums of money to friends and acquaintances, was a good orator, and knew how to show off his nice clothes and expensive technological gadgets, he sometimes appeared insecure about his political ambitions. After spending more time in Pipeline, however, I realized it was not Benson's character or conduct but rather the urban environment of the estate and its character as a place of transit that had few historically deep kin or kin-like political ties that made his activities appear pointless. Whenever I discussed my living conditions with others by, for instance, trying to convince them that it was my right as a tenant to have water delivered as outlined in the rental agreement, most suggested I should vote with my feet and move to another plot. Some male migrants like Samuel and Arthur even embraced the estate's challenging living conditions as an ordeal on their way to a better life, chiming in with the widespread narrative that if you make it in Nairobi, you can make it everywhere. Benson, I realized, was shouldering an almost impossible task, one that the authors of the 1948 master plan had called the main 'problem of sociology', namely, how to 'convert a conglomerate of individuals into a functioning community' (White et al. 1948: 9).

In light of these ethnographic observations, I refrain from agreeing with Mary Njeri Kinyanjui's diagnosis that economic livelihoods in Nairobi are characterized by a humanistic '*utu-ubuntu* business model' that 'refutes and resists western culture's exaltation of individualism and its veneration of wealth and technology as solutions to human problems' (2019: xiii). Though I observed a few 'grassroots and friendship-based initiatives among tenants' (Huchzermeyer 2011: 246), such as HoMiSiKi or WhatsApp groups in which neighbours shared complaints about the housing conditions, capitalistic, materialistic, and individualistic assumptions about what constitutes success in life dominated the discourse and influenced economic and social practices in Pipeline far more than in any other place in which I have lived. Most male migrants had an opportunistic attitude toward the estate and its residents. They considered Pipeline as a place to advance their economic careers and instil their romantic schemes. Aware of the estate's problematic living conditions and infrastructure, they did not plan to stay in Pipeline forever (Maina and Mwau 2018: 221). Nobody, as Samuel observed once, considered the estate his or her home. Any investment of financial resources or political energy that would not create more money or transform into transportable consumer goods appeared futile to most of my male interlocutors. If the 'neighbourhood unit' of the 1948 master plan was assumed to have the potential to produce an upwardly mobile class of Africans, the dark and poorly ventilated single rooms of Pipeline crammed with consumer goods and indices of success helped reproduce the middle-class aspirations of migrant men and their families by reminding them that a man's stay in Pipeline should be nothing more than a short interlude on his way toward economic success.

The two chapters that follow explore some of the more deplorable economic and social effects of migrants' lack of personal investment in, and their instrumental attitude toward, the estate. By considering Pipeline a place to become economically successful without striving to turn the estate into their home, Pipeline's inhabitants intensified migrant men's pressure to perform well economically. If they did not make money in Pipeline, male migrants had no reason to be there. The expectations of being economically successful and providing for their girlfriends, wives, as well as their urban and rural families, created and exacerbated economic and romantic pressures, leading to a demand for masculine spaces where men could decompress, find new and promising solutions to their problems, or just escape the agonizing experience of constant pressure.

2

Economic Pressure and the
Expectation of Success

Thinking ends in money. (Dholuo, *Paro ogik e pesa*)

Samuel Onyango

As I branched into the street leading to the No Mercy Gym on a sunny morning, I encountered a circle of roughly 100 people. Forcing my way through the crowd, I caught a glimpse of a body lying in the middle of the small crowd. At the end of the street, I could see Carl, Godwin (one of our training partners), and Carl's wife sitting opposite the gym. 'What happened?', I inquired when I reached them, and Carl answered: 'The guy came to fetch water. He wanted to cook for his children, then he collapsed, and it seems that he is dead. There is no pulse.' The crowd was agitated, wondering why it had happened and what should be done. Much of the wild chattering suggested that it must have been Corona. After what struck me as a very long time, a healthcare professional arrived, asked bystanders to stop taking pictures with their phones, checked the body for signs of life, raised his hands to indicate that there was nothing that could be done, and declared the man dead. 'Does anyone know him?', I asked Carl and the others. 'Nobody knows him. We looked through his pockets, but there was nothing apart from some slips from the pawn shop. He had many debts. It seems that he died of pressure.' We continued to discuss the possible identity and fate of the unknown guy who might have died of high blood pressure, excessive stress, or a combination of both. When the crowd began to disperse, we entered the gym and went through our routines as if nothing had happened.

Though life in Pipeline could be anonymous, especially when a recently arrived migrant was not keen on forming social bonds, livelihoods in the estate were, largely as a consequence of widespread economic pressure, influenced by a myriad of social obligations between relatives, friends, and colleagues (see Shipton 2007). These landscapes of entrustment, which were reproduced by a multitude of transactions across Pipeline, Nairobi, and the whole of Kenya, had massive effects on the estate's infrastructure and how migrants socialized. Beneath the smooth flow of daily transactions, not only of money but also of sexual favours, words, food, and other forms of hospitality, lay a carefully balanced web of latent economic and social obligations whose threads crisscrossed social, spatial, and ethnic boundaries. The flow of money, goods, and promises organized relations between friends, family members, neighbours, and colleagues. While migrants came to Pipeline with the aspiration to progress economically as individuals or individual families, economic and social pressures would form obligations to others. It was indeed hard to find a migrant who was not a debtor to some and a creditor to others.

Many debts and social obligations remained dormant until a situation forced male migrants to claim them. The measures put into place to curb the spread of COVID-19 created such a situation during which many male migrants felt compelled to try to make use of some of these dormant obligations by asking for a favour or demanding repayment. The sudden increase in these demands had dramatic social effects. An increase in social atomization, coupled with an overburdening of the nuclear family, led to a spike in gender-based violence and mistrust between spouses, neighbours, and friends. Financial obligations, in other words, not only created and maintained social relations, but also threatened them. In an environment where 'everyone was crying', as a friend phrased it, it was difficult for people to ask for money successfully. The pandemic had equipped everyone with a handy excuse to reject requests, and hence it was hard to be sure who was sincere about his or her inability to help. In the end, everyone could blame COVID-19. The most drastic economic change was a rush toward formal loans offered by banks, shop owners, credit sharks, pawn shops and, most importantly, mobile loan apps (Donovan and Park 2022). Landscapes of informal social entrustment transformed into landscapes of formal economic debt (see Shipton 2010).[1] Unsurprisingly, those offering loans were well aware of the local importance of pressure. An advertisement for Kenya Commercial Bank's mobile loan made the connection clear: 'Need cash? *Usitense!*' (Kiswahili, 'Don't tense' or 'Don't feel pressured'), advice that no longer applied to the man who died of pressure just up from the gym.

Money, pressure, and expectations

Despite its analytical potential, and in contrast to buzz words such as poverty or economic marginalization used by politicians, aid agencies, and NGOs to formulate political claims, pressure as a factor has largely been ignored by

---

[1] These formal debt relations were not treated in a purely instrumental or impersonal way. Employees of mobile loan companies, for instance, reminded debtors of their patriotic duties toward other Kenyans or pressured them to accept loans from friends.

scientists and policy-makers alike. This is surprising, given that the concepts of aspiration and stress have been receiving increasing attention from anthropologists (Appadurai 2004, see Izugbara and Egesa 2020 for men in Nairobi, and Di Nunzio 2019: 82–3 for a recent critique), the development aid sector (Haushofer and Fehr 2014), and the discipline of development economics (Genicot and Ray 2020). In an attempt to fill this scholarly gap, chapters 2 and 3 zoom in on how the feeling of being under pressure emerged at the interface of the economic, the romantic and the social, and how it reproduced prevalent notions of masculinity and male success among migrant men in Pipeline.

Although male migrants sometimes blamed greedy politicians as well as corrupt police officers and employers for their lack of economic success, they felt that these external factors were ultimately beyond their control. Instead of critiquing, or even attempting to improve, the wider Kenyan political-economic constellation, migrant men situated the cause of their inability to meet economic expectations inside of their most intimate social relations. Be it rural kin who asked for remittances, girlfriends who wanted to be taken out for dinner, or wives who demanded their husbands find jobs despite the lack of opportunities, male migrants' economic misfortunes were aggravated by what others expected of them. The gap between their economic situation and their own and others' expectations was an existential challenge that created sometimes almost unbearable somatic reactions such as sleeplessness, depression, hypertension, increased aggressiveness, ulcers, and suicidal thoughts. During the pandemic, men in Pipeline found it increasingly difficult to succeed in 'balancing on the edge of a knife between success and failure, between maintaining an affective sense of forward momentum in their everyday lives, and sinking into a sense of stagnation' (Fast et al. 2020: 1). As an effect of their inability to provide for their families, men's self-esteem diminished. More and more male migrants felt that they were no longer of use to anyone.

The concept of expectation helps analyze men's fear of their expendability caused by the experience of pressure because it straddles the normative and the epistemic, the individual and the social, as well as the moral and the ethical. While many male migrants believed that society at large, as well as their most intimate others, held the opinion that they should (normative dimension) and will be (epistemic dimension) successful providers, they also wanted (ethical dimension) and felt obliged to (moral dimension) have economic success. Migrant men and women had internalized the expectation that men should be economically successful, or at least stable, through decades of being told that education and migration would turn dependent boys into providing husbands and fathers. This expectation of economic success exacerbated feelings of pressure and individual failure. The fear of being unable to meet personal, familial, and public expectations created a fertile ground for the emergence of practices for depressurizing and for pretending to be successful that momentarily alleviated the negative feeling of pressure without permanently changing its cause.

Many male migrants embraced forms of short-term depressurization by resorting to activities provided by financially capable investors who had realized the economic potential of pressure-releasing valves. Alcohol, betting on football games, dancing to the newest *ohangla* music, watching movies and TV shows the whole day, smoking weed, spending time in the gym, taking painkillers and other pills, engaging in male-to-male and gender-based violence against their wives, or having sex with sex workers were among the most common forms of letting off steam among male migrants in Pipeline. Migrant men also engaged in what I call 'practices of pretence' (see Archambault 2017) that allowed them to pretend to already be wealthy. Contrary to male migrants' intentions, practices of pretence that 'simulated' wealth (Lockwood 2020: 46) tended to increase pressure because they led to expectations that spiralled out of control, which was one reason why Samuel called them 'acts of bravado'. Since most migrant men pretended to be better-off, smarter, stronger, or wealthier than they were, the economic, social, and romantic expectations of friends, spouses, and relatives increased even more.

Practices trying to attenuate the experience of pressure involved the need to acquire, spend, and invest money. Migrant men needed money to present themselves and act as capable providers and breadwinners. The extent to which money defined masculinity and encompassed other values in Pipeline becomes manifest in a proverb Samuel mentioned when pondering his lack of economic progress: *Paro ogik e pesa* (Dholuo, 'Thinking ends in money'). Only money's 'generative potential' (Green 2019: 109) could permanently reduce pressure and bring planning and structure into a male migrant's life. With money, men could give their daily lives *form* (Sheng, 'plan, agenda'), or, as another male migrant from western Kenya phrased it: 'Money is the denominator, money is everything, other than God, money is the second thing, [...] *kionge pesa, to ionge ngima*' (Dholuo, 'if you don't have money, you don't have a life'). Every migrant man in Pipeline was thus judged and valued against the amount of money he had or, at least as often, pretended to have.

Aspirations and landscapes of debt

When I met up with Samuel and Cliff Ocholla, another migrant from western Kenya, at a corner close to Milele Flats on a sunny August morning in 2019, I had no idea what ordeal was awaiting me. All I knew was that we were going to Athi River, a small industrial town close to Nairobi, to collect some sacks of potatoes, and that this was to be the beginning of a business collaboration between Cliff and Samuel. Cliff had experience of distributing potatoes wholesale in Pipeline's informal economy, and a friend of Samuel's called Barbara oversaw a factory in Athi River where different vegetables and potatoes were sorted and packed. For a small fee, Barbara would allow Samuel to channel off a few sacks of potatoes for 1,500 KSh each. Cliff and Samuel would then sell each sack for 3,000 KSh to people preparing chips in Pipeline.

Arriving at the factory, we encountered around ten men waiting in front of the gate, still expecting to be called in for a casual job for the day, a common practice throughout Kenya. Upon entering her office, Barbara greeted us and then, to our surprise, gave us overalls and empty sacks and led us into a large hall where workers were sorting and packing potatoes and cabbages. Pointing to massive heaps of potatoes at the other end of the hall, Barbara told us we could collect our potatoes from there. When we got closer to the potato heaps, it dawned on us that we were going to have to search them for usable discards, as they had already been sorted by the factory workers. While none of the potatoes looked appealing, we worked out which ones were still edible. After all, they were going to be made into chips, so their appearance was unimportant. Eight long hours later, we had filled eight sacks, heaved them onto a handcart, hauled it outside the factory, where we waited for the friend whom was coming to collect us. After loading the vehicle, I sat in front with the driver, and Samuel and Cliff lay down on top of the potato sacks. However, before we had even turned onto the main highway, we were pulled over by the police, who wanted to charge us with two offences: transporting commercial goods in a private vehicle and violating laws regulating the safe transport of passengers. Samuel bribed the police officers with 2,000 KSh to prevent the vehicle from being impounded and the driver being arrested.

When I met Samuel the next evening, he looked devastated. Cliff had sold the sacks of potatoes without a problem, but upon passing a betting shop, he decided to try to double the profit, as the extra money would enable him to pay off his debts. Unfortunately, he lost the bet. Enraged by Cliff's action, Samuel called a few friends and went to Cliff's house to take some of his household property to regain his own share of the potato sale. Upon entering the house, however, he saw that Cliff had already sold most of his furniture. Cliff then told Samuel that his wife was pregnant and pleaded with Samuel to give him some time to find the money. Pitying his friend whose ancestral home was close to his own, Samuel decided to let things be for now and focus on finding another way to pay back his wife the 10,000 KSh she had lent him to start the potato business.

A few days later, Samuel asked me round to discuss a way forward. While the potato business with Cliff had not succeeded, he felt that selling chips was a good idea. He had established the links to Athi River and starting the business would not require much capital if we did it together. All we needed was a fryer (19,000 KSh), a screen to sell the chips (6,000 KSh), and a cutter to slice the potatoes (4,500 KSh). Moreover, Samuel had already identified a spot where we could tap into an illegal electricity line for an informally negotiated monthly fixed rate. I agreed that the spot was well-chosen, especially in the long-term, as some plots were being constructed nearby. We could sell the machines at a minor loss if the business failed. If the business succeeded, we would split the profit. We decided to try it, bought the equipment, and opened our outlet a day before I left for a conference in Germany. My presence caused curiosity, and we had underestimated the work involved, but customers did buy our chips. Stepping onto the plane to Germany, I was confident that the business would succeed.

A few days before I returned to Pipeline, Samuel told me that he had been forced to close. Electricity had been off for a week, and he had not saved enough money to cope with the blackout. He had handed over the equipment to Eric, the migrant from Nakuru County who had advised Samuel and Arthur to move to Pipeline and sold chips adjacent to his vegetable shop. As his own equipment had been forcefully taken by some of his creditors, he could make good use of ours. Samuel agreed that Eric, who did not have enough money to buy the machines, would pay Samuel half his daily profit until the debt had been cleared. A week later, we realized that Eric had stored the equipment in the back of his shop because the price of potatoes had risen sharply, making selling chips unprofitable. 'I can't raise the price of chips; people won't buy them,' he explained. As Eric could no longer pay Samuel because his profits had declined dramatically and Samuel had not yet found a willing buyer for the equipment, Samuel was forced to take a loan from a mobile money loan app to repay his wife, who was under pressure to settle the loan she had taken from her *chama* (Kiswahili, 'savings group'). Although only two men had decided to invest in a business, around a dozen people suddenly found themselves involved in a network of debts: Cliff, Samuel, Eric, Immaculate, myself, the mobile money loan app and its debt collectors, Cliff's pregnant wife, Barbara, and the driver who had helped us to transport the potatoes. While everyone had got involved in the business in an attempt to reduce their day-to-day pressures, the result had only intensified their economic problems.

Samuel's failed business offers important insights into Pipeline's economy. First, migrant men did not lack what Arjun Appadurai called the 'capacity to aspire' (2004). If anything, their aspirations were too high. Becoming a small business-owner was a widely shared goal among male migrants (Dolan and Gordon 2019), and everyone could narrate detailed business plans and ideas with ease. Successful business models were available and could be copied, but the fundamental problem was the lack of capital. Second, even if capital was available, hopes were often shattered by external factors that could not be controlled, such as corrupt policemen, an unexpected increase in the price of potatoes, or a global pandemic. Third, as illustrated by Eric's inability to translate the price increase of potatoes into a price increase of his chips, Pipeline's economy was a 'zero-balance economy' (Donovan and Park 2019). Customers could not risk incurring what could be called 'marginal losses' (Guyer 2004). Even a one Kenyan Shilling increase in the price of an egg caused concern among customers, and entrepreneurs like Eric had to persevere through hard times without increasing prices by, for example, diluting the tomato sauce with water or reducing the number of chips per bag. Last, failures to transform one's 'capacity to aspire' (Appadurai 2004) created personal problems that were integral to the creation of Pipeline's landscapes of debt.

Migratory expectations and the experience of pressure

> When I was in school, I was told, '*Bwana* (Kiswahili, 'boss, sir, friend'), you have done mechanical engineering and you have advanced (Kiswahili, *umefanya mechanical engineering na umeadvance*), you will be paid a hundred and twenty thousand.' Yes, I was told that *bwana*, you are going to be paid one twenty (Dholuo, *in idhi chuli one twenty*).
>
> *Joel Opiyo, migrant and* ja-pap *from Migori County*

After being forced to leave Pipeline due to the COVID-19 pandemic in March 2020, I joined an interdisciplinary research project on the economic effects of the pandemic. Trying to understand how the pandemic influenced the lives of Nairobians living in different parts of the city, three of our long-term research assistants interviewed around a total of 150 people living in Pipeline, the wealthier estate Kileleshwa, and the well-known informal settlement of Kibera (Stephan et al. 2021).[2] During the same time, I cooperated with a group of political scientists and anthropologists, the main goal being to take a serious look at economic actors' experience of pressure (Wiegratz et al. 2020). Respondents and our daily interlocutors expressed that they felt 'stressed', 'depressed', 'under pressure', that things 'disturb their mind' (Dholuo, *chapo paro*), that the 'world weighs heavy on them' (Dholuo, *piny pek*, see also Schmidt 2017a), that they 'think too much' (Dholuo, *paro medre*, see also

---

[2]   Comparing Pipeline and Kibera was particularly illuminating. When we asked interview respondents to rate their feeling of pressure on a scale from one to ten, respondents in Pipeline reported higher scores than those living in Kibera, alluding to a lack of reliable, long-term kin- and friendship networks, pressure from mobile loan apps and the expectations of rural relatives, among other things (see Yose 1999). Considering that inhabitants of Pipeline were economically better off than those in Kibera, this was a surprising finding.

Osborn et al. 2021, *paro mang'eny*, 'many thoughts'), or that 'all ways are completely blocked' (Dholuo, *yore odinore te*), among other things. Male migrants in Pipeline juxtaposed these and similar discursive descriptions of stress, pressure, and depression with reports about somatic symptoms such as fatigue, restlessness, insomnia, headaches, high blood pressure, and ulcers.

Unpacking migrant men's experience of pressure and their 'idioms of distress' (Nichter 1981) is important because they lived a life that could too easily be portrayed as bordering on a successful middle-class life in terms of the amount of money some had at their disposal. With the average formal wage being around 20,000 KSh or slightly less, many policy standards would not deem Pipeline's inhabitants as poor. However, with monthly rent, electricity and water costing around 5,000 KSh, food at least 2,000 KSh per week for a family of four, and transportation often requiring another substantial share of a man's salary, 20,000 KSh was not enough to quench male migrants' thirst for middle-class success and economic development. It was not surprising that some male migrants quit their formal jobs to try their luck in Pipeline's informal economy. They no longer lost time and money on transport and could mingle with other migrant men during the day. After all, they had not migrated from the village to Nairobi to suffer and barely make ends meet.

Joel Opiyo, 25-year-old migrant from Migori County, is a good example. A mechanical engineer, he had come to Nairobi a few years ago with salary expectations hovering around 120,000 KSh. He had been lucky to find a job in the nearby industrial area during the COVID-19 pandemic but his salary was only around 16,000 KSh per month. As he had to pay roughly 6,000 KSh for his single room and electricity, 6,000 KSh for his Higher Education Loan Board loan, and buy food for himself and his girlfriend, his monthly salary was almost consumed by necessary expenses. However, known as employed in his rural home and among friends in Pipeline, he was often asked to buy drinks for *jo-pap* or to contribute financially to the education of his younger siblings.

Most male migrants, more so those with jobs or businesses such as Joel, did not go hungry. Nonetheless, the expectations they were confronted with exceeded the bare minimum, such as the provision of food and rent. The experience of pressure, in other words, was not an effect of a migrant man's absolute monetary wealth but resulted from an assessment of an imbalance between, on the one hand, his and other actors' economic expectations and, on the other, the ability to fulfil them. In contrast to mere stress, pressure was furthermore based on an underlying attachment to its cause. Migrant men were not simply annoyed, overwhelmed, or stressed by their and others' expectations. They were under pressure to meet these expectations because they agreed that while quantitatively unreasonable, they were qualitatively justified. After all, it was a migrant man's job to provide and carve out a good life for his rural and urban family. Joel, for instance, did want to help pay his siblings' school fees, but what was requested of him was just too much to manage.

Two types of expectations were particularly pressure-inducing for migrant men in Pipeline. They felt their families in Nairobi, as well as their rural kin, expected their essential needs satisfied as well as a continuous display of newly purchased signs of economic progress and success. Whenever I ate at a friend's house, for instance, his wife would remind him to buy a new dining table in a joking but serious way. From the wife's perspective, welcoming guests in a house without a beautiful table was inappropriate.[3] On the other hand, it was hard for men to save money as three 'crisis-inducing financial burdens' (Smith 2017: 96) repeatedly demanded large lump sums of money: school fees for one's own children and those of relatives, healthcare emergencies, and funeral costs. Male migrants felt that these obligations were exclusively placed on them as household heads and were significantly larger if the man was the first-born son, like Joel. Focusing on the experiences of pressure thus helps us to grasp the intimate links between life's temporal, sensory, and spatial dimensions. Circulating economic deadlines, such as the payment of school fees or the monthly rent, as well as social and romantic expectations, created an encompassing atmosphere of pressure exacerbated by a dense, anonymous, noisy, and congested urban architecture and geography neglected by the Kenyan state (Rose and Fitzgerald 2022).

As most migrant men depended on their salaries and profits, or on money being distributed to them by relatives or friends who had jobs or successful businesses, any economic recession and the resulting unemployment and business meltdown caused serious financial throwbacks. The example of Victor Omollo indicates what could happen to a male migrant's life in Pipeline if he lost his job or if his business collapsed. Although his story is drastic, most respondents faced similar problems during the period of our interviews, coinciding with the time when the Kenyan economy was hit hardest by the COVID-19 pandemic (June to November 2020), which threatened to derail Pipeline's 'zero-balance economy' (Donovan and Park 2019). In the wake of the pandemic, pressure became almost unbearable.

[3]   Such female demands clashed with migrant men's pride in being able to survive with makeshift furniture and simple utensils. When moving in with a girlfriend after living alone or together with other male migrants, men had to change their perspective on what commodities counted as signs of economic progress. While male migrants who lived alone or with other men could use their money on clothes, alcohol, and electronic gadgets, many men who had begun to live with their girlfriends or wives suddenly faced different demands, such as the expectation to buy expensive furniture.

A pressured man

There is pressure in rent, pressure in what we will eat, pressure on what people will eat back in the village, my mother and father, now that they are aged, they no longer work, so, all that is pressure.

Victor Omollo

Victor Omollo was born near Asembo, a small and quiet market centre along the shores of Lake Victoria, roughly 30 kilometres from Bondo. Like many rural *jo*-Luo, he had dropped out of school before finishing his primary education due to financial burdens. The second eldest son in a monogamous family, and with four siblings, Victor described his family as living in poverty and narrated how he had to take on responsibilities early in life. Instead of enjoying a carefree childhood and youth, he had to look for casual jobs, such as herding cattle, to assist his parents and younger siblings. After spending some time in the homestead of an economically better-off family friend, Victor began working as a moto-taxi driver in the area around Asembo. This brought him into contact with well-off migrants whom he picked up and transported to the main road at night so that they were not confronted with financial demands of other villagers. Victor shared his challenges and dreams with one of these customers, who subsequently invited him to learn how to repair cars and lorries in a small town not far from the Ugandan border. Having mastered the techniques involved, Victor returned to Asembo and found a job as a car mechanic. After repeatedly being denied payment by his employer, Victor became increasingly frustrated with his life in the village, where his progress was stunted. Luckily, friends told him that a company in Nairobi was looking for mechanics to maintain their fleet of lorries. After taking a bus to Nairobi, he found a place to stay in an informal settlement along Mombasa Road and began to work for the company. Shortly after settling in Nairobi, Victor married Elizabeth, a Kisii woman from Nyamira County, and they moved to a house in Pipeline in 2016. Life was good, Victor had made progress, and his development (Dholuo, *dongruok*) was visible.

Victor was almost 30 when I met him for the first time in 2019. This tall, physically intimidating and boisterous man, whose smooth voice could be misleading, was living with Elizabeth and their three children and worked as a forklift operator for a cargo company at JKIA. Like many other migrants working at the airport, or in Nairobi's transport or hotel sector, Victor was hit hard by the measures enacted to curb the spread of the COVID-19. Soon after the pandemic reached Kenya on the 13 March 2020, all inbound and outbound flights were banned, schools, hotels, restaurants closed, and all of Nairobi went into near-lockdown. In the first two months of the pandemic, Victor's salary was slashed by 50 per cent, and soon after he was asked to work only two or three times a month. When my long-term research assistant Jack Omondi Misiga interviewed Victor in July 2020,[4] his savings had been wiped out, and he was surviving by relying on friends and members of the HoMiSiKi investment group (see chapter 4). His wife had also been forced to close her business selling clothes due to a lack of capital and the need to buy food and necessities for the family.

Victor summarized his problematic situation by concluding that the amount of pressure he experienced was 'comparable to the distance between heaven and earth'. His carefully balanced life had been derailed by the pandemic; he was unable to meet the expectations of his landlord, his wife, his children, his creditors, and his rural kin. This forced him to adjust mundane day-to-day practices. As he owed money to several shops and food vendors, he had to vary his walking routes to try to avoid being seen by his creditors. The relationship with his wife had deteriorated in tandem with his economic decline, and he reported that he had stopped smiling when his children were around because he feared that they would approach him and ask for money to buy chips or sweets. In an attempt to force Victor to pay the rent, the landlord had not only threatened to throw him out but also disconnected the electricity.[5] To avoid being locked out of the house, he constantly had to plead with the caretaker and ask for more time to find money. He was also under increasing pressure from his rural kin as he could no longer send remittances and couldn't spare the money to buy airtime to call them. Victor had to choose between buying food for his urban family or phoning his kin back home. Moreover, he had taken out loans using different mobile loan apps, whose employees were either calling or sending him text messages almost daily to remind him to repay what

---

[4]   Because I could not travel to Kenya during the first months of the COVID-19 pandemic, Jack Misiga conducted the qualitative interviews for the project on the economic effects of the pandemic. Of the 50 respondents he interviewed in July and August 2020, seventeen were interviewed again in November or December of the same year. In addition to the interviews on the pandemic, I rely on seven one-on-one interviews with men working out in gyms, six interviews with men who betted on football games regularly, six biographical interviews with *jo-pap,* and roughly a dozen interviews with men and women focusing on gender relations in Pipeline. While most interviews were between 60 and 90 minutes long, some of the *jo-pap* interviews lasted three or more hours. The interviews were conducted in Dholuo, Kenyan Swahili, Sheng, and English. They were audio-recorded, and then transcribed and translated by my research assistant Isabella Achieng Oluoko. Due to my knowledge of Kiswahili and Dholuo, I was able to doublecheck and, if necessary, adjust the translations.

[5]   Disconnecting electricity forced tenants without solar-powered lights to use candles, which made neighbours aware they had not paid their rent. By inducing feelings of shame, landlords thereby increased pressure on their tenants. In an aspirational place like Pipeline, nobody wanted to appear poor.

he had borrowed. When the debt collectors of one mobile loan company who were, as he phrased it, 'waiting with an open mouth to devour me', called while Victor was sitting with other *jo-pap,* one of them grabbed the phone and told the debt collector that Victor had died in a road accident and that his corpse was in the city mortuary. If anything, Victor's friend suggested, the mobile loan company should contribute to the funeral expenses. To make matters worse, monetary flow in and out of two financial cooperative groups had run dry due to the pandemic, and friends were increasingly hesitant to help. As Victor put it, 'ninety-nine per cent of them are no longer there, it is only one per cent that has remained.' The situation so intensified pressure on Victor that he had to ask his family to leave him alone when he was at home so that he could sleep for long hours.

When re-interviewed in November 2020, Victor and his first-born son had moved to a house in Fedha, on the other side of Outer Ring Road, leaving behind his wife and the other two children. He had a more regular working schedule that had reduced the economic pressure on him. Despite this financial 'recovery', which also allowed him to support Elizabeth and the children, he had decided that things had become too much with his wife and that he would never return to his marriage. Pressure, in other words, had destroyed his family.

Some statistical observations

The vast majority of the 50 respondents whom my research assistant Jack Misiga interviewed for the interdisciplinary research project on the economic effects of the COVID-19 pandemic were migrants. Thirty-two were male and eighteen were female. Slightly over half of the respondents were ethnically Luo, the others were Kisii, Kamba, Kikuyu, and Luhya. The average age was 30 (22 to 55), and 35 identified as married (one polygamist), four as divorced or separated, and eleven as unmarried.[6] Thirty-nine had children, and four were single parents (with an average of 1.87 children across the sample). The average household comprised 3.25 members, and twenty households sheltered at least one relative who did not belong to the nuclear family. Twelve respondents were involved in Pipeline's informal economy, twelve were formally employed, and nine engaged in informal labour arrangements.

---

6   The high number of people who self-identified as married could lead to the conclusion that respondents perceived their romantic life rather positively, which would be an incorrect assumption (see chapter 3). Moreover, self-identifying as married did not necessarily mean that relatives knew about the relationship or that bride-wealth had been paid. More often than not, couples simply began to self-identify as married once they were living or raising children together.

Many migrants, however, alternated between formal and informal working arrangements or added a small business to their formal jobs. This diversity was an effect of Pipeline's volatile economy. Migrants felt that they had to rely on different income-generating activities so that they still had access to cash if their main strategy failed. The livelihood activities of the respondents included being a security guard, a bouncer, a *boda-boda* driver, a shop assistant, a teacher, a data clerk, an owner of a child day care centre, working in a café, owning a grocery store, selling chips, or trying to get day jobs in the industrial area. Of the seventeen migrants without stable income-generating activities, only one did not blame the COVID-19 pandemic for their situation. Unsurprisingly, considering Kenya's transformation into a 'debt society' (Kusimba 2021: 45), 38 respondents reported having debts ranging from bank and mobile loans, soft loans at shops, to money taken from a merry-go-round or other such financial self-help groups. Our sample of 50 Pipeline residents thus corroborates the perception of the estate as a place for young families with a migratory background who had aspired to start a promising life in the city but were struggling to meet their own and others' expectations of economic success.

Most migrants felt that their economic and social life had deteriorated massively due to the COVID-19 pandemic. They reported incidents that spoke of increasing social atomization and mounting levels of pressure that had become almost unbearable. In addition to the problems of paying rent, and electricity and water being cut off, respondents told us about deteriorating relations with rural kin and neighbours, collapsing investment and saving groups, restlessness, taking long walks through Pipeline to avoid spending time with their families, headaches, sleeplessness, keeping phones turned off to avoid calls from debt collectors, the feeling that friends from the city were not to be entrusted with personal problems and frustrations, skipping meals, shaving off their hair to avoid having to go to a salon, and an increase in gender-based violence. One migrant woman mentioned a neighbour whose husband had choked her until she had passed out, and another reported that her husband slept with a knife under his pillow to instil fear in her and their children.

In light of the widespread feelings of pressure and collapsing landscapes of social obligations, one might assume that male migrants would have taken their frustrations to the street, joining some of the protests organized in Nairobi's CBD against the economic consequences of the COVID-19 lockdown measures. However, instead of contributing to political mobilization, the dire economic situation and the conflict between costly practices of depressurizing and the need to meet expectations of success led to intensified fights and arguments between family members. The wives of some *jo-pap,* for instance, had to deal with their husbands' growing aggression, which often caused fights with other migrant men in bars and on the streets, their increasing alcohol consumption with other *jo-pap*,[7] as well as their failure to provide for their families. In response, some decided to make use of what one wife of a *ja-pap* called her 'hidden mind' (Kiswahili, *akili zingine hidden*), referring to the common practice of asking one's husband for more money than was actually needed to buy something and keeping the change. However, this practice sowed the seeds for further mistrust when husbands began to suspect that their wives were using the money for unnecessary purchases. Instead of bringing families together, ongoing expectations of success coupled with the challenging economic situation further intensified migrant men's pressure to provide, enhanced the mistrust inside families, and compelled male migrants to pretend that they were already or soon would be financially successful.

Practices of pretence as acts of bravado

Bravado, 1a: blustering swaggering conduct, b: a pretence of bravery, 2: the quality or state of being foolhardy.

Merriam-Webster Dictionary

When I landed in Nairobi in February 2020 after spending Christmas at home, I realized I had forgotten the key to my apartment. Unable to get hold of Arthur, to whom I had given my spare key, I sent Samuel a text message asking him about our friend's whereabouts. While I was waiting for my luggage, Samuel called to tell me that a group of police officers had stormed their apartment a few hours ago. They had found Arthur in possession of a stolen phone and a detailed map of Pipeline that I had asked him to draw. The police officers had accused Arthur of being the mastermind behind the theft of a box of expensive smartphones from a warehouse and had confiscated the phone as well as the map that Arthur allegedly had used to navigate the maze that is Pipeline. Despite Samuel's pleas, the policemen had taken Arthur to the police station and thrown him into a cell that had previously been a pit latrine. Though Samuel and Eric had managed to pool 8,000 KSh to pay the bail, Arthur would only be released the next morning, with the order to return to the police station for further interrogation.

---

[7] In an environment where one beer cost as much as a meal for an entire family, buying alcohol for oneself or for others was an ambivalent form of conspicuous consumption or 'conspicuous redistribution' (Smith 2017: 18-19) inside each male's peer group (see chapter 4).

When Arthur returned to the police station the day after he had been released, I accompanied him, partly out of curiosity and partly because I felt somewhat to blame. After all, the police officers had used the map I had asked Arthur to draw as evidence of his guilt. On our way to the *matatu* stage, Arthur spotted a pair of used leather shoes, went to the vendor, and returned to me with a broad smile and his new shoes: 'Only 1,000 *bob*' (Sheng, 'Kenyan Shillings'). Not knowing that Arthur would be let off the hook, I felt that he should have saved the money. I asked him if he thought buying these shoes with his remaining money had been a good idea, to which he responded: 'Of course, I will wear these shoes when I am rich.'

This incident is another example illustrating the drastic influence that external and, to a large degree, uncontrollable factors had on the lives of male migrants in Pipeline. Arthur had done nothing wrong. He had simply bought a used phone that turned out to be stolen. Yet, within an hour after being arrested, he found himself in a dirty cell being bitten by mosquitoes, his phone confiscated, and with new social obligations toward Eric and Samuel. However, the fact that Arthur purchased new shoes with his last money gives me the opportunity to elaborate on how practices of pretence helped migrant men to simulate success in front of others, whereby they simultaneously convinced themselves of their future economic achievements. Arthur was far from the only male migrant who spent his meagre resources on expensive consumer goods such as an Apple Magic Mouse or a tailor-made suit. These and other commodities, which often cost more than a migrant man's monthly income, did more than match their consumerist desires and signal their economic success to others. Talismans of future success, they also enabled male migrants to cling to their own migratory dreams and expectations.

Purchasing consumer goods that they could not actually afford was not the only way male migrants tried to convince themselves and others of the certainty of their financial prowess and their ability to comply with the ideal image of 'a hardworking, focused, fashionably dressed attractive young man' (Spronk 2012: 187). Young men working out in gyms, for instance, took pictures in which they held weights that were too heavy for them to perform a proper lift. In these cases, other gym members helped to lift the weights to the perfect position so that a photograph could be taken quickly. Others used photographs of a friend's child to seduce women by portraying themselves as responsible fathers, or took pictures in front of an expensive motorcycle or car and pretending that it was their own. These practices resemble the 'photographic self-creations' observed by Heike Behrend on the Kenyan coast, where actors used photographic self-portraits to communicate their 'true' selves to others (Behrend 2002). To identify the social factors that produced these and comparable practices of pretence, it is helpful to know a bit more about

Arthur's biography, a poignant example of what happens when rural expectations and individual achievements become unsynchronized.

Born close to Chabera in 1995, Arthur came from one of the area's more affluent families. In contrast to most children, for instance, Arthur went to a private academy for his primary school education. Due to his outstanding performance in the Kenya Certificate of Primary Education exams, a nationwide test conducted in all primary schools, Arthur was invited to a prestigious boarding school in Nakuru, from which he emerged with the highest score in all subjects in the exams for his Kenya Certificate of Secondary Education (KCSE). This gave him the chance to choose from the most respected university courses, thus promising him a well-paying job and financial success. Being a remarkably good student, Arthur was the subject of much celebration when he returned to Chabera. Both his family and the rural community were expecting miracles from one of their brightest members. According to a linear understanding of the path from educational to financial success still prevalent in rural western Kenya, his KCSE results had secured his own and the economic future of his rural kin. Fuelled by his educational achievements, and looking forward to a successful life in the city full of romantic adventures and economic success, Arthur began to study digital marketing at the Jomo Kenyatta University of Science and Technology, a course that combined economics, statistics, marketing, and computer sciences, which meant it was promising in terms of employment opportunities in Kenya's booming financial technology sector.

Arthur had yet to graduate when I got to know him in 2019. Already under economic pressure, he took the advice of Samuel and other friends and applied for a job at a supermarket in Nairobi's CBD in 2020. When the employer saw Arthur's KCSE certificate, he laughed and told him to stop wasting time and finish his university degree. Not only was Arthur effectively overqualified for the job as a cashier, the erstwhile employer also expected more of Arthur. By that time, some people in Chabera had begun to spread rumours that Arthur could have only achieved his KCSE results by cheating. Although Arthur had failed to meet the expectations of some, he, and those who knew him better and could therefore vouch for his intelligence, still believed in his potential. According to him, and his close friends and family, he still had the opportunity to prove the others wrong. To use his own words, he would start wearing those nice leather shoes when he was rich.

When I asked Samuel what he thought about practices of pretence that more often than not involved deception or lies, he told me that migrant men living in Pipeline were inclined to engage in what he called 'acts of bravado' whereby he hinted at three characteristic traits. First, they were based on a superficial demonstration of an alleged underlying financial success. Second, these acts risked being discovered, which, third, made them dangerous and potentially foolish. Despite Samuel's critique, which mirrored how women discussed migrant men's behaviour, he too engaged in practices of pretence, such as walking around in expensive suits when he was unemployed (see chapter 1). Individual instances of practices of pretence were thus like double-headed figures. While some saw them as rightful appropriations of a successful future, others considered them deceitful or foolish frauds.

In contrast to the young and economically disadvantaged men in Abidjan's low-income estates who embrace 'bluffs' as social practices that pretend without disguising and thereby both imitate and criticize social hierarchies (Newell 2012, see also, for instance, Gondola 1999, Masquelier 2019, Weiss 2009), my male interlocutors' practices of pretence were built upon their sincere belief that they would soon be successful. By 'inhabiting the fantasy' (Weiss 2002) and the expectations of others and themselves through, for example, posing in suits on their Facebook profiles, migrant men complied with and circumvented prevalent notions of masculinity based on economic success. They emulated the narrative of the man as the economically capable provider, which was good enough until an intimate other, such as a wife or a close male friend, demanded material proof. Expecting to achieve financial success in the near enough future, therefore, also bore the danger of being too ambitious. It could lead to shameful exposure, thereby adding more impetus to the vicious cycle of aspirational expectations, increased pressure, feelings of looming failure and depression.

Practices of pretence perpetuated the image of Pipeline as an aspirational place imbued with the potential for economic success. Though most male migrants worked in the industrial area or Pipeline's overcrowded informal sector, some did have well-paying white-collar jobs or ran thriving small-scale businesses. At the same time, the prevalence of acts of bravado made it hard for migrant men and women to assess with certainty if signs of success reflected actual economic achievements. By reproducing Pipeline as an aspirational place, practices of pretence thus also created an atmosphere of mistrust toward one's own economic success and that of others. It was hard to distinguish between 'realistic fictions' and 'fictitious realities' (Newell 2012: 101), a difficulty that was also responsible for how male and female migrants viewed me. It remained unclear for many if I was an authentic *odiero* (Dholuo, 'white man', Kiswahili, *mzungu*, Sheng, *mlami*, from Kiswahili, *lami*, 'asphalt') with a lot of money or a *mzungu mwitu*, a 'savage' or fake white person whose financial abilities were not in line with what his skin colour promised.

From hustling to pressure

The literature on African urban livelihoods rarely zooms in on the experience of economic pressure. Rather, scholars have focused on creative practices through which their interlocutors make ends meet in an uncertain present while criticizing the political elite and hoping for a better future. Recently, for instance, the widespread use of the term 'hustling' in Nairobi has been identified as a key entry point for a conceptual debate on economic livelihoods. The editors of a special issue published in *Africa*, for example, describe 'hustling' as 'an agentive struggle in the face of harsh circumstances, where opportunism, playfulness, fierce persistence [...] generate particular logics and localized practices of adaptation and improvisation' (Thieme et al. 2021: 7). This focus on hustling and uncertainty has done more than help to analyse the livelihoods of unemployed male youth born and living in sub-Saharan Africa's informal settlements. It has also shed light on hope as 'an existential force of productive uncertainty and indeterminacy' (Lockwood 2020: 46).[8]

Migrant men in Pipeline rarely mentioned their hustles or the practice of hustling when they discussed their current or future economic situation. The reason for that might lie in their lack of interest in being identified as hustlers. A statement about men in Pipeline that Caroline Mwangi made during an interview on gender relations in Pipeline corroborates this assumption. Being asked how men of Pipeline differ from men in the village, Caroline, a shop owner and migrant from central Kenya in her thirties, concluded that migrant men in Pipeline 'have relaxed' (Kiswahili, *wamelegea*) and 'don't want to be associated with hustlers'. Due to their immense expectations and aspirations, migrant men in Pipeline did not have a reason to piggyback on the hustling discourse to create a form of 'cultural intimacy' (Herzfeld 2016) with Nairobi's poor, like its middle-class, or, like Nairobi's poor, to present themselves as hustlers in front of other actors who might be willing to enter into patron–client relationships based on pity for their struggles or admiration for their ingenuity.

Instead of imposing the hustling analytic on migrant men's economic livelihoods in Pipeline, this chapter ethnographically described their experiences of pressure caused by circulating expectations of economic success, which they perceived as reasonable in kind but not always in degree. It showed how mostly well-educated male migrants from western Kenya dealt with their own as well as other actors' expectations, which had started to develop when they were still attending school in their rural homes. Rather than embracing uncertainty and employing 'a political-economic language of improvisation, struggle and solidarity' (Thieme et al. 2021: 2), most male migrants clung to the certainty of their future economic success and used a capitalist language of persistence, material wealth, as well as individual accomplishment and

---

8   Some languages use the same word to express the theological concept of hope and the more secular concept of expectation. In Dholuo, for instance, 'to hope' is translated as *geno*, which can also be translated as 'to expect' or 'to trust' (Odaga 2005). In contrast to the concept of hope, though, the concept of expectation does not point toward an uncertainty mediated by a third, such as God or luck.

responsibility. Following Pete Lockwood's apt critique of anthropology's understanding of 'hope as an existential force of productive uncertainty and indeterminacy' (2020: 46), I propose assessing migrant men's expectations as an existential force of unproductive certainty and determinacy. Male migrants in Pipeline, in other words, were certain that they would be economically successful one day, which supported them in their decision to remain in Nairobi despite their blatant lack of success.

Migrant men's attitudes toward their future thereby stand in stark contrast to how Naomi van Stapele described the life of Fake, who lived in Mathare:

> His imagined pathways were not intentional, single or linear routes that were obvious in direction and had clearly defined destinations, but unfolding, multiple, ambiguous and diverging imaginings without fixed outcomes. [...] The metaphor used by Vigh to describe social navigation, namely as the ship that sails through dark and unpredictable waters towards still invisible, and thus imagined, and shifting horizons, aptly fits the deep uncertainty that marked Fake's daily deliberations and everyday life. (Van Stapele 2021b: 138, see also Vigh 2009)

Rather than comparing male migrants' lives with a ship sailing through 'dark and unpredictable waters', I suggest imagining them as standing on a ship's deck with a detailed map and a functioning compass trying to reach a desti-nation decided upon a long time ago. They had migrated to Nairobi to find a permanent and well-paying job or to start a business that would produce enough profit to provide for their urban and rural families. When they were lost at sea, they fell into depression and slept in their berths until it passed, after which they returned to the deck with new energy. Instead of adjusting the course in order to reach their destination, they continued to follow the same route, relying on the map they already had. This is unsurprising considering that, being well-educated migrants from rural homes without electricity and running water, they felt that they had already accomplished much more compared to people born in or close to Nairobi. Living as eternal apprentices of a better future that they and their relatives and friends from the village had always dreamed of since childhood, they believed that they were on the track toward modernity and economic success (see Ferguson 2006: chapters 6 and 7).

The concepts of pressure and expectation help in understanding the vicious cycle of depressive passivity and aspirational activity in which some male migrants were trapped. The interplay of shame arising from failing to meet the expectations of their intimate others and the lack of self-efficacy caused by the failure to live up to their own expectations produced feelings of excruciating pressure and led to practices of pretence that created a fleeting sense that things were not always as good as they seemed. Though providing the daily necessities proved challenging to many male migrants during the COVID-19 pandemic, they remained preoccupied with assuring themselves and others that they were on the brink of an economic and personal breakthrough. They were, in other words, at least as much pressured by their attempts to reach a future in which they would be responsible and wealthy husbands and fathers as they were pressured by the demands of the present.

The next chapter analyses how the experience of pressure, the expectation of economic success and the fear of staged wealth influenced sexual and romantic relations in Pipeline by catalyzing an increasingly ambivalent communication between romantic partners, resulting in the erosion of trust in committed relationships and marriages. While husbands justified their practices of pretence as 'a display of potential' (Newell 2012: 1), whereby they invested in and showcased their future success, wives viewed such practices as lies or as unnecessary spending of money needed for food, rent and school fees. A similar logic was observable in the initial stages of romantic relationships as well as friendships. While men engaged in practices of pretence to impress potential friends and romantic partners, once they were in committed relationships, they started to complain that their partners and friends did not understand that their careers and businesses needed more time to develop. Men who had pretended to be more successful than they were to impress a woman or another male migrant were suddenly confronted with the justified demands of intimate others who expected to benefit from their alleged economic wealth.

3

Romantic Responsibilities
and Marital Mistrust

Dating a woman from Nairobi is like buying a swamp with the intention
to build a house.

Proverb circulating on Kenyan social media

The romantic relationship between Immaculate Chepkemei and Samuel
Onyango began where many romances in Pipeline begin: on the balcony.[1]
Samuel was living with Arthur in a single room when Immaculate and one of
her younger sisters moved into an apartment on the same floor. After flirting
for a while whenever they were both out on their balconies, their relationship
turned more intimate and Immaculate soon began to spend most nights with
Samuel in his and Arthur's flat. Though common, such arrangements can lead
to conflicts between male friends. In this case, for instance, Arthur either had
to sleep at another friend's apartment, wait on the balcony, or roam around
in Pipeline whenever the couple wanted to be intimate. Trying to ease these
tensions, Samuel and Immaculate decided to find a place of their own and
moved into a single room in the plot that was directly opposite. Samuel
continued to pay half of Arthur's rent to avoid straining their friendship, as
it would have been difficult for Arthur to meet the costs on his own. A few
months into their new life as a couple, Immaculate was pregnant.

---

[1]   While men and women flirted on balconies, communal bathrooms were places for
extramarital affairs (Kiswahili, *kugeuza diet*, 'to change diet') or quick sex between
neighbours. They were also potentially dangerous zones for women, who were at risk
of being sexually harassed there. The anonymity and sexually heated atmosphere of
Pipeline was indeed uncomfortable for many women. A friend's girlfriend, for instance,
expressed in an interview that men in Pipeline were too aggressive in their sexual
advances, often refusing to leave a woman alone if she let them know that she was
not interested: 'They try to give you their line, you say that you are not interested,
they extend to a point of, you are like, sometimes you start to feel like it is a threat to
you [...], the way he is pursuing you, it's like he has a hidden agenda or something
until you start to be scared.'

Their love story is not only typical in terms of how marriages developed in Pipeline, but it also illustrates some of the differences between contemporary urban marriages and the rural marriages of my interlocutors' parents. Most obviously, Samuel and Immaculate's marriage was interethnic: Samuel was a *ja*-Luo, Immaculate was a Kipsigis. Though rural marriages between these two ethnic groups were not completely unheard of, partly because the ancestral land of the Kipsigis bordered Kisumu County, most rural *jo*-Luo felt that marrying a Kipsigis man or woman was risky due to linguistic barriers and cultural differences. Interethnic romantic relationships in Pipeline had little in common with the trans- or post-ethnic relationships between young professional Nairobians who strove to overcome or downplay each other's ethnic backgrounds in order to paint the picture of a modern, post-ethnic Kenyan couple (Spronk 2012). For male migrants in Pipeline, the ethnic background of romantic and sexual partners was a constant topic of conversation that emphasized the importance of skin colour. They also discussed the sexual preferences and performances of women from different ethnic groups. Young migrant men were, for instance, curious to know how it felt to have sex with a circumcised *nyar Kisii* (Dholuo, 'a daughter of Kisii') or a brown-skinned Kamba woman (Dholuo, *lando*, 'brown-skinned woman', in contrast to *dichol*, 'dark-skinned woman'). Many sexual and romantic relations in Pipeline were thus 'ethno-erotic' encounters (Meiu 2017).

Another important difference between traditional and contemporary marriages was that potential spouses among *jo*-Luo were traditionally scrutinized by *jogam* (Dholuo, 'marriage mediators', see also Evans-Pritchard 1950). Though the final decision rested with the two individuals, who only had to come from different clans due to the norm of exogamy, marriage had always been a social affair. *Jogam* informed each partner about the potential spouse's background and character, and the woman would end up leaving her parent's home after successful bride-wealth negotiations to move in with her husband in his father's home, where she entered the vicinity of what Michael Dietler and Ingrid Herbich called the 'long arm of the mother-in-law' (2008, see also Schellhaas et al. 2020). In contrast, many contemporary urban 'come-we-stay' marriages (Neumark 2017: 750) began with chance encounters and flirtatious exchanges on the balcony or the street. Moreover, and enabled by Pipeline's anonymity, young male migrants could hide their marriages and children from rural kin if they felt that disclosing this information would lead to unsolicited advice or criticism.

'Double-Double', a popular song by *ohangla* artist Prince Indah, contrasts these different approaches to marriage by celebrating romantic love, which has become a strong trope across sub-Saharan Africa (see, for instance, Smith 2001, Stasik 2016), and highlighting the fact that the strong bond between two individuals will always produce jealousy and conflict between the couple and their rural relatives.

Safar mar hera, wachako ji ariyo kodi.	We started the journey of love, the two of us.
Ang'o makelo mor maloyo hera?	What brings more joy than love?
Herawa kodi biro kelo koko e kinda gi anyuola.	Our love will cause conflicts between me and my family.
Herawa kodi biro kelo koko e kinda gi mama.	Our love will cause conflicts between me and my mother.
Herawa kodi biro kelo koko e kinda gi baba.	Our love will cause conflicts between me and my father.
Ni hera mit kiparo mapariga.	Love is sweet when you think of someone who thinks of you.
Ni hera mit kileko malekiga.	Love is sweet when you dream of someone who dreams of you.
Miya double-double marito herawa.	Give me double-double that protects our love.
Kata e chan, kata e dhier, jaber, wenda nobed wendi, oda nobed odi.	Even in poverty, beauty, my guests will be your guests, my house will be your house.
Asingo tho kende emapogowa kodi.	I promise only death can bring us apart.

Since many of the problems that young couples and marriage partners faced revolved around economic hardships, Prince Indah's suggestion to love one another unconditionally regardless of the financial situation struck me as naïve. Despite the widespread romanticization of love, dating had not become a purely romantic issue. Rather, it was still shot through with economic considerations. In the eyes of many migrant men in Pipeline, dating, courtship, and marriage had potentially devastating financial and personal consequences. As alluded to by the proverb equating a potential wife with a piece of swampy land, a woman might turn out to be an investment that demanded continuous but ultimately fruitless reinvestment. The lyrics of another song that was popular during my fieldwork, Brizzy Annechild's *Hera nyalo sandi* (Dholuo, 'Love can punish you'), illustrate migrant men's fear that romantic love might not only demand material resources but could also lead to financial bankruptcy.

Hera nyalo chandi kendo hera nyalo sandi [...],	Love can trouble you, and love can punish you […],
saa miyudo pesa, iluongi honey [...],	when you have money, you are called honey […],
saa ma pesa onge, hera onge,	when there is no money, there is no love,
ok ocham alot, odwaro smokie [...],	she does not eat vegetables, she wants sausages […],
kok itang', onyalo negi.	if you are not careful, she can kill you.

After analyzing how migrant men and women conceptualized the relationship between sex, money, and love, this chapter examines the different categories men used to classify women. Male migrants assumed that these categories threatened to collapse into one another unexpectedly due to money's corrosive influence. This produced stereotypical narratives and rumours that revolved around wives who go out during the night as sex workers (Dholuo, *ochot*, Kiswahili, *kahaba*), naïve village girls who turn out to be dangerous 'slay queens', or teenage schoolgirls who become single mothers shortly after arriving in Nairobi and are subsequently forced to 'sell themselves' (Kiswahili, *kujiuza*). The sections after that illustrate the structural importance of the house (Dholuo, *ot*, Kiswahili, *nyumba*) and how living under one roof stabilized gender roles while increasing the expectations husbands and wives had of each other. This spiralling of expectations was further catalyzed by new and often ambiguous forms of digital communication between men and women, resulting in a further escalation of male migrants' experience of pressure. Finally, the chapter concludes with a brief discussion of how Samuel and Immaculate's marriage failed due to incompatible expectations and the interference of neighbours and relatives.

Sex, love, and money in Pipeline

You meet a girl […], you don't even know her second name, and you tell her to come to your house, as long as she sees that you have bought her chips and soda, she will come and you will have sex. I think here in Nairobi, sex is rampant (Dholuo, *Aparo ni Nairobi kae, sex is rampant*).

Wellington Ochieng

Wellington Ochieng, a 33-year-old casual labourer and moto-taxi driver from Migori County, was not the only inhabitant of Pipeline who commented on the estate's unrestrained sexuality. Many male migrants made the availability and transactional nature of sex responsible for infidelity, gender-based violence, single parenthood, homosexuality, and the materialism of women. A member of the No Mercy Gym even went so far as to compare Pipeline to the biblical Sodom and Gomorrah: 'This place is Sodom and Gomorrah. Where else in the world do you see teenagers carrying their babies proudly in front of them and mother and daughter fighting over the same guy? I witnessed that. Such things really happen here.' Sex and love were indeed tragically involved in many, sometimes deadly, events. On a September morning, for example, a friend sent me a text message saying nothing but 'Romeo & Juliet are dead!' After inquiring what had happened, he told me that one of his neighbours had 'slaughtered his wife like a chicken', after which he critically injured himself in a suicide attempt. This incident was the most dramatic of many atrocious ones during which love had turned into its opposite: a drunk *ja-pap* who did not realize that he brought his equally intoxicated girlfriend to the conjugal bed until his wife started screaming, a man who committed suicide by jumping from the seventh floor because his wife had left him, or a friend's girlfriend who had aborted their child without telling him, fearing that giving birth would only make their dire economic situation worse.[2]

Male migrants frequently engaged in conversations about these and similar events, which often ended in debates about the alleged materialism of women and the impossibility of having a functioning marriage without money. Migrant men, in other words, felt that the intricate relation between love and money threatened the stability of their romantic relationships (see, for instance, Cornwall 2002, Cole 2010, Smith 2017). Insufficient economic and emotional support, as well as a lack of romantic affection, could, so the stories went, impel a wife to become unfaithful, and the sexual offers by slay queens and sex workers could compel a migrant man to start a 'side project' (Kiswahili, *mpango wa kando*, used to refer to sexual affairs). The intimate connection that male migrants assumed existed between romantic love and the expenditure of money becomes palpable in the translation of 'romance' as *duso hera* (Dholuo, 'to decorate love'). Victor's answer to the question of how he displays romantic affection toward his wife Elizabeth, for instance, was that 'you are only going to be romantic as long as you have Shillings' (Dholuo, *ubiro duso herano so long as un gi shillings*).

---

[2] I do not mention these incidents to refuel debates about an African sexuality characterized by permissiveness, promiscuity, or the virility of black men (Ahlberg 1994, Ndjio 2012). Such racist discussions rightfully have been discarded because they perpetuate colonial discourses about the alleged savage nature of black men and women. While male discussions about the frequency of sex and the number of sexual partners seemed to be guided by what migrant men considered society's standards of masculine virility, remarks about Pipeline's unrestrained and 'rampant' sexuality allowed female migrants to distance themselves from such immoral acts (Spronk 2012: 118-9).

Migrant men thus did not interpret romantic love as an ideology of equality and emotional support (Spronk 2009, see also Illouz 2008). Rather, they felt that women had embraced romantic love in the form of consumerist expectations, which required men to provide expensive commodities to demonstrate their genuine and exclusive love. Spending money on a woman marked a man's romantic interest as serious and distinguished it from mere sexual interests hidden beneath meaningless palaver. From the perspective of many migrant men, women's evocation of romantic love, therefore, had only generated new financial responsibilities. They complained that they were no longer merely responsible for providing material things necessary for the upkeep of their families but now also had to surprise their wives with romantic things, such as expensive clothes, flowers, or invitations to eat out. In addition, they were confronted with the expectation to adopt romantic and erotic techniques that they had not heard of in their rural homes,[3] such as cuddling or oral sex, which further increased their experience of pressure. Wellington, for example, criticized women's romantic expectations in an interview on gender relations by claiming that they would hinder male migrants from meeting other men as well as from focusing on their professional careers:

> When you come to Nairobi, our girls want that you hold their hands when you are going to buy chips, you hug them when you are going to the house, I hear there is something called cuddling (Dholuo, *awinjo nitie gimoro ni cuddling*). [...] at what time will you cuddle and tomorrow you want to go to work early? [...] you don't go to meet your friends so that you show her that you love her, you just sleep on the sofa and caress her hair, to me, this is nonsense because that is not romantic love. I think that romantic love, so long as I provide the things I provide, and we also sire children, I think that's enough romance (Dholuo, *Aparo ni romantic love en so long as aprovide gik ma aprovide to nyithindo be wanyuolo, aparo ni mano romance moromo*). [...] Another girl told me to lick her, and I asked her 'Why do you want me to lick you?' She said that she wanted me to lick her private parts. Are those places licked? [...] Those things are things that people see on TV, let us leave them to the TV people (Dholuo, *jo*-TV).

As a consequence of the lasting influence of the narrative of the male breadwinner who was increasingly expected to also provide expensive consumer goods to signal genuine love, migrant men not acting in compliance with these

---

[3]   Migrants often juxtaposed narratives about an urban sexuality out of control with 'a romantic iconography of rural African life' (Callaci 2017: 29) as sexually modest. By invoking this contrast, they painted a picture of themselves as less promiscuous than men and women who had grown up in the city.

economic–romantic expectations were described as 'useless', whereby women stressed men's financial inabilities, or as 'dogs' (Dholuo, *guok*, Kiswahili *mbwa*) interested in nothing but sexual seduction. Considering these circulating stereotypes, many migrant men concluded that they would remain without a long-term partner if they did not become economically successful and therefore felt compelled to resort to practices of pretence to convince women to have sex with them. While most men agreed that they should provide food, clothes, shelter, and education for their wives and children, they were overwhelmed by women's economic-romantic 'over-expectations' that increased their experience of pressure, as Wellington diagnosed during the aforementioned interview on gender relations:

> Over-expectation is where you find someone who maybe has just graduated, he is out of campus, you expect that he is going to get some big job and you live happily ever after (Dholuo, *Over-expectation en moro miyudo ng'ato saa moro koka ograduate, oa campus, iexpect ni odhi yudo tich moro maduong' and you live happily ever after*). [...] like when COVID came there was no one who knew that COVID is coming. The job that you used to have and that paid you that little money has ended, now you are laid off, life must change. Maybe you lived in a bedsitter or one-bedroom, now you are forced to go back to a single room, because life needs to continue, and you find that your wife does not want to understand that life has changed. It is her expectation that life must move forward (Dholuo, *En expectation ne en ni ngima nyaka move forward*).

Subtle changes of the narrative of the man as the breadwinner were also highlighted by the semantic difference between 'providing' and 'spending on'. While most male migrants used the English word 'provide' to describe their duties, women sometimes replaced 'provide' with 'spend on', thereby signalling a shift from the provision of necessities that kept social groups, such as families, intact to conspicuous expenditure that only benefited individuals. Breadwinners, in other words, were under pressure to become 'sugar daddies' or sponsors. What migrant men perceived as the increasingly difficult task of balancing economic, romantic, and sexual expectations furthermore became manifest in discussions and rumours about four female archetypes that encapsulate some of the challenges that male migrants lamented upon when they talked about love, sex, and marriage: the slay queen, the village girl, the single mother, and the prostitute.

Of slay queens, prostitutes, single mothers, and village girls

I have heard of slay queens and I think that Pipeline has many of them, more than any other estate. Slay queens are those girls that have long nails, right? And they have painted their mouths red, and they have plaited their hair, I don't know, green. [...] Even in the plot where I used to live, what made me move was because my wife felt that there were slay queens living nearby and she felt, maybe, when she was away, I was looking at them. [...] I have not been with one, but I think when you look at the life they live and the clothes they put on and how their nails are long, they have nails that look like the nails of the devil. [...] If I stay with someone like that for two days, I will be finished, my friend.

Wellington Ochieng

Wellington was trying to eke out a living in Nairobi's east, working hard but also taking loans and placing bets. He had been living with his wife, three children, and a sister-in-law during our first interview in August 2020, but economic circumstances during the COVID-19 pandemic and insurmountable marital disagreements had forced him to relocate to the informal settlement Viwandani, taking with him his two older children, and leaving behind his wife and the youngest child in Pipeline. Though confessing that he regularly visited sex workers whom he described as 'curing him' – he had even saved the phone number of his favourite under *daktari* (Kiswahili, 'medical doctor') – his attitude toward slay queens was dismissive.[4] Their desire for expensive commodities such as phones, televisions, western food, wigs, make-up, perfume, and designer clothes could 'finish' (Dholuo, *rumo*) men and leave them penniless. Slay queens were only interested in men's economic wealth and offered nothing in return apart from sexual adventures and fake love. In contrast to sex workers, about whom migrant men rarely talked in a negative way, slay queens pretended to be in love with a man while having other sponsors on the side who also contributed money to their limitless desire for material goods. The fact that slay queens financially relied on men but

---

[4]   Though the term 'slay queen' arose during the last decades, the history of the social character it describes goes back well into the middle of the last century. In the Ugandan poet Okot p'Bitek's famous *Wer pa Lawino* (Acholi, 'Song of Lawino') published in 1966, for instance, Lawino describes her husband's girlfriend Clementine in a way resembling Wellington's portrayal of slay queens: 'the beautiful one aspires to look like a white woman; her lips are red-hot like glowing charcoal, she resembles the white cat that has dipped its mouth in blood [...] Tina dusts powder on her face and it looks so pale; she resembles the wizard' (P'Bitek 2008: 37, see also Emily Callaci's description of *kisura*, Kiswahili, 'good looking girl', in Dar es Salaam in the 1970s, 2017: 136–7, similar descriptions can be found in Powdermaker 1962: 163).

did not express any interest in getting married was perceived as a sign that they lacked a proper plan for their lives.[5] Though exclusively referring to slim women, the term *GB moja* (Sheng, 'one gigabyte') encapsulated slay queens' focus on western ideals of beauty, commodities, and technology by drawing a parallel between the lack of sustainability of one gigabyte of data with a slay queen's petite body and unreliable character. If at all, slay queens should – this was the moral lesson – only be entertained for a short period and without wasting any money on them.

In contrast to a slay queen, a *nyar agweng'* (Dholuo, 'village girl') was considered sexually inexperienced, generous, obedient, easy to satisfy, and pious. *Ohangla* artist Odongo Swag's song *Nyar Agweng'*, for instance, praises a village girl whom the musician loves, 'because she does not bring losses' (Dholuo, *nikech oonge hasara*). In contrast to 'city girls', who 'disgust' him (Dholuo, *nyi town ojoga*) by asking for money for chips and soda when they visit (Dholuo, *saa ma obiro wendoni, soda gi chips nyaka ing'iewo*), the village girl does 'not even ask for transport money' (Dholuo, *kata fare ok okwa*). To protect her from the corruptive influences of the city, the best trajectory for a village girl was, therefore, to be taken as a wife by an experienced city dweller as soon as possible after she had arrived in the city. By providing for her, the husband would ensure that the village girl dropped her superstitious beliefs, learned proper English and Kiswahili, and kept her good qualities, such as showing respect to her husband and guests, keeping the house tidy and clean, and being faithful in front of God. The husband would, in the local idiom, 'straighten' her (Dholuo, *rieyo*, see also Hunter 2010: 171–3), which was also the framing men and women used to justify some forms of gender-based violence, such as slapping, which many approved of as a way of reprimanding the behaviour of women who failed to behave in accordance with their husbands' expectations.

The categories of the slay queen and the *nyar agweng'* did threaten to collapse into one another. Many circulating stories about women's individual

---

[5]   From the perspective of some women, the lifestyle of slay queens was the result of a correct assessment of contemporary gender relations. Because most men were 'dogs' and players, it was rational to exploit them financially by turning them into sponsors as long as one's beauty lasted. In line with the observation that economic uncertainty forces people to 'cultivate relationships of dependence and mutual obligation with more than one person [...] as insurance against the loss of patrons' (Scherz 2014: 25, see also Ferguson 2013, and Hunter 2015), one *ja-pap* commented on the habit of slay queens to 'have five or ten men, one paying the house, one buying food, the other doing what and what.' The structural similarity between slay queens' practices and men's practices of pretence was, despite being obvious, neither commented upon nor even recognized by most male migrants.

lives even suggested that, without the guidance of a male, most village girls would inevitably turn into slay queens. If not transformed into a responsible wife by a man, a naïve village girl would be seduced by Pipeline's sexual atmosphere and the allure of consumer goods. Pressured by her sexual and economic desires, she would try to find male sponsors to support her financially. Due to the unsustainable lifestyle of a slay queen, which required multiple and changing sexual partners, one of the sponsors would impregnate her at some point and then 'throw her away' (Dholuo, *wito*) because he had no interest in providing for a child. Being left to live the life of a single mother, the village girl of a few years back would then be forced to start selling her body in the dark bypasses of Pipeline. The corruptive influence of Nairobi and money, in other words, could turn a naïve *nyar agweng'* into a cold-blooded sex worker.[6]

This male narrative concealed the economic opportunities single mothers had and embraced. Most single mothers did not engage in sex work but worked hard to provide for themselves and their children. Moreover, male migrants relied on this narrative to portray single mothers as morally dubious and as entirely responsible for their status, allowing men to deny responsibility for any pregnancy resulting from a sexual affair. The characterization of single mothers as morally inadequate also helped justify all kinds of male misconduct. Instead of blaming men for their actions, their problematic behaviour was explained by alluding to the possibility that they had been brought up without a disciplinary father, a common trope in globally circulating self-help narratives about the crisis of masculinity (see chapter 6, see O'Neill 2018: 131–2 for a British discourse on single mothers).[7]

The classification of women as either a slay queen, village girl, prostitute, single mother, or responsible wife corresponded with a 'love continuum' (Archambault 2017: 104) ranging from feelings of paternal care toward a younger female migrant, sexual lust toward an attractive, but dangerous slay queen, and true love toward one's wife. The instability of this 'love continuum' and the ambiguity of men's classification of women was reflected in rumours about wives who secretly worked as sex workers while their husbands worked night shifts or male fears about wives being seduced by other men on balconies

---

6   The corresponding narrative for male migrants assumed that economically unsuccessful men would turn to petty crime, become gambling addicts, or join a gang such as the *Mungiki*.

7   Characterizing women as slay queens, 'daughters of Jezebel', or irresponsible single mothers resonates with men's portrayal of progressive women who defy traditional gender roles as 'wicked' in different locations and during other historical periods (Hodgson and McCurdy 2001, on single mothers in postcolonial Kenya, see Thomas 2003: chapter 5).

or in Pipeline's bypasses, where flirtatious comments and flings were common. As a consequence of these ambiguities and fears, marriages depended upon stabilizing practices, which were not only viewed as securing marital peace but also as paving the way for financial success, as illustrated by the proverb *pesa oluoro koko* (Dholuo, 'money fears noise').

Gender roles and the house as a female sphere

> When someone is living with a woman in the house, you find that issues are many because money is little (Dholuo, *weche ng'eny nikech pesa tin*), and sometimes she finds men outside there who court her. She believes that she is very beautiful and should not be suffering.
>
> *Wellington Ochieng*

Joel Opiyo, a *ja-pap* and member of HoMiSiKi, lived in one of Pipeline's older plots with his wife Faith. The single room's wallpaper was peeling in some places, and the couple had partitioned their room into a sleeping area and a sitting area, where they welcomed guests. As in many apartments, the walls were decorated with posters, one of which depicted a white family next to a big car in front of a beautiful house. Joel had invited Arthur and me for lunch after we had spent two months training together in the No Mercy Gym. When we arrived in the apartment with Joel, who had picked us up in front of the plot, he asked his wife in a commanding tone why she had not cleaned the sitting area. Faith quickly wiped the table and removed some pieces of cut tomatoes and onions before she disappeared behind the curtain to finish cooking. After around 30 minutes, during which Joel, Arthur and I had exchanged stories, Faith brought us water to wash our hands, and we drank tea and ate the *chapo mayai* (Kiswahili, 'flatbread rolled in fried eggs') Faith served us. When we had finished, we thanked Joel's wife, left the dirty plates and cups on the table, and went to play some pool.

The communication and division of labour between Joel and his wife hints at a structural dichotomy between the house and the world outside. This dichotomy influenced most practices and discourses around marriage and love in Pipeline. In analogy to the female body, migrants conceptualized the house as a container into which the husband was obliged to deposit not sperm, but money, which was then transformed into marital peace through female reproductive practices such as cooking, washing clothes, mopping the floor, being sexually available, and taking care of the children. While the man put the house and its inhabitants in order through the flow of money and by giving moral advice, the woman's job was to clean it and act in morally exemplary ways by being a good host, caring mother, and faithful wife. At the same time, the house was viewed as the primary place of romance and sexuality. It was the only place where most migrant men felt comfortable enough to show signs of affection toward and sexual interest in their wives. The house was thus marked as a female sphere, and the presence of the husband inside of it was considered aberrant unless he was eating, sleeping, or having sexual intercourse with his wife.[8] The underlying expectation was that men were at work or, if they did not have a job, engaged in what was known as 'tarmacking'. Instead of sitting in the house, men should, quite literally understood, walk on the streets 'hunting' for jobs in the industrial area or elsewhere in Nairobi.

Mama Cyrus (Kiswahili, 'mother of Cyrus') was a woman in her mid-twenties who had migrated to Nairobi from western Kenya. She had a small shop next to Milele Flats that sold daily necessities such as, among other things, milk, tea, bread, and eggs. Her marriage offers a good example of how the enactment of strict gender roles allowed men and women to live a peaceful marital life. One of few interlocutors who described their marriages positively, Mama Cyrus had met her husband when she was still going to school in her rural home. She was only sixteen when he impregnated her, but instead of leaving her alone with the baby, he ensured that she had everything she needed to raise the child. Throughout their relationship, her husband had accepted his responsibility to provide for Mama Cyrus and their child. He paid rent, bought clothes and electronic gadgets, refilled the cooking gas, and paid the school fees. He had even decided to rent and stock the shop for Mama Cyrus so that she could earn some money for herself. Consequently, Mama Cyrus respected her husband by being what she called a 'good wife' (Kiswahili, *bibi mzuri*). She cooked, washed clothes, cleaned the house, took care of the child, was sexually faithful, and made sure that her husband never came home without finding her there waiting for him. Mama Cyrus concluded that although being a wife was 'not an easy thing', once a woman had decided to be a wife, she was supposed to 'sit in the house' and subordinate herself to her husband. Instead of going to birthday parties and visiting clubs like an irresponsible slay queen, a wife should prioritize her family, her house, and her business activities.

When asked about the role of money in her marriage, Mama Cyrus claimed that for things to 'run smoothly', money had to be there. According to her, money was 'everything, this house needs money, the TV needs money, utensils and what else.' Yet, the money she earned and the money that her husband earned were not supposed to be treated equally. Reminiscent of what male migrants criticized as Kenyan women's financial motto of *pesa yangu ni*

---

8   If male friends lived together, they shared domestic duties. In case of a hierarchical relation between male kin, for instance when an elder brother hosted a younger sibling, the hierarchically inferior man often took over more female tasks.

yangu, pesa yako ni yetu (Kiswahili, 'my money is mine, your money is ours'), Mama Cyrus voiced the opinion that a husband should not 'control' his wife's income. While men had clear duties such as paying rent and school fees, women were only responsible for buying 'small things' such as kitchen utensils. Other than that, they were free to use their money in any way they felt was the most appropriate.

This 'ideal image of urban life as shaped around [...] the male being responsible for income and the female for the domestic realm' (Neumark 2017: 759) seems to resonate with how gender relations were organized in migrants' rural homes. Even so, these superficial resemblances are misleading because, in Pipeline, the social organization of space did not mirror kin relations as it does in the village, where brothers build homes next to one another and women move into the homesteads of their husbands' families. Instead of a few brothers and their families who speak the same language, share a past, and are bound to one another through practices establishing kinship, social life in Pipeline meant being surrounded by thousands of unknown neighbours of different ethnic and cultural backgrounds. While the rural public space was congruent with the husband's kinship order and wives could be controlled comparatively easily through the gaze of the husband's family (Schellhaas et al. 2020), the public space of Pipeline was perceived as impossible to survey. Pipeline's anonymity thus threatened to destabilize male control. This led some men to discourage or even forbid their wives from leaving the house or spending time on the balcony where they would only 'gossip', compare their hairstyles and clothes with those of better-off neighbours, and become susceptible to the seduction of migrant men with 'deeper pockets'.

Money and mistrust spiralling out of control

Women are the reason why men have changed because women are hard on men. [...] The expectations they come with into a relationship (Dholuo, *Expectations ma gibirogo e relationship*), and generally how they have been brought up, or the life they live, that is what gives some men stress (Dholuo, *ema miyo chuo moko stress*).

Wellington Ochieng

Mama Cyrus' remark that money 'smoothens' marriages exemplifies the fact that a stable marital life in Pipeline required money. Few husbands could refer to paid bride-wealth, crops that were harvested on their fields, or a house that they had built for their wife if they wanted to reap the 'patriarchal dividend' (Connell 2005 [1995]: 79). Unable to point to past economic transactions, male migrants felt compelled to leave the house to make money. Men could only justifiably expect that their girlfriends and wives would take care of the house, wash their clothes, cook, and raise the children if they continuously proved their willingness and ability to provide money for rent, food, gas, school fees, and other things. If men failed to provide money, their wives accused them of not keeping their material promises. As illustrated in the last chapter, many male migrants painted a picture of themselves as already or soon-to-be financially successful, which further raised their partners' expectations and fuelled the vicious cycle of high expectations, mounting pressure, and mistrust. As described by David Parkin in reference to Luo migrants living in Nairobi in the late 1960s, 'wage dependency' was still a 'seed of uncertainty' (1978: 120).

The common understanding of men as providers created and reinforced a situation where male migrants expected themselves to be able to provide and women pegged the quality of their romantic relationship to their partner's financial capabilities. Stereotypes about men as rotten dogs uninterested in providing economically and women as materialistic and money-minded slay queens shifted the focus away from structural problems such as the dire state of Kenya's economy, which had been destabilized by the COVID-19 pandemic and then by the start of the war in Ukraine. Rumours and narratives, as well as accusations and unfulfilled expectations, fed into a spiral of mutual mistrust where men feared that their wives would look for men who were more financially capable and women started to suspect that their allegedly successful husbands were spending money on extramarital affairs or sex workers. Consequently, men like Wellington perceived women's demands for public displays of affection as part of an urban set of economic–romantic practices that only increased their pressure.

The narrative of the male provider, moreover, obscured the importance and often even the existence of female labour. Many migrant men, for instance, discouraged their wives from working or downplayed the importance of female labour to emphasize their own financial contributions. However, the bleak economic situation left most women no choice but to try to use their economic power to help to sustain the household. Most had small businesses, were employed in town, took on minor jobs such as washing clothes, or used their kinship networks to get financial help (Kusimba 2018). Despite their vital contributions to the household, many women felt compelled to engage in something similar to what Hanna Papanek called 'covert integration' (1979: 777). They hid their financial contributions in public because they did not want to put shame on their husbands or boyfriends by suggesting that the latter were unable to provide. Rather than presenting themselves as economically capable providers, they whitewashed their marriages or relationships as functioning according to local standards that took for granted that the husband was the main breadwinner.

Comparable to what Mary Moran (1990) observed among migrants in south-eastern Liberia, both migrant men and women in Pipeline strove for the same middle-class lifestyle. By respecting their husband as the main provider and taking care of all domestic duties, women such as Mama Cyrus were able to fulfil their middle-class consumerist aspirations without the risk of appearing financially independent or too modern, which could not only be interpreted as disrespectful but also trigger migrant men's fears about their expendability. The subordination of wives under their husbands, whereby 'gender-sensitive positions within the hierarchy' were 'conceptualized as complementary rather than parallel' (Moran 1990: 169), was thus not unconditional. Most women were only willing to subordinate themselves in their marriage if their husbands provided financially or did, at least, try to find new money-making opportunities.

As shown by the demise of the marriage between Victor and Elizabeth (see chapter 2), 'the script of male generosity and female dependence' could quickly become 'strained in the context of economic crisis' (Callaci 2017: 140). Women were only willing to be dutiful housewives who understated their financial contributions to the household if their husbands provided the financial means to meet their consumerist desires. Expecting men to be providers helped women participate in the economy of middle-class consumption whilst appearing respectful and submissive, unlike wives who were wealthier than their husbands. If men were unsuccessful, however, women felt confident to look for someone else or to leave the relationship to start providing for themselves. The complexities of male–female relations, and the fact that mistrust had become the norm rather than the exception, were also visible in how couples communicated about and inside their relationships with the help of modern communication technology (see, for instance, Archambault 2017, Nassenstein and Storch 2020).

The public and secret negotiation of sex and love

In March 2021, a meme depicting a handwritten love letter was shared in the WhatsApp chat group of *jo-pap*. Phrases such as *chunya oheri to kendo ber bende iberna maka apari to kata nindo tamore tera* (Dholuo, 'my heart loves you and you are also good for me, when I think of you, even sleep refuses to take me') exemplify that the letter was hopelessly romantic, and the discussion that followed in the chat group reflected migrant men's nostalgic longing for their rural youth, during which women were allegedly not yet materialistic and romance still pure (see Parikh 2016). In the last decades, however, love letters were almost completely substituted by communication through social media apps such as Facebook, Instagram, and, most importantly, WhatsApp. While migrants used WhatsApp for sending each other sexual invitations, nude pics, pornographic material, or romantic greetings, they used the WhatsApp status feature to share messages on a public wall that was immediately visible to all their contacts. These messages could be texts, pictures, or short videos, and were not automatically integrated into the private chat of all contacts, who could comment on it in a private message.

While love letters directly addressed a specific person and were only meant to be read by him or her, a WhatsApp status update thus addressed a large group of people at the same time. It was, for instance, very common for younger women to post status messages such as 'birthday loading' or 'only a few days left until I turn 25' and to upload pictures of beautifully decorated houses, expensive restaurants, and cars. Male migrants interpreted such status updates as a more or less subtle way in which women demanded monetary or other gifts from potential boyfriends and husbands. After proudly announcing that he tends to forget his own birthday, Samuel once summarized these female practices under the label of an 'extortion racket' fuelled by women's unrealistic consumerist expectations (see Newell 2012: 135).

The WhatsApp status option also allowed migrants to indirectly criticize intimate others in order to create public awareness of private issues. After a friend's relationship with a single mother called Martha had gone sour, for instance, she posted new status updates daily that everyone in her contact list, including myself, was able to see and comment on:

> Some people think I hate them, but I don't even think of them. Relax.

> When you needed me, I was there, when I needed you, all of a sudden you are busy.

> Never hide your kid just to save a new relationship! If you love the mother, also love the child, or just leave!

While these status updates revealed Martha's emotions to everyone in her contact list, including her estranged boyfriend, who was supposed to see her status as well, they did not address anyone in particular. Though Martha thereby dragged a private issue into the public sphere and implicitly accused her ex-boyfriend of not having shown enough affection for her daughter, she did so in a manner that allowed immediate disavowal. If approached by her ex-boyfriend, Martha could pretend that her status updates were just general comments about love and romantic relationships.

Updating their WhatsApp status enabled women to indirectly articulate expectations toward men and to launch ambiguous forms of critique directed at intimate others that everyone in their contact list could see and comment on. Such digital forms of gossip fostered social relations between women and reminded men of their moral duties (Gluckman 1963). A further advantage of the WhatsApp status feature was that it allowed women to upload messages no matter where they were. Unlike their movement in and out of the house, this could not be easily controlled by men. It was, in other words, impossible for male migrants to completely curtail female gossip, and the creation of anonymous communities of communication via women's WhatsApp status was one way that mistrust became socially productive (Carey 2017). For example, after a friend from Siaya County had left a girlfriend, the latter kept uploading photographs of a male *mzungu* (Kiswahili, 'white person') posing half-naked in bed, standing on a rock, and in other heroic postures along with pictures of expensive food and drinks. She commented on her status by writing how she had been lucky, and how her *mzungu* had helped her to heal and move forward from a toxic relationship with one of those Kenyan 'dogs'. The message was clear. She was living a good life thanks to the economic prowess and romantic inclinations of a white man, and Kenyan men should watch and learn how to treat a woman.

WhatsApp was not the only technology that helped migrants avoid direct confrontations with their romantic partners. Several of my male interlocutors, for instance, had installed an unremarkable app that looked like it was for recording and editing audio files. The app's icon was entirely misleading; it actually enabled users to receive and then hide messages from specific phone numbers. This allowed men with 'side projects' to let their girlfriends or wives scan through their phone's contacts and messages in case they were jealous or suspicious, a common demand in romantic relationships. WhatsApp and this fake audio app thus gave men and women the ability to engage in carefully orchestrated games of pretence. Mobile phone users could pretend to be faithful, show off signs of their alleged financial success, and navigate 'the tensions between display and disguise' (Archambault 2017: 21) by sending potential partners ambiguous offers to engage in sexual affairs that could easily be withdrawn if necessary.[9]

The presence of rural kin and Pipeline's 'micro-politics of proximity' (Bjarnesen and Utas 2018: S4), however, risked rendering such practices of carefully balancing social distance and proximity futile. The physical presence

---

[9]   A less refined practice of coordinating 'display and disguise' was to delete messages if the other person did not respond as expected. Migrant men, for instance, could receive invitations of a sexual nature that were *ex post* deleted by the woman who had sent them if they had not shown any interest. Local notions of respect were thus not only influenced by considerations of doing or being morally good, but also by attempts to appear to be morally good (Archambault 2017: 60–2).

of relatives and neighbours, some of whom were viewed as misleading role models and potential witnesses of marital conflicts, made it difficult to negotiate romantic feuds privately. Though Pipeline's population density and chaotic high-rise architecture appeared to grant anonymity to the estate's residents, tenants were actually continuously challenged to 'negotiate the transparency imposed by dense housing arrangements' (Bjarnesen and Utas 2018: S5). This was something I became aware of during the collapse of Samuel's marriage to Immaculate.

The demise of a marriage

Their marriage had, from the very beginning, been marked by misunderstandings typical of interethnic relationships in Pipeline. Samuel, for instance, often complained that Immaculate spoke her mother tongue Kipsigis and not Kiswahili with her sisters and female cousins, thereby excluding him from the conversations, which left him feeling disrespected. Immaculate, on the other hand, appeared to be disappointed by the fact that Samuel's promises of a good life had yet to materialize. Though Samuel had embarked on a promising career path as a lawyer, Immaculate still had to work six days a week as a sales agent for a travel company to help support their young family. As Arthur and I feared that the arguments between Samuel and Immaculate could soon get worse if they stayed in the same apartment, we convinced Samuel to move back into Arthur's single room until things had calmed down. As Immaculate left Pipeline early in the morning and returned from town late in the evening, Samuel's young son stayed with his father and Arthur during the day. The spatial separation seemed to ease some of the tension, but Samuel and Immaculate continued to exchange bad words. The situation escalated when one of Immaculate's neighbours falsely claimed that, looking into Arthur's house from her balcony situated directly opposite, she had seen us drinking whiskey with a group of known slay queens while Immaculate's baby was crying in the corner.

Probably aware of the limited chances of finding a new romantic partner as a single mother of a son and, more importantly, still in love with Samuel, Immaculate continued to try to fix the relationship.[10] Samuel, on the other hand, no longer believed the marriage could be repaired, but remained committed to

---

[10] Due to the patrilineal regulation of kinship among *jo*-Luo, single mothers with sons were considered difficult marriage partners because of the fear that the biological father would later lay claim to his son or that the son would demand inclusion into his biological father's family. It was thus not easy to find a man willing to 'wash the seeds' of someone else (Dholuo, *luoko kodhi*).

his responsibilities as a father by providing financial support and spending time with his son. His behaviour stood in stark contrast to the attitude of many of our male friends, who advised Samuel that he should withdraw from spending time with his son to avoid getting emotionally involved.[11] When he returned to Immaculate's house a few weeks later to pick up his son, Samuel encountered one of Immaculate's female cousins and an argument broke out between the two. Alerted by the ongoing commotion, as Samuel had recounted to me later on, a Luo male neighbour of Immaculate and acquaintance of Samuel intervened, dragged the cousin to the staircase, gave her a slap, and lectured her that she was not supposed to disturb him or other neighbours. Neither, he concluded, should she cause problems in the house of her cousin's husband.

These incidents were the final blows to the marriage of Immaculate and Samuel. In addition, they also illustrate how difficult it was for the inhabitants of Pipeline to fulfil a model of romantic love based on 'the sovereignty of the individual above and against the claims of the group' (Spronk 2012: 232). In contrast to this romantic ideal, which had been adopted as a sign of migrant modernity by many of my interlocutors and was celebrated in *ohangla* songs such as Prince Indah's 'Double-Double', relations between relatives, neighbours and members of different ethnic groups continued to affect Samuel and Immaculate's marriage and, as a result, the lives of Samuel's friends, such as Arthur, who had to be careful when conducting his day-to-day activities. After the rumour about the party with slay queens, for instance, he now kept his curtains closed during the day. Though apparently offering anonymity, Pipeline's density was thus shot through with the potential of unwanted sociality, meaning that the estate's residents had to carefully navigate the 'micro-politics of proximity', where 'practices of alliance, respectability and display intersect with strategies of avoidance, accusation and deceit' (Bjarnesen and Utas 2018: S4). Gossip circulated offline as well as online, and ungrateful gazes were exchanged across balconies, solidifying what Patrick Desplat aptly called 'closed circles of mistrust' (2018).

Male migrants ascribed their experience of pressure to the unreasonable nature of women's expectations, which they perceived as insatiable and thus

---

[11]   Some migrant men confided to me that they lacked the instinct for dealing with younger children. In case of a separation from his wife, it would therefore be best for a father to provide financially from a distance until a child started primary school. In light of these assumptions, it is thus unsurprising that Samuel felt that other men looked down on him because he was involved in the upbringing of his baby despite having left his wife: 'Typical Kenyan gentlemen would just leave the child alone and let the woman suffer. Then tell themselves that they come back after the child has grown. You know men think that Immaculate rules and dictates me because I take the baby in the morning. A man is not supposed to carry a baby like I do.'

impossible to meet. It is therefore unsurprising that many of them developed what John Remy called 'an extra-familial, extra-patriarchal impulse' (1990: 48). The next two chapters explore this impulse by describing how migrant men related to one another in two different homosocial spaces where they tried to evade the encompassing atmosphere of pressure created by women's expectations. It is important to emphasize that men did not try to get rid of pressure. Precisely because they viewed women's expectations as unreasonable only in degree, but not in kind, they used these male spaces to momentarily evade pressure, not to shake it off completely. Comparable to other practices of depressurizing (see chapter 2), visiting male spaces gave migrant men time to take a deep breath and refuel their energy. While chapter 5 zooms in on how recreational weightlifting helped to build a feeling of close-knit brotherhood among the members of a local gym, chapter 4 recounts the establishment and demise of an economic investment group and an associated circle of friends who, although mostly married, addressed each other as 'bachelors' (Dholuo, *jo-pap*). Scrutinizing practices that created a social arena for acting out impulses of wastefulness, violence, and raw masculinity gives ethnographic flesh to the observation that the demands of being a good father and husband sometimes conflicted with the demands of being a good friend. Feeling under pressure to provide and perform as married men, some male migrants decided to let off steam as *jo-pap*.

PART 2

EVADING PRESSURE

4

Investing in Male Sociality and
Wasteful Masculinity

Re: *Pap onge kun* (Dholuo, 'No hard feelings on the playing field'). In the
aforementioned, *pap* means an open field for celebrations and fun-making
such as dancing, feasting, wrestling [...] with the expected results being
joy and laughter such that no one is expected to frown even if you lose
a wrestling match, dance competition, athletics, etc.

Quote from a WhatsApp chat with Arthur

'Ho ... Mi ... Si ... Ki'. While we walked through the muddy streets of
Pipeline, Patrick Ouko pronounced the syllables carefully, and with a small
break between each one:

It stands for Homa Bay, Migori, Siaya, and Kisumu. We, the young
Luo of Pipeline, had to come up with our own investment group. [...]
By now, we have around 30 members, all men apart from one, but we
are expanding. [...] One day we will buy a minibus and join the matatu
business.

With a few exceptions like Patrick, who was born in Pipeline (see chapter
1), most of the 30 or so members of HoMiSiKi had grown up in western
Kenya and come to Nairobi as migrants full of expectations of a better life.
What united Victor, Joel, Patrick, and the other members, apart from being
ethnic Luo, was a sense of being overlooked by politicians, invisible to the
international aid sector, and excluded from municipal initiatives. Pressured
by the expectations of their rural and urban families, they had sensed the
need to experiment with communally organized attempts to achieve economic
progress and forms of male conviviality that allowed them to briefly forget
their economic pressures and romantic frustrations.

Theories of gift exchange, corruption, and patronage show that the degree
to which actors make productive use of their social network influences their
economic success (Berman 1998, Blundo and Olivier de Sardan 2006). Economic
wealth, in other words, emerges from what Jane Guyer (1993) has called 'wealth-
in-people'. The interactions and debates I observed during HoMiSiKi meetings,

however, suggest a reversal of this causal relation between the social and economic spheres. Against the background of narratives circulating nationwide about entrepreneurship and self-employment, talking and meeting under the banner of the investment group's future economic success allowed members to engage in socially approved forms of male bonding. HoMiSiKi's use of economic buzzwords such as 'skills', 'self-employment', 'insurance', 'capital', and 'investment' should thus not only be interpreted as a naïve rehearsal of Kenya's new economic paradigm celebrating the skillful entrepreneur (Dolan and Gordon 2019). Rather, the members of HoMiSiKi employed such a rhetoric to justify to themselves, as well as to their wives and girlfriends, why a group of male strangers stranded in the liminal and aspirational space of Pipeline socialized with one another. It was in the shadow of the economic rationality of the official investment group HoMiSiKi that its members created and maintained a space for wasteful masculinity they called *pap* (Dholuo, 'arena, playing field'). In *pap*, migrant men behaved in ways that were structurally opposed to the expectations of their rural and urban families. Instead of being responsible boyfriends, husbands, sons, and fathers, they acted as irresponsible 'bachelors' (Dholuo, *jo-pap)* 'transgressing' (Groes-Green 2010) the prevailing norm of the male breadwinner.

Simultaneously pretending to be economically successful as members of HoMiSiKi and embracing wasteful masculinity in *pap* depended on carefully negotiating conflicting notions of masculinity and was, therefore, a delicate affair. *Jo-pap,* for instance, were well aware of the fact that by diverting resources from their families, they risked being more intensively criticized for not providing enough. Achieving the balance between providing for one's family, investing money in HoMiSiKi, and wasting resources in *pap* was already difficult before the COVID-19 pandemic reached Kenya. Together with political frictions caused by the general elections of 2022, the economic effects of the pandemic led to the breakdown of HoMiSiKi as well as increasingly violent and socially problematic behaviour in *pap*. In other words, while HoMiSiKi was collapsing, *pap* was steadily getting out of control. Before taking a closer look at this dynamic, it is helpful to narrate the historical emergence of *jo-pap* and HoMiSiKi, which was characterized by violence, political opportunism, and male camaraderie, and thereby exemplary for Pipeline's transformation into one of the world's most densely populated high-rise settlements.

A history of violence and hospitality

While walking through a bypass on my way to meet some friends in late August 2021, I heard a familiar voice calling my name. Turning around, I saw Thomas Okeyo, a member of HoMiSiKi and *ja-pap*. After exchanging pleasantries and greetings, Thomas invited me to his single room, which he shared with his wife, children, and nephew. While drinking *nyuka* (Dholuo, 'liquid grain porridge'), I inquired about the violent past of some *jo-pap* I had heard about. Thomas broke out in laughter before he answered: 'That is just diplomatic chaos. We stay up the whole night before the election and make sure that our people are the first in line. Ochieng in the first line, Omosh in the second, and Ocholla in the third.' After enough votes had been cast for their preferred candidate, *jo-pap* would start fighting with one another to scare other voters away. During the nomination for the Orange Democratic Movement's contestant for the position of the Member of the County Assembly of Nairobi representing Kware ward in the 2017 general election, for instance, *jo-pap* had stirred up such 'diplomatic chaos' to help their favourite candidate to win. Relying on a strong ethnic network of Dholuo-speaking migrants, *jo-pap* continued organizing political campaigns for their candidate, thereby crucially contributing to the candidate's electoral victory. While such an instrumentalization of carefully planned and orchestrated electoral violence has remained a common political strategy in twenty first-century Kenya (Klaus 2020, Mueller 2008), here I want to highlight the personal and social effects that were at stake for those male migrants who participated.

During the time when Victor Omollo, the migrant from Asembo I introduced in chapter 2, was taking care of the fleet of lorries for the transport company, other young men alerted him about the opportunity to earn extra money by becoming a member of a youth group that protected illegally acquired land for wealthy politicians and businessmen. Lured by promises of substantial material and financial rewards, Victor joined without hesitation and employed violence against members of rival youth gangs trying to encroach on the land of his patron, who was rumoured to be a close associate of a prominent Luo politician. When reflecting on this period of his life, Victor expressed regret for the violence he had witnessed and participated in. In the end, most material promises had never been fulfilled. Soon after he moved to Pipeline, however, Victor's violent involvement in the defense of the economic interest of his political patron caught up with him in the form of Leonida, who had also been a close political acquaintance of Victor's patron.

Holding a high position in a parastatal, Leonida, who also hailed from western Kenya, had acquired enough money to invest in the construction of a plot in Pipeline. In 2016, her yet-to-be-finished building already housed a small restaurant on its ground floor that was run by a male Luo migrant known for his hospitable character. The restaurant was visited almost exclusively by other migrant men from western Kenya who came there to drink porridge, eat something small, and meet other male migrants. Casual workers constructing the plot's upper floors and migrants telling each other stories in the restaurant soon realized that they shared the same ethnic background and began to meet informally in front of the plot, where they installed a wooden bench to hang out together without having to visit each other's houses, whereby the 'base' of *jo-pap* was born. Through sharing and listening to amusing stories and political debates, more and more migrants joined and helped to expand the network of *jo-pap*, which turned into what one male migrant described as 'a market for friends to get acquainted with one another' (Dholuo, *market mar osiepe mar ng'erwuok*).

Being interested in supporting a friend who was vying for a seat in Kenya's national parliament at that time, and recognizing the political potential of an informal group of Luo supporters, Leonida decided to tap into this human infrastructure of migrant men (Simone 2004) by regularly giving small handouts to *jo*-base (Dholuo, 'members of the base'). In an attempt to secure their political loyalty, she offered *jo*-base around 10,000 KSh and suggested that they establish an investment group. After heated debates among the members of the base (while many felt that an investment group would be beneficial, some preferred to use the money to buy drinks), the majority decided to go along with Leonida's suggestion. They founded HoMiSiKi at the end of 2016, after which the members of the group began to meet once a fortnight on the fifth floor of Leonida's plot, which also housed Patrick's barber shop (see chapter 1).

The genesis of HoMiSiKi and *jo-pap* was characterized by fraternal hospitality and political opportunism. While male migrants' violence helped some rich patrons to acquire land in Nairobi's east, Leonida relied on a group of young migrant men to support her political ally in the elections. At the same time, the restaurant and the base also served as spots where Luo migrants exchanged news, shared meals, offered advice about jobs and urban life to recently arrived migrants, and planned nocturnal escapades sweetened by alcohol and scantily dressed Kamba women exposing their exoticized brown thighs. A support group for aspiring politicians, as well as an ethnically based association for wasteful and misogynistic conviviality, on the one hand, and an investment group trying to become economically successful, on the other, HoMiSiKi's economic goals and the social and political practices of *jo-pap* had a tense relationship from the outset.

HoMiSiKi as an institution of pretence

As he did every other Sunday, Benson, the aspiring politician and chairman of HoMiSiKi introduced in chapter 1, had invited all members of the investment group as well as myself to meet on the balcony of the fifth floor of Leonida's unfinished plot. While a few members stood, the rest sat on chairs, empty plastic buckets, the rail of the balcony, or half-empty sacks of cement. Before officially starting the meeting, Benson explained the rationale of the investment group to me. He and the other founding members had started HoMiSiKi to raise financial assets to support its economic growth and the professional success of its members. Benson emphasized that members should learn new skills and attend seminars and workshops during which they would hear about new business ideas for the group, thereby copying Kenya's ubiquitous discourse on self-employment and entrepreneurialism. Comparable to Benson's suggestions, many local politicians and NGOs also propagated, alongside other neoliberal strategies, the acquisition of new professional skills and saving money to start a 'micro-enterprise' as the most appropriate methods to overcome the staggering level of youth unemployment (Dolan and Gordon 2019).

Being a member of an investment group was thus far from extraordinary. During the time of my fieldwork, almost every Kenyan was a member of at least one rotating savings and credit association (ROSCA), a savings and credit cooperative (SACCO, government-registered), or an accumulating savings and credit association (ASCA). These organizations enabled members to save, lend, and invest money. Though comparable organizations have existed in sub-Saharan Africa for centuries (James 2012, see also Carotenuto 2006 for a history of welfare groups among Luo migrants), they received a boost after the development aid sector began to advertise them as a bottom-up and infra-structurally simple way of financializing the poor in the second half of the twentieth century. Like other investment groups, HoMiSiKi depended on its members making regular contributions. It was therefore unsurprising that most HoMiSiKi members had been formally employed when I encountered the group for the first time in 2019. Among the members were, for instance, a salesman for an insurance company, a lorry driver, a forklift operator, a teacher, a hotelier, and an electrician.

HoMiSiKi's official goals were to offer social and economic assistance to its members and to provide a platform for discussing business ideas that would benefit the group as a whole. The constitution, over ten pages long and written in formal English, clarified the responsibilities of the chairman, secretary, treasurer, and auditor. After being vetted as eligible for membership, new members registered by paying 5,000 KSh and providing a photocopy of their ID, a valid email address, a phone number, and the personal details of a relative. The constitution also specified the amount of the monthly contri-butions, different fees, and how much money every member had to pay if a member or a relative of a member died, thereby doing justice to the high costs of transporting a corpse to the family's ancestral home in western Kenya, where members of HoMiSiKi, as *jo*-Luo, were supposed to be buried. While the constitution thus clearly defined how members had to behave in case of a member's death, it described HoMiSiKi's business agenda only in very vague terms by mentioning that the group should 'do business as much as possible to achieve its development dreams'.

Comparable to the formal character of HoMiSiKi's constitution that entailed precise protocols, such as those outlining the requirements for membership, the group's meetings were well-structured and followed agendas that had to be officially sanctioned by the chairman before each meeting. Moreover, in contrast to the use of Dholuo in their daily lives, members tended to switch to English when they discussed issues related to HoMiSiKi. The highly formalized structure of their meetings and their constitution, as well as their use of English, which many Kenyans considered the language of politics and business, echo Maia Green's observations about saving groups' 'public performance of social and developmental responsibility' (2019: 110) that creates 'an institutional space in which persons assume an identity as "savers"' (2019: 105), or, in the case of HoMiSiKi, as prudent investors and cosmopolitan businessmen. However, despite the important role the group played in the lives of its members, who contributed financially and invested a lot of their time, HoMiSiKi did not yield any economic profit. Though its members helped one another to find jobs or training opportunities, it would be a stretch to conceive of HoMiSiKi as being engaged in a form of 'solidarity entrepreneurialism' (Kinyanjui 2014: 90). After all, the dream of buying a bus to join Nairobi's thriving matatu economy remained just that, a dream. The group was, in other words, first and foremost a burial society.

Considering the investment group's lack of economic growth, I suggest that HoMiSiKi's official financial development agenda and its high level of formalization helped to transform the investment group into an institution of pretence. By framing the group as an economically serious and prospectively successful initiative, members who talked about HoMiSiKi primarily as an investment group and not a burial society retained 'the mystique of the project' (Smith 2008: 65) and convinced themselves, their wives, and their families that they would be successful. Furthermore, understanding and portraying themselves as businessmen who had founded and contributed to an investment group made it easier for these men to participate in social activities that their wives and girlfriends considered an unproductive waste of time and resources. The 'norms, values, attitudes and beliefs' members of HoMiSiKi displayed overtly thus acted as a 'banner' (Kapferer 1969: 209) in the shadow of which migrant men could engage in wasteful forms of masculinity. HoMiSiKi, in other words, helped cover up migrant men's irresponsible and wasteful behaviour on what they called their 'playing field' (Dholuo, *pap*).

Wasteful masculinity

Men of the past provided, but with those of today, there is no providing (Kiswahili, *Wanaume wa zamani walikuwa wanaprovide, lakini wa siku hizi kuprovide hakuna*). […] if they see expenses, they think that they have to escape to a place that has no expenses.

Joy, 23-year-old migrant from Transmara, pregnant and married

When I returned from the gym on a scorching hot afternoon in April 2021, I saw some men sitting in front of a plot being constructed not far from my apartment. From a distance, I mistook them for day labourers who were working at the construction site and taking a break. Approaching the group, however, I soon spotted the familiar faces of several *jo-pap* relaxing on cement bricks and enjoying rum mixed with energy drinks. After buying a bottle of Captain Morgan, I joined them, and we exchanged stories until the atmosphere suddenly changed. An alert had gone out that a *ja-pap* needed help somewhere in Kware. Gulping down their drinks, a few *jo-pap* started running toward the place where their help was needed. Still unsure what was happening, I followed the others and, after walking deeper into Kware for a few minutes, I recognized a handful of *jo-pap* patrolling the area carrying wooden and metal sticks. Concerned for my safety, some *jo-pap* urged me to stand by the side as they searched for a man who had stolen some goods and vandalized the pawn shop of Geoffrey Ochieng, an aspiring politician, businessman, and *ja-pap*. After a while, two *jo-pap* dragged a bleeding individual out of a plot and brought him to the pawn shop, where he tried to explain his actions and begged for mercy. Shortly thereafter, two police officers arrived and agreed that *jo-pap* should help them to escort the thief to the local police station. Once the suspect was handed over to the authorities, we headed to Patrick's barber shop, which was located opposite the base and was a vantage point for *jo-pap* to watch two of the estate's main roads (see figure 7). Feeling that Pipeline's anonymity required a communal response, and being aware that their power lay in their number and solidarity, *jo-pap* had declared an area around the base a no-go zone for thieves and members of the Kikuyu-dominated cult and youth gang *Mungiki*, which extorted money from informal businesses in the estate (Frederiksen 2010).

Adeline Masquelier's ethnography of young male Nigeriens' experience of boredom and belonging describes how unemployed men in Niger prepare and drink tea while sitting around at so-called *fada*, makeshift meeting places where they discuss politics and other issues concerning their lives (Masquelier 2019). Comparable things took place at *jo-pap*'s regular meeting point. Migrant men could be found at the base every day, but most came at the weekends and in the evenings after returning from their jobs, and discussed politics, bought

Figure 7   View into one of Pipeline's main streets. Photograph by the author, 6 June 2022.

and drank tea, porridge, or alcohol, enjoyed the free Wi-Fi from a nearby shop, went out to get some food at a small restaurant owned by the wife of a *ja-pap,* and discussed news, gossip and important information about Pipeline or rural western Kenya. If a *ja-pap* was not in the house or at work, he was, most probably, at the base.

In contrast to a typical day at a Nigerien *fada*, sitting around at the base was not perceived as excessively boring. Rather, spending time at the base exposed *jo-pap* to a temporal rhythm characterized by unexpected and sudden shifts between relaxation and excitement. Discussions about politics were punctuated by catcalling passing women with beautiful tooth gaps (Dholuo, *rambanya*) or big buttocks, and the relaxed sipping of hot porridge could anytime be interrupted by a *ja-pap* calling for help, as in the case of the vandalism of Geoffrey's store. Most importantly, the base was where *jo-pap* thought about and planned their evenings and weekends. They discussed where to drink alcohol, or which *ohangla* concert to attend, and how they would enjoy the fruits of what they called 'back' and 'through passes', the former being the informal exchange of previous sexual partners (also known as 'recycling second-hand goods') and the latter the setting up of a one-night-stand or a sexual affair with a female friend for another *ja-pap*. In *pap*, as Victor phrased it, thereby summarizing *jo-pap*'s wasteful conviviality, men had to realize that 'an antelope is nobody's goat, if you find an antelope, you can eat it, and then you carry it back to the bush so that another man will find it.'

Though *jo-pap* also acted as a local vigilante group, the primary social function of the base was to offer male migrants a public place outside their houses where they did not have to fear being confronted with the expectations of their wives and children. The base was, in other words, the structural antidote to the house. Though comparable, this binary spatial partition was not congruent with how social space was organized in rural western Kenya, where *pap* was not only opposed to the female-dominated house, but also the male-dominated homestead, which was owned and controlled by the husband. While the rural homestead was overseen by the homestead head (Dholuo, *wuon dala*), who decided what happened and who was welcome in the homestead (see Dietler and Herbich 2009, Schmidt 2020), the rural *pap* used to be a social arena where predominantly unmarried men and women from different local areas met to enjoy dances, traditional wrestling matches, music, sexual encounters, and other recreational activities.

By introducing 'an imaginary village space [....] into the neighbourhoods of the townships' (Pype 2007: 266), *jo-pap* reduced the tripartite structure of social space prevalent in rural western Kenya to a binary one. This reduction of complexity did, however, intensify the contrast between the two social spheres of the 'house' and the 'playing field'. Migrant men who lacked the social prestige and recognition of a *wuon dala* but felt increasingly pressured by their wives, girlfriends, and rural relatives to provide economically also began to seek solace in *pap* simply because there was no other public space to which they could go. A migrant man who lost his job during the pandemic could decide to spend most of his days at the base because the house had turned into what Victor once described as a 'battlefield' (Dholuo, *ka lweny*), where one had to behave like a cunning 'leopard' (Dholuo, *kwach*)[1] in order to avoid fights and arguments. As most social contacts of a *ja-pap* were in one way or another related to *pap,* hanging out at the base even made sense economically. Instead of sending a résumé to an unknown human resource manager, it was more promising to sit at the base inquiring about job openings or waiting for the chance to be taken along by a friend to a factory in the industrial area for a day job, thereby at least earning a few hundred Kenyan Shillings.

The contrast between *ot* (Dholuo, 'house') and *pap* (Dholuo, 'playing field') comes into even sharper relief when taking a closer look at how social relations were conceptualized inside *pap.* While the house was perceived as a place of pressure and unrealistic expectations (see chapter 3), *pap* was understood as a place where no grudges should be held and where men should not expect much from each other. *Pap* was thus not only differentiated from the house but also from the HoMiSiKi investment group, whose members were contractually bound to one another and had to pay contributions and fees. These differences became manifest in what could be called the unofficial constitution of *pap*: eight 'principles' that circulated as a meme in *jo-pap*'s WhatsApp group, of which six are quoted here:

Principles mag pap (Dholuo, 'principles of the playing field')

Pap onge kun.	No hard feelings on the playing field.
Pap onge ritaya, once ja-pap, forever ja-pap.	There is no retirement on the playing field, once a *ja-pap,* forever a *ja-pap.*
Pap iye tin, ji tuomre.	The playing field is small, people bump into each other easily.
Ja-pap ok landre, your record will speak for you.	A *ja-pap* does not broadcast himself, your record will speak for you.

---

[1]   Migrant men addressed each other using names for wild animals, such as *kwach* (Dholuo, 'leopard'), *rwath* (Dholuo, 'bull'), or *ondiek* (Dholuo, 'hyena'), which carried positive connotations and created feelings of brotherly relatedness (comparable to *omera*, designating a friend or 'brother', and *owadwa*, 'brother'). Correspondingly, women were called *mwanda* (Dholuo, 'antelope') or, in a more romantic register, *atoti* (from Kiswahili, *mtoto*, 'child', meaning 'babe' or 'beautiful one'), *aswito* (from the English word 'sweetheart'), and, more ambivalent, *jaber* (Dholuo, 'beautiful one'). In an ironic twist on the perception of Luo women as materialistic, the female comedian Adhis Jojo demanded to be called 'my bungalow', 'my car keys', or 'my cheque book' instead of *aswito* in a sketch during which she responded to the comment that Luo women have high expectations with a rhetorical *Ni kweli?* (Kiswahili, 'Really?') Interestingly, local minibuses known for reckless driving, loud music and rough conductors were known as *manyanga*, a Sheng word for 'girl' that a Luo friend translated as *nyar pap* (Dholuo, 'daughter of the playing field').

Pap ji tee singul.   On the playing field, everyone is single.

Ja-pap nyaka bed gi nying' mar pap.   A *ja-pap* must acquire a *pap* name.[2]

Jo-pap did not expect to smoothly progress along the linear trajectory toward economic success, which was the official aim of HoMiSiKi and what men felt their intimate others demanded of them. The temporal rhythm of *pap* was rather a circular repetition of the same activities, such as talking about politics, drinking, catcalling women, having sexual affairs, fighting, and dancing to *ohangla* music. Life in *pap* was deliberately constructed as a celebration and performance of wasteful, sexually potent, and sometimes violent masculinity. Spending time in *pap* thereby allowed men to temporarily evade the pressures produced by modernity's promise of economic progress. In contrast to the house as a place focused on the reproduction of the family and the continuous accumulation of commodities that marked the economic achievements of a migrant man, *pap* was a place of excessive and wasteful consumption and non-reproductive sexuality. Here, married men could once again behave like irresponsible teenagers living in the rural hinterland.[3] Considering that experiencing oneself as masculine is a socially produced and validated feeling, it is unsurprising that *jo-pap*'s practices of violent and wasteful masculinity took the form of staged performances. Through engaging in the practices of *pap,* men assured each other and the wider public of their masculinity, even if the traditional dances and wrestling matches of the past (Carotenuto 2013) had been replaced by carefully orchestrated political campaigns and staged barfights.

---

[2]   One *ja-pap,* for example, was known as *Pump Mkubwa* (Kiswahili, 'big pump'), or *Agwata Mzinga* (from Dholuo, *agwata,* 'calabash', and Sheng, *mzinga,* 'large bottle of spirits'). Other examples of a *nying' mar pap* were *Brigadier, Kauzi* (Sheng, 'thief'), or *Martial* (after the football player Anthony Martial).

[3]   While *jo-pap* exhibited a form of what could be called 'conspicuous rurality', many migrant women avoided showcasing their rural background by, for example, preferring to speak Sheng or Kiswahili instead of Dholuo. This was probably caused by differences in how men and women planned their futures. While many women had migrated to Nairobi with the intention to stay, most men considered their migration to Nairobi a temporary adventure and wanted to return home later in life, which intensified their motivation to mingle with other Luo men who would remain part of their social networks in rural western Kenya. Many migrant men interpreted women's rejection of rurality as a rejection of 'hard work' (Dholuo, *tich matek*) and neglect of their kinship obligations. Patrick, for instance, called women in the village 'women of development' (Dholuo, *mon mag development*) and women in the city 'women of anti-development' (Dholuo, *mon mag anti-development*).

Staging masculinity

When you dance, drink, and make stories, you don't feel heavy, you feel light.

A ja-pap

On a weekend in October 2021, and in preparation of the general elections 2022, *jo-pap* had invited several politicians who planned to contest for the seat of the Member of the County Assembly of Nairobi representing Kware ward to the base. Unsatisfied with the incumbent whom they had helped to win and who had announced to run again as the candidate of the Orange Democratic Movement party, most *jo-pap* had not yet openly declared whom they would support. Among the aspiring politicians eager to tap into the power vacuum were Benson, HoMiSiKi's chairman, and Geoffrey Ochieng, owner of the pawn shop. In the days before the meeting, aspirants adorned the base and surrounding plots with stickers and posters, thereby officially starting to vie for political support among Kware's inhabitants.

Prior to the meeting, Patrick emphasized that the people of the base invite politicians in Kware ward and not the other way around. Without the support of *jo-pap* – this was the implicit message – no Luo politician could be successful in the upcoming elections. Though not based on what Kenyans called the 'tyranny of numbers' but rather on the ability to tap into and activate social networks structured around Luo male migrants, the historical success of *jo-pap* proved Patrick right. Although Kamba outnumbered *jo*-Luo in Kware, a Luo candidate had won the last election.

During their speeches in front of *jo-pap* and other interested inhabitants, all aspirants presented political programmes focused on 'community development', the 'youth', and 'jobs', echoing the language used during official meetings of HoMiSiKi. Though all politicians thereby denounced the culture of corruption and monetary handouts, an influential *ja-pap* disappeared with each one of them for a few minutes after their speeches to receive a financial contribution in a nearby plot or dark bypass. Comparable to the way in which HoMiSiKi's rhetoric of economic success and investment covered up the wasteful masculinity of *pap*, politicians' official anti-corruption agenda thus allowed them to secretly channel material support to *jo-pap*, who then redistributed it in their networks.

Though they had yet to openly declare their support for a specific politician in order to continue to financially benefit from all candidates, most *jo-pap* had already decided to support Geoffrey, who appeared to have the resources to help *jo-pap* and to acquire connections among Nairobi's political-economic elite, which were necessary to secure more financial support for his campaign.

When Geoffrey arrived at the base in a private vehicle, a sign of his economic potential, he heartfully greeted some well-known *jo-pap* and gave stacks of his business cards and whistles to others, who distributed them to the men standing around. After Patrick and Geoffrey had sorted out some things, Geoffrey gave a short speech and then *jo-pap* launched a political rally that had likely been prearranged.

While walking through Kware ward, we danced, sang, and praised Geoffrey while handing out his business cards. As we marched through the estate, we stopped at meeting points for Luo youth, such as a pool hall, where other young migrant men joined us. The crowd had soon swollen to several hundred men who ensured that the people standing on the balconies and walking around the streets were aware of Geoffrey's candidacy. During the almost three-hour walk through Kware ward I realized that the almost exclusively male supporters of Geoffrey relished being part of a political mass. Resembling what Émile Durkheim called 'collective effervescence' (1995 [1912]: passim) and Wandia Njoya described as the 'political energy' of Kenyan men that was 'harvested by politicians' during elections (Njoya 2022), male migrants enjoyed the tumult, dancing, loud whistling and singing, and acting as Geoffrey's bodyguards, clearing the roads and making sure nobody interfered with the campaign's progress. Walking with them, I saw men who were proud of the fact that a politician would achieve nothing without their support. In *pap*, they decided who ruled.

After the campaign had ended, I met Joel Opiyo, who confided to me that Geoffrey had given *jo-pap* a mere 4,000 KSh, of which I would later receive one hundred from Patrick, and concluded that this amount was not enough for their 'work'. Joel's use of the term 'work' illustrates that *jo-pap* understood the campaign as a form of 'relational labour' (Baym 2015). Patrick, having grown up in Kware, had the deepest connections among Pipeline's inhabitants, and had so assembled hundreds of supporters with ease, and the assistance of fellow *jo-pap* which had helped to make Geoffrey a known figure among a substantial share of Kware's inhabitants. Furthermore, the term 'work' points to the fact that the relationship between politicians and supporters, some of whom would later put-up Geoffrey's posters all over the estate (figure 8), was a contractual one. While *jo-pap* could withdraw their political support, politicians might stop giving out handouts as soon as they were elected, which *jo-pap* bitterly reminded each other about when they talked about the incumbent.

Local politics was not the only arena where *jo-pap* staged performances of masculinity. After we had drunk several rounds of beer and spirits in a bar not far from the base, an argument broke out between two *jo-pap*. While one suggested it was time to go home, the other one kept telling us to continue

Figure 8   Campaign posters at a makeshift dumpsite, Kware. Photograph by the
author, 24 July 2022.

drinking. The discussion got more heated and the two started to push each
other around until another man noticed and tried to intervene. In a few seconds,
around ten *jo-pap* were on their feet and had started a bar brawl, everyone now
united in their fight against the man who had tried to appease the two *jo-pap*
as well as against a few of his friends. Slaps and blows were exchanged until
one *ja-pap* managed to calm down the others, and we left the bar. Outside we
found a *ja-pap* shouting that he was *kwach, wuod Awiti* (Dholuo, 'leopard, son
of Awiti') while threatening to attack bypassing men. After we had quieted him
down, we walked home together, laughing about what had happened, shouting
pap onge kun (Dholuo, 'no hard feelings on the playing field'), which was the
informal motto of *jo-pap,* and reassuring each other that in Pipeline nobody
could disturb a *ja-pap*. When returning from the gym the next day, Joel and
I were approached by a group of youth, some of whom had been threatened
by the *ja-pap* outside the bar. Feeling tense about a potential rekindling of the
aggression, I was relieved when Joel and the guys laughed about what had
happened. The incident, it seemed, was already forgotten. Bar fights, mostly
ignited by minor issues, are thus best understood as forms of public violent

behaviour by which *jo-pap* performatively reassured one another and others of their masculinity and control over *pap*.

Being a *ja-pap* entailed observing the city with a male gaze and making sure that the residents of Pipeline viewed *jo-pap* as masculine. It meant forcing one another and others to look at and deal with violent, sexualized, and wasteful forms of masculinity. *Jo-pap* created an audience for their displayed masculinity by catcalling bypassing women, discussing politics and organizing political campaigns, surveilling the area, and drinking and fighting in bars. These and related practices relocated the source of their masculinity from the house to *pap* and helped migrant men forget about their economic pressure and domestic frustrations. Though their wives and girlfriends might bicker about their inability to provide, in *pap* where the group was the 'bearer of masculinity' (Connell 2005 [1995]: 107), male migrants reassured one another that they were more masculine than those men who just sat in their houses and had forgotten that men excelled at being men around other men.

COVID-19 and the collapse of HoMiSiKi

I have taken *pap* to be something just to pass time, because there is nothing it helps with.

A ja-pap

The success of investment groups such as HoMiSiKi depends on accepting 'calculative rules' that make the private relations between group members irrelevant and fully 'determine whether and how actual money from some individuals returns to others in the group' (Green 2019: 117). Fragile ties of friendship and brittle political alliances can thus be detrimental to an investment group's economic success. In the case of HoMiSiKi and *jo-pap,* the goal to invest and the goal to provide a cover for male socializing were in conflict with one another from the beginning. The wasteful masculinity celebrated in *pap* furthermore opposed the narrative of the prudent male provider that dominated in the domestic sphere of the marital house. Though migrant men tried to keep these three 'communities of practice' where different types of masculinity were performed (Paechter 2003) strictly apart, their boundaries remained porous. This was unsurprising, as male migrants attempted to square the circle of successful masculinity by striving to be economically prudent investors in HoMiSiKi, sexually virile, generous, and wasteful men in *pap,* and romantic breadwinners in the house. While HoMiSiKi meetings, for instance, often struggled with drunk members who came late or interfered with the meeting's organizational structure, the activities of *jo-pap* were more calculative than narratives about *pap*'s conviviality and generosity suggested. This becomes clear when one looks closely at how the social consumption of alcohol was organized.

Going out for drinks either developed spontaneously from sitting together at the base or was initiated by a *ja-pap* who had some spare money to spend on the first rounds of drinks. In both cases, *jo-pap* had to engage in careful calculative considerations. For example, to avoid criticism from their wives, and to prevent themselves from spending too much money on alcohol, *jo-pap* often sent some money to their wives before starting to drink. *Jo-pap* also had to decide who would be included in the drinks besides those present, and how the drinking would continue after the initial contribution had been depleted. These two questions were officially answered according to the principles of *pap*. Everyone should be included and, once *jo-pap* required money for another round, everybody should contribute according to his financial ability so that a new bottle of spirits could be purchased and then shared among those present.

In reality, the bleak economic situation often forced *jo-pap* to exclude some members. When I, for instance, once told some *jo-pap* that I had only 1,000 Kenyan Shillings to spare, we decided to go to a bar located far from the base so that we would not be spotted by other *jo-pap* and each of us could drink enough alcohol to enjoy its relaxing and depressurizing effects.[4] *Pap*'s ethos of generosity and conviviality was thus threatened by migrant men's limited economic resources. Carefully balanced relations of alliance and distance and the subtle economic hierarchies between *jo-pap* risked becoming publicly visible when other *jo-pap* found out they had not been invited for a round of drinks.[5] Though nobody was to hold grudges in *pap*, nobody wanted to be

---

[4]   The degree to which *jo-pap* considered drinking alcohol and spending time in bars as a way to reduce the pressure caused by the expectations of women was captured by a meme that circulated on WhatsApp: 'Pls whenever u feel overloaded by your wife's issues, rather than engaging in domestic violence, kindly go to the nearest (Biological Anxiety Relief) (BAR) center or place and order for any 1 or more of the following antidotes: 1. Wife Irritation Neutralizing Extract (WINE), 2. Refreshing Unique Medicine (RUM), 3. Bothersome Estrange-wife Elimination Rebooter (BEER), 4. Vaccino Officio Depression-Killing Antigen (VODKA). 5. Wife High Infusion Suspicion Killing Energy Yeast (WHISKEY). Make yourself happy. There's more to life than domestic violence at home. This is issued by the Federal Ministry of Happiness (MoH).'

[5]   Alcoholic drinks were categorized according to their price. Imported beers and spirits were the most cherished, followed by Kenyan beers and spirits, and then locally brewed alcohol, which was ranked the lowest. Cans or bottles of beer were rarely drunk because they were individually consumed and more expensive than spirits.

excluded either. In as much as drinking alcohol helped to unite *jo-pap,* it could also stir up negative emotions and lead to social schisms among migrant men.

Local politics also united and divided HoMiSiKi and *jo-pap.* After Benson decided to follow the COVID-19 containment rules and thus cancelled all meetings of HoMiSiKi from around March 2020, some members united in an attempt to overthrow him around the beginning of 2021. Feeling that HoMiSiKi's savings were sitting idle in the group's bank account, though nobody could pinpoint the exact amount, they began to demand that the investment group be liquidated and its members receive their respective shares. The HoMiSiKi secretary responded that such a decision must be reached during an official meeting, which could not be held because of the COVID-19 regulations. Instead of further arguing with the group's members, he presented a list of individual members' payment arrears, which showed that most had failed to pay contributions during the COVID-19 pandemic. Some members reacted to this with rage, threatening to come to the houses of Benson and the secretary to demand their shares using force. While many members feared that Benson would use their money for his political campaign, some even suggested that embezzling the funds had been Benson's intention from the beginning. When I discussed the issue with Benson, he alerted me of the possibility that the request for liquidation was a staged attempt to get him arrested for violating the COVID-19 regulations by organising the meeting. If this happened, it would open the way for his political competitor Geoffrey Ochieng, whom Benson rightly suspected had more support from *jo-pap.*[6]

Though I did never find out what the true intentions of each party were, this incident exemplifies the fragile nature of friendship bonds developed in Pipeline. However, it would be misleading to interpret the feelings of brotherhood that emerged in *pap* and HoMiSiKi's atmosphere of potential economic success as simple delusions. Rather, participating in *pap* and in the activities of HoMiSiKi offered migrant men relief from their boring and repetitive

---

[6]   At a later stage of the political campaign period, Paul Okumu, an acquaintance of Leonida and migrant from Homa Bay County, entered the race. Probably due to Leonida's ongoing influence, many *jo-pap* started to support Paul. Because Benson had decided to forego his candidacy a few months before the general elections in August 2022, voters could thus choose between three Luo candidates on the voting day, namely, Geoffrey, Paul, and the incumbent, who still had considerable support in the northern parts of Kware ward. This led to a split in the Luo vote and helped a Kamba candidate to win the election. Though the split of the *pap* vote led to serious arguments and even fights between the supporters of Paul and Geoffrey, such confrontations were quickly forgotten once members of the base met in a bar or bumped into each other on Pipeline's streets. This exemplifies that, in *pap,* male sociality encompassed what many *jo-pap* considered as nothing more than the dirty game that was politics.

wage labour as well as from the suffocating atmosphere of pressure in their marital homes. They had tried to attenuate their experience of pressure by joining HoMiSiKi, which allowed them to view and present themselves as serious businessmen. Unfortunately, the economic effects of the COVID-19 pandemic further increased their experience of pressure and compelled them to look for ways to depressurize in *pap,* an arena of wasteful, and sometimes violent, masculinity. As they immersed themselves in *pap,* HoMiSiKi fell apart because the COVID-19 regulations had banned public meetings and most members had stopped paying their monthly contributions due to the dire economic situation brought on by the pandemic. Drinking, fighting, and politicking in *pap,* however, were not the only remaining options to evade the increased economic pressure. Some *jo-pap* and many other migrant men also sought solace in hardening their bodies in one of Pipeline's many gyms.

5

Lifting Weights and the
Performance of Brotherhood

You can't be there just alone.

No Mercy Gym member

The No Mercy Gym was basic: two adjacent single rooms with wooden doors, peeling paint, no mirrors, no advertisements, a pungent smell emanating from the communal latrines, rats running around, mould on the walls, and the irritating beeping of electricity meters announcing the upcoming disappearance of *stima* (Kiswahili, 'electricity') if not fed with money soon. The gym was located on the ground floor of one of Pipeline's older plots. While the upper floors housed tenants, Carl and his wife had rented the entire ground floor and converted it into one of Pipeline's many private primary schools. Walking to the gym, therefore, meant being warmly welcomed by troops of schoolchildren who ran around during their breaks, peeped out of their classrooms smiling, or gathered in front of the gym's window to catch a glimpse of adult men lifting weights.

The school consisted of ordinary single rooms that would otherwise be used as housing units. Yet, in as much as they offered enough space for a bunch of children to hunch over their schoolbooks, Carl had figured that they were spacious enough for a gym focusing on the essentials of weightlifting. He had been forced to close his old gym soon after the Kenyan government had prohibited social gatherings in response to the COVID-19 pandemic. Instead of renting another single room to reopen the gym once the pandemic restrictions were relaxed, Carl and his wife decided to squeeze a few more children into one of the other rooms so that two of the school's single rooms could be used as a gym. There were few jobs available, and diversifying the family's income by training migrant men who wanted to become stronger would assist Carl's family financially and keep him occupied.

While one of the rooms was also used as a storage room for school furniture and utensils, it primarily functioned as a training room for beginners who needed to learn the exercises Carl considered essential for the development of a naturally strong body. These included squats, deadlifts, and bench presses. The second room was reserved for more advanced lifters who could perform these exercises with good form and had reached a basic level of strength. Though the weights and machines in both rooms had been built by local craftsmen according to Carl's instructions, the second room was better equipped than the one for novices. Apart from different barbells and dumbbells, the room had a more stable rack, a refurbished bench that included the possibility to perform leg extensions and curls, a machine for pull-down exercises, weights ranging from 500 grams to 30 kilogrammes, and a jerrycan with water that members drank using the same cup. COVID-19 could not, according to the gym's members, affect strong and healthy men.

The limited space of the No Mercy Gym forced members to synchronize their training routine and adjust to one another's movements, making it compulsory for them to interact. This was one of the reasons why members considered the No Mercy Gym less competitive and antagonistic than other gyms 'where the big guys take all the weights and don't care about you', as one member put it. In as much as male migrants who came to the gym wanted to transform their individual physical bodies, these training conditions also led to the development of the members' social body. In the No Mercy Gym, male migrants concentrated on becoming stronger under the sympathetic gaze and with the help of other migrant men. Lifting weights made members not only physically stronger, but also created an atmosphere of brotherhood which allowed migrant men to momentarily forget about the social and economic pressure they experienced in their marital homes.

Weightlifting in Pipeline

Carl was a quiet and caring, and occasionally even shy, 40-year-old migrant with the sturdy look of a man who had lifted weights and had worked hard physically throughout his life. He had come to Pipeline when he was around twenty. Comparable to the trajectory of other male migrants, his first jobs in Pipeline involved exhausting manual labour, but Carl soon discovered the economic potential of a big body. Being drawn into the world of squats, barbells, and bicep curls, Carl realized that it was profitable to combine lifting weights with being a bouncer in one of Nairobi's clubs and hotels, where 'bodybuilders were paid a lot of money,' as he remembered nostalgically. Reflecting on his days as a bouncer, he laughed and told me how applicants for positions were not interviewed but just had to really fill out a T-shirt. Being big was good enough to make money. When Carl started lifting weights, the gym scene had been more closely connected to the security business and the economic activity of being a bouncer than it was today. Around ten to twenty years ago, almost no one viewed lifting weights primarily as a recreational activity. Neither did Carl and his friends start 'carrying stones'

(Dholuo, *ting'o kite*) to become physically more attractive. Though it helped migrant men to remain healthy and allowed them to spend time with male friends while working out, lifting weights was first and foremost considered a necessary qualification for the job of a bouncer or bodyguard. Paying the daily or monthly fee was thus an investment in one's professional career.

After his daughter was born in 2007, Carl stopped working as a bouncer. Despite having gone through a range of self-defence classes, he no longer felt safe. He had witnessed people being seriously injured with fists, guns, knives, and glasses. As a former instructor in the Power Iko Gym, one of Pipeline's oldest gyms and, in the early 2000s, the estate's only one, he understood both the intricacies and the economic potential of owning a gym. He had already advised men on how to train, watched out over the property, and collected entrance fees if the owner was not around. Carl realized that as an instructor he had basically run the gym. He might as well have his own, he thought. Following his instincts, he opened the No Mercy Gym not far from the Power Iko Gym at the end of 2008. This entrepreneurial move negatively impacted his friendship with John, the owner of the latter. While members of the Power Iko Gym still trained with barbells and dumbbells to which they had attached self-made cement blocks, members of Carl's gym, to quote a famous Arnold Schwarzenegger documentary from the 1970s, 'pumped iron'. To make matters worse, the roof of the Power Iko Gym leaked and the floor was not made of concrete. Its members thus had to put up with rainwater dripping into the gym and turning the floor to mud, which made it difficult to remain stable during exercises.[1] By opening the No Mercy Gym, Carl had taken advantage of a solid business opportunity that gave him an income to raise his daughter and provide for his family.

Carl's pragmatic understanding of weightlifting was reflected in his gym's minimalistic furnishing. Its makeshift and run-down atmosphere stood in stark contrast to some of Pipeline's newer gyms that carried flamboyant names such as Phenomenal Gym, Springfield Gym, or Digital Fitness Centre.[2] Although these gyms could not compete with the quality of those located in Nairobi's more affluent neighbourhoods, they were certainly more spacious and better-equipped than the No Mercy Gym. Many of them had mirrors as well as photographs of famous bodybuilders on their walls and sold nutritional supplements, such as whey protein powders, creatine, or amino acids. In addition, they used sound systems to entertain members with the latest

[1]   Carl and John's relationship improved once John had managed to upgrade his gym. During the time of my fieldwork, both gyms coexisted peacefully.
[2]   Carl and I identified roughly a dozen gyms in Pipeline, but probably missed several others that, like Carl's own, did not advertise their existence with a sign.

Kenyan and US-American hits. Almost impossible to find as it was not situated adjacent to one of Pipeline's main roads, the No Mercy Gym had none of these. Operating without official opening hours, the gym, furthermore, had to be opened by the caretaker of the plot if Carl was not around. To make matters worse, we were regularly forced to train in the near-dark, using candles or the lights of our mobile phones, if the area was experiencing one of the frequent blackouts or the electricity meter had not been fed. In short, nothing made the No Mercy Gym an attractive place to work out in from an outsider's perspective. It was a business run by Carl for people he knew and for those who were brought to the gym by other members. The only thing that the gym had to offer, besides the minimal equipment to perform the essential lifts, was the presence of other men and the total absence of women.

Leaving aside these differences, the development of Pipeline's gym landscape mirrored the history of recreational weightlifting in other places of the world. Weightlifting began as a circus attraction in the late nineteenth and early twentieth century and remained a niche sport for bouncers, prison inmates, and competitive Olympic weightlifters and bodybuilders until the 1980s. Since then, weightlifting and strength training have become recreational activities for a broader audience. Being pushed by the fitness boom and the rise of Hollywood's action stars (one member of the No Mercy Gym was nicknamed 'Commando' after a famous Arnold Schwarzenegger action movie), weightlifting was forced out of its niche in the 1980s. During this time, more and more men and women started to engage in strength training for a variety of reasons ranging from achieving a higher level of fitness, becoming physically more attractive, or wanting to compete with other athletes in feats of strength and endurance. The global south was no exception to this trend. Since the early 2000s, people across the globe have flocked to gyms and sparked a worldwide 'fitness revolution' (Archambault 2021: 521, see also Baas 2020 for an analysis of bodybuilding in India and Quayson 2014: chapter 6 on gyms in Accra).

The inclusion of weightlifting into the everyday routine of actors from different socio-economic and cultural backgrounds increased economic competition between gyms, forcing them to either focus on a specific group of athletes or to diversify their training programmes in order to remain attractive to a variety of customers. While some gyms in Europe, for instance, only accept female athletes, others try to create an atmosphere in which women feel comfortable enough to train alongside men (see, for instance, Sehlikoglu 2021). Though some gyms in Pipeline attempted to tap into a female customer base by offering aerobics classes, an activity considered decisively female, most men and women viewed lifting weights as a masculine practice and gyms as male spaces where men discussed their romantic frustrations and latest sexual escapades. During the course of more than 150 training sessions in the No Mercy Gym, I only saw one woman come for a training session, but she never returned. It is thus fair to assume that nobody went to the No Mercy Gym to present his chiselled body to, or flirt with, women. Several of its members emphasized that they had come to Carl's gym after feeling too intimidated by physically bigger and aggressive men who took up all the space and kept the equipment for themselves. Caleb, a friend of mine from western Kenya we got to know in the introduction, for example, was surprised about the tight-knit sociality of the No Mercy Gym and compared it favourably to other gyms where, as he described it, men trained while listening to music through earphones, ignoring everyone else. While most gyms in Pipeline did indeed radiate an anti-social and aggressive atmosphere, the No Mercy Gym was a hospitable and non-antagonistic space where migrant men could meet to lift weights together and forget about their economic challenges and romantic frustrations.

The No Mercy Gym was thus neither a space for masculine competition nor an arena to start a sexual affair or relationship. Rather, joining the No Mercy Gym promised new members a transformation of their physical bodies as well as an integration into a tight-knit group of male friends. In contrast to *jo-pap,* however, the social body of the gym members was not formed along ethnic lines. Though most members were born in former Western and Nyanza provinces, the gym attracted male migrants from all over Kenya. Regular members included Anthony, an electrician who worked for the Kenyan railway and hailed from the former Western province, Andrew and Isaac from Kisii County, Arthur from Chabera, Joel, a *ja-pap* from Migori County, Edward, a manual worker from Kenya's coastal region, Carl from Ukambani, and Godwin, part-time DJ and former owner of a cybercafé born in Bomet. While these migrant men went to the No Mercy Gym to acquire a stronger and more muscular body, the big bodies men showcased in Pipeline's streets and bars were, despite a superficial resemblance, far from the same. Many men just appeared strong because their huge but weak muscles, like the astonishing wealth of some landlords, had been built with the help of illicit shortcuts and corrupt behaviour.

Big but weak and small but strong bodies

The social sciences have developed a keen interest in the body over the last three decades. Initially viewed as 'a social skin' (Turner 2012) on which society inscribes its authority and notions of masculinity and femininity, recent scholarship has shifted attention to the body's potential to influence individuals and societies through its material agency (Mol 2002). During the same period, anthropologists and other social scientists alike have increasingly focused on competitive and recreational forms of athletic activity in order to shed light upon how societies produce and stabilize gender notions and what it means to be masculine (Messner 2002). This scholarship has emphasized that the employment and alteration of human bodies through what Marcel Mauss called 'techniques of the body' (1935) speak to larger contemporary political, social, and economic debates (Besnier and Brownell 2012). Realizing that a theory of the body must be complemented by a methodology that does not shy away from 'deploying the body as tool of inquiry and vector of knowledge' (Wacquant 2004: viii), it is also unsurprising that social scientists took boxing lessons (Lockwood 2015, Hopkinson 2022), mastered Olympic weightlifting (Sherouse 2016), or engaged in capoeira (Downey 2005).

Bodybuilding, fitness, and weightlifting have drawn the particular attention of scholars interested in understanding how neoliberal logics of self-perfection reflect in athletic activities. Katie Rose Hejtmanek, for instance, suggests that the rise of functional fitness in the US gym landscape and the accompanying practices of 'self-governance' and 'auditing' of one's training progress were a direct reaction of athletes' fears of a 'pending death world [...], where a racialized Other is intent on bringing death, or zombie apocalypse, by upending the current world order' (2020: 872). Focusing on the specific role of masculinities, Alan M. Klein's ethnography of bodybuilders along the US-American West Coast, *Little Big Men. Bodybuilding Subculture and Gender Construction*, proposes that male weightlifters transform themselves into 'bodily fortresses' to protect their 'vulnerability inside' (1993: 3). Feeling under siege by feminism and a crisis of masculinity, the bodybuilders interviewed by Klein had turned away from an increasingly feminist society and a ruthless capitalistic economy to focus on, and achieve full control over, their bodies.

Though I shy away from transferring such psychologically inspired diagnoses to the members of the No Mercy Gym, it cannot be denied that male migrants' interest in increasing their muscle mass emerged against the background of Pipeline's geography of urban exclusion and men's experience of pressure caused by what they perceived as women's distortion of the narrative of the male breadwinner. In the No Mercy Gym, migrant men's masculinity was not evaluated by economic criteria. Members were not interested in how much money others provided for their families or spent on their girlfriends. Rather, a man's masculinity depended on the size of his biceps, the weight he could push off his chest, and his willingness to persevere despite physical discomfort and pain. Working out in the No Mercy Gym thus constituted an opportunity to critique notions of masculinity that exclusively focused on material wealth.

However, to the regret of some members of the gym, the size of a man's body did not always correlate with his strength. While walking to a local restaurant that served huge portions of 'natural' and 'libido boosting' porridge in traditional calabashes, I shared a story with Carl that illustrated how difficult it was to rely on physical size alone if one wanted to estimate a man's strength and masculinity. The day before, Arthur and I had visited a gym that Carl had shown us a couple of weeks before. While warming up in a corner of the gym, we saw a muscular guy with big arms and a mighty chest who appeared to be using heavy weights in an exercise known as 'rowing', during which an athlete bends over until his torso is parallel to the floor and pulls a loaded barbell to his stomach. As Arthur felt curious and intimidated at the same time, I pushed him to ask the guy if he could try to lift the weight. Arthur went to the guy, discussed something with him, grabbed the barbell, and lifted it easily. Though he had laughed heartily about the incident, Carl responded more seriously after I had finished telling the story: 'That is unproportionate. You shouldn't be big and weak, being strong and small, that's better, like Bill. Bill just needs to eat more, but being big and weak, that is not good.' While the guy Arthur and I had seen in the gym appeared strong because of his big and muscled body but actually lacked strength, Bill (a member of the No Mercy Gym) was slight but, as we all knew, definitely strong. Asking Carl about what he thought caused such paradoxical appearances, he replied that the muscles of some men were 'big but soft' and that 'you can't expect results without energy. They use steroids and supplements.'

Disapproving of injecting steroids and taking supplements, Carl emphasized the need to train hard and eat natural food rich in protein like *omena* (Dholuo, 'freshwater sardines'), porridge (Kiswahili, *uji*), eggs, groundnuts, *mboga kienyeji* (Kiswahili, 'indigenous vegetables'), and *ugali* (Kiswahili, 'stiff grain porridge').[3] Carl's training philosophy was equally simple and straightforward. Members should arrive at the gym after breakfast and focus on the major compound lifts such as bench presses, squats, rows, and deadlifts. After lifting as much weight as possible, they should go home, eat well, and rest. For a strong and big body, men only had to eat plenty of good food, be patient, and persevere through painful, long, and exhausting exercise sessions. 'No pain, no gain', as members of the No Mercy Gym reminded each other if someone complained about sore muscles or any other discomfort.

---

3   Carl also rejected taking drugs for minor illnesses such as coughing, light fever, or headaches. After telling him that I had tested positive for COVID-19 and wondered whether I had been infected in the gym, he remained calm and urged me to take garlic, lemon, ginger, and honey.

Figure 9   Sign giving direction to the Phenomenal Gym. Cartoonish figure with emphasized arm, chest and abdominal muscles, the so-called 'Johnny Bravo look'. Photograph by the author, 2 February 2022.

Carl contrasted his training philosophy with the one he believed most weightlifters in other gyms adhered to. His philosophy emphasized a balanced diet, natural strength, health, and a simple but physically and mentally taxing training that focused on the development of the body's larger muscles. The style of training he criticized was determined by the attempt to achieve a specific physical appearance characterized by a big chest, defined abdominal muscles, and muscular arms, the so-called 'Johnny Bravo look' (figure 9). To achieve such results quickly, and without effort, many men, according to Carl, embraced the use of machines and, in addition to supplements such as protein shakes and creatine, the use of steroids allegedly illegally imported into Kenya by Cuban doctors who had arrived in the country as part of a health cooperation agreement between Kenya and Cuba.

In contrast to the Georgian weightlifters studied by Perry Sherouse (2016) who classify bodies and the techniques used to create them as either male or female, Carl distinguished between two types of male bodies resulting from different training philosophies. While Carl's training regime could lead to small bodies that were hard and strong but would become big if the athlete started eating more, the other training regime produced big bodies that were weak and soft and would become wrinkled if the athlete stopped training. A man who looked strong might thus be a weakling trying to impress women without putting his energy into hard and painful training. In other words, a man's outer appearance was an inaccurate measure of his body's actual strength. Being just big did not prove a man's masculinity. In as much as fast wealth depended on the willingness to sacrifice one's own or the reproductive power of relatives, taking steroids furthermore damaged men's virility. While working out with heavy weights was seen as increasing sexual stamina and performance, taking steroids reduced men's ability to perform sexually. Supplements, in other words, caused men to be 'flat'.

Local notions of masculinity, and the bodies into which these were inscribed, grappled with what Achille Mbembe has characterized as the postcolonial decoupling of the sign from the thing it signifies (2001). While the economic success of young politicians and landlords with large potbellies did not signify decades of hard work but merely their capacity to gain wealth through illicit and occult means, the big but soft and weak muscles of steroid-users evoked the physical strength and sexual energy of a massive male physique without actually embodying these properties. According to my male interlocutors, it was women's naivety and thirst for short-term gratification that made them fall for such deceptions, even though the material excesses of fake muscles and fast money did not signify anything real and sustainable. Rather, they were based on 'summoning up the world of shade' (Mbembe 2001: 145) populated by members of the satanic Illuminati who sacrificed children and suspicious doctors who sold steroids that led to erectile dysfunction. Working out in accordance with Carl's training philosophy forestalled such a loss of reproductive agency. In contrast to the injection of steroids, training in the No Mercy Gym even offered recreational weightlifters an experience of increased control over their lives by giving their days *form* (Sheng, 'plan, agenda') and a proper structure. Instead of promising fast results, Carl continuously advised members to accept that the goal of having a massively muscular body that not only looked but actually was powerful and strong could only be achieved after years of hard work.

The promises of a big body and the temporality of physical success

> I can't say that there is something I can achieve in one month because I am aiming higher. You know when you are aiming higher, you are supposed to train for some period.
>
> *Isaac, No Mercy Gym member*

Godwin was a 24-year-old migrant from Bomet who had started lifting weights a couple of years ago in order to lose some weight and lead a healthier life. When I met him in the No Mercy Gym in 2020, however, his motives had changed, and his main goal was to acquire what he described as a 'big, and more muscular' body. Asking him about his role model, Godwin mentioned the actor and former wrestler Dwayne Johnson, also known by his stage name The Rock. Although Godwin, who came to the gym every day, was strong and, being around six feet, comparably tall, he still had a rather lean appearance. Weighing around 80 kilogrammes, he did not look massive, especially when wearing his favourite clothes that were rather baggy. If he wanted to achieve a body comparable to Dwayne Johnson's, he would have to gain around 25 or even 30 kilogrammes of muscles which would be an impressive accomplishment and could take years even if Godwin ate well, trained hard, and had enough time to rest.

Most members of the No Mercy Gym shared Godwin's goal. They all agreed that women preferred muscular men over skinny or overweight ones. Women, so the narrative went, would feel more comfortable with a physically intimidating man who could provide security so that they, as Godwin concluded, could 'disturb everyone else' when going out. A big body would thus not only increase a man's sexual success with women, but it would also enhance the respect of other men in bars, clubs, and on the streets. While reinforcing the notion of ideal men as physically strong and composed, this narrative also relied upon stereotypes of women as physically weak, hysterical, and in need of being protected. Furthermore, a big physique opened up financial opportunities, which was important in the context of Kenya's economy as it lacked employment opportunities. If a job required physical strength and there was an oversupply of potential workers, a big body could prove advantageous. Bouncers and bodyguards, for instance, were still required to have massive physiques. Gym members, in other words, mostly viewed the enlargement of their muscles as a means to improve their relations with others and not as a way to increase their self-esteem (Klein 1993, Wacquant 1995).

However, when I asked Godwin and Carl what it meant to be a man in contemporary Kenyan society during an interview on their lives and attitudes toward lifting weights, Godwin concluded that 'you must have money, and you must have a very nice house'. Reproducing the narrative of the male provider, Carl added that if the woman paid the rent in a relationship, she would become 'bigger' than the man. Despite clinging to the physical transformation of his body, Godwin was thus certain that money trumped physical appearance and strength any time. Although he was aware of his inability to do justice to the prevalent narrative of the wealthy male provider, Godwin refused to embrace a life that stood in contrast to this narrative. He had once observed how a close friend tried to be in a relationship with a wealthy woman, but it had taken such a toll on his friend that he felt compelled to end the relationship: 'He had a girlfriend, she had money, she wanted to control him […]. He couldn't move around by himself, if he wanted to move around, she had to be there, if he wanted to buy something, he had to tell her how much. I could never live like that.'

The intricate relation between money, the male body, and a migrant man's prospects of finding a wife also crystallized in one of Jacob's WhatsApp status updates. Jacob, a migrant from western Kenya and member of a gym located not far from the No Mercy Gym and the Power Iko Gym, had posted pictures of his muscular body alongside images of him repairing cars. Below the pictures, he had written: 'Wife material is not looking for a wealthy guy, she's looking for an ambitious guy, hard-working, warm, available'. This statement contrasted Jacob with an emotionally distant man who was always on the move, wealthy without working hard, and thus probably involved in occult activities. By presenting himself as ambitious and hard-working, traits that his muscular body seemed to attest to, Jacob suggested to women in his contact list that he had a bright future and soon would be ready to provide for a family. After all, however, the focus on the 'promise of a big body' that 'is almost preinterpreted as strong' (Linder 2007: 464) remained a subordinated and fragile attempt to be respected by women and other men. While becoming physically big and strong put one in an advantageous position compared to a man who was weak and poor, a migrant man's impressive muscles and physical strength could not compete with the thick wallet of a wealthy man who proudly paraded his potbelly. In the end, it was money and not muscles that made men big.

Godwin and other unemployed gym members did not feel that they could influence the fate of Kenya's economy, and they believed that sustainable romantic relationships and progress in their professional careers were beyond their control. In such a context, adhering to Carl's training philosophy and engaging in systematic weightlifting provided structure to their lives. Lifting weights six days a week to progress continuously toward, for instance, the body of The Rock or comparable role models was a goal-oriented, structured, and meaningful activity that helped migrant men to 'embody themselves as capable and agentive persons' (Lockwood 2015: 5). Whilst they perceived cause and effect to be disentangled in the economic and romantic spheres, with slay queens having ugly sponsors and hardworking men remaining poor, they could exert near complete control over their individual physical success in the intimate and homosocial space of the No Mercy Gym. Yet, the marginal utility of lifting weights drastically reduced after an athlete had achieved what was sometimes referred to as 'beginner gains'. Progressing from deadlifting 60 kilogrammes to deadlifting 120 was much easier than progressing from 160 kilogrammes to 220 and, leaving aside genetic factors or questions of technique, lifting heavier weights translated into having bigger muscles. Members of the No Mercy Gym, therefore, had to persevere through months without getting significantly stronger, which was the reason why they were convinced that merely maintaining their level of strength by going to the gym regularly was a respectable accomplishment in itself. While their intimate others expected continuous economic growth, other gym members understood that lifting weights was a mentally challenging practice that demanded patience and perseverance.

As 'a never-ending activity' (Pype 2007: 251) whose objective remained 'always "just out of reach"' (Archambault 2021: 534), working out in the No Mercy Gym was premised on an extended temporality of delayed physical success and thereby constitutes an example of what Jane Guyer called the 'evacuation of the near future' (2007: 410). While lifting heavy weights demanded total concentration on the moment, its ultimate aim lay in the far future. Strengthening one's body, however, was not a solitary accomplishment but involved communicating, meeting, and working out with other migrant men. It was intimately related to and depended on the construction of a male 'community of practice' (Wenger 1998) or, as Andrew phrased it more emphatically, 'brotherhood' among the members of the No Mercy Gym.

The interactional construction of brotherhood

> In the No Mercy Gym, guys are like family. When you are there, you feel much comforted because, inside and outside the gym, we support each other. When you have an issue, you find guys who give you a helping hand.
>
> *Edward, No Mercy Gym member*

Most of the days I worked out in the No Mercy Gym followed a similar rhythm. Around ten a.m., I left the house, talked to a few friends I met on my way, and branched into the small road leading to the gym. Arriving in front of the plot, I was greeted by Carl and one or two members waiting outside the primary school, basking in the warm but not yet scorching sun. Exchanging news and reminding each other which body part we would be training, we waited for a while, phoning those members who were not yet there to ask if they still intended to come. Anywhere up to 30 minutes past its official starting time of 10.30 am, we would enter the gym and begin training. Following a routine that focused on a different body part every day, we worked on our chests (Kiswahili, *kupiga kifua*, or *kupiga chest*, literally, 'beat the chest'), arms (Kiswahili, *mikono*, alternatively *kupiga bi* for biceps, *kupiga trayo* for triceps), backs (Kiswahili, *mgongo*), legs (Kiswahili, *miguu*), or shoulders (Kiswahili, *mabega*). This training routine created a five-day rhythm from Monday (back training) to Friday (arm training), with Saturday being a day for warming up the muscles and Sunday reserved for resting.

A typical training session included around five exercises and lasted up to two hours. After warming up our muscles, we started with the most fundamental exercise for developing the body part we were training. In the case of legs, for instance, this would be weighted squats. After loading the barbell with weights, one person started the first set of twenty repetitions and the other members waited for him to finish.[4] After everyone had finished their first round, we increased the weights and did eighteen repetitions for the second set, until we reached the final set of around twelve heavier repetitions. By thus progressively increasing the weight while reducing the number of repetitions, we went through so-called 'pyramid sets'. After the main exercise, we moved on to supplementary exercises; in the case of the legs, for example, these being lunges, dumbbell and reverse squats, or leg extensions and curls.

The limited space of the gym, the number of weights available, and the number of people training – most of the time around three to six but sometimes more – made it almost impossible to train more than two compound exercises simultaneously. Depending on the body part and the equipment involved, we would at most engage in three different exercises at a time: one compound exercise requiring a lot of weight and two supplementary exercises that required less weight. As the second room of the gym was rarely occupied, especially during our morning routine, restricting us to one room was, however, a choice. Arranging ourselves in the cramped room not only increased the temperature that members believed would keep the muscles active and prevent them from cooling down, but also raised the humidity level, which our bodies responded to by increasing sweat production, reassuring us that we were working hard. Rather than an externally imposed constraint, training together among friends was a deliberate attempt to create an intimate atmosphere where 'you just feel the psyche', as Godwin explained.

When lifting heavy weights we employed 'an array of tactics that include ridicule, encouragement, harassment, and direct physical assistance' (Klein 1993: 68) to reassure each other of our strength. It was, for instance, common to 'psyche'[5] each other by shouting positive remarks such as 'Big legs! Big legs!',

---

4   A repetition is one completed movement. In the case of a barbell squat, it means starting while standing, lifting the barbell onto the back, squatting down until the upper thighs are below parallel to the floor, and standing up again. A set is a number of completed repetitions, after which the athlete rests for a specific time. The duration of the break and the number of sets and repetitions depend on the training style.

5   I could not establish how the concept of 'psyche', which also circulated in the bodybuilding scene of the US-American Westcoast in the 1990s (Klein 1993: passim), ended up being used in Pipeline's gyms.

'Strong! Strong!',[6] 'Power *iko*' (Kiswahili, 'Power is there'), or 'Light weight, light weight!' These remarks were meant to increase the confidence of the lifter and to assure him that he had the strength to 'squeeze the weight' (Kiswahili, *kufinya weight*) to complete the lift. Frequent misogynistic comments further contributed to an atmosphere of masculine bravado and male power, thereby boosting members' confidence. These comments included ridiculing someone for not properly getting into what was known as the 'polluting position' (pushing back the hip and bending over one's torso to start rowing a heavy weight), comparing a 50-kilogramme weight to a petite slay queen to motivate the lifter, or accusing a gym member of having recently engaged in sexual intercourse with a woman if he was weaker than the week before. While such accusations perpetuated the image of women as drawing away male energy both in the form of money and physical strength, the equation of weights with women signalled a male control over the female body. Apart from calling weights 'sexy' when psyching oneself or others, Joel, for instance, used to shout 'Yes, madam', 'Yes, sweetheart', or 'Yes, *jaber* (Dholuo, 'beautiful one')' after every repetition.

As communicational cues encouraging oneself and others (Sherouse 2016), practices of increasing 'psyche' are best understood as positive forms of putting pressure on members attempting to lift heavy weights. By psyching each other, gym members expressed the expectation that the person trying to lift a weight would manage to finish the repetition. At the same time, they were ready to support the athlete if he could not manage to complete the lift on his own. In contrast to their friends at the gym, who understood that a man was sometimes unable to push a heavy weight off his chest without support, male migrants often expressed that their wives and girlfriends were unwilling to offer sympathy and emotional support when they failed to progress economically. Instead of being ridiculed as 'useless' despite working hard and trying their best, migrant men wanted to be psyched by their intimate others as well. They desired to be praised for their economic potential and work ethic and to receive emotional support whenever external constraints impeded their economic progress. When asked about the most important character trait of a woman during an interview, Godwin thus unsurprisingly answered that a girlfriend or wife should 'understand you [...]. Understanding meaning, if you have money or you don't have money, she will understand.'

Weightlifting has been depicted as a heroic fight between man and iron, an 'intra-relational contest' (Lockwood 2015: 15) in anonymous gyms that are 'no place for sociability' (Wacquant 1995: 164). It has been suggested

---

[6]   'Strong' also functioned as a form of greeting and, more common, of saying goodbye.

that the sole social component of lifting weights lies in the competition with other weightlifters (Klein 1993: 54). In contrast, working out in the No Mercy Gym depended on adapting one's movements and training routines to those of others. Working out well meant working out well with and caring about others. Even setting up the gym and loading weights on barbells depended on cooperative practices. Shifting equipment around and looking for weights hidden beneath each other or behind something else required members to move their bodies carefully to not disturb anyone already lifting. Just standing or sitting somewhere blocked space and the crowdedness of the gym forced us to avoid any movement not specifically aimed at facilitating the training.

Moreover, members seldomly engaged in individual exercises. If we trained the legs by doing squats, everyone trained their legs by doing squats. Even more remarkable, we did not use different weights while working out together. Despite the strength differences between the five or six men who regularly attended the morning routine, we started and finished each exercise with the same weights. Those unable to finish their set were supported and psyched. If we were bench-pressing and progressed from 50 to 110 kilogrammes, everyone had to persevere, or at least try to lift the heavier weights. The chain was considered to be as strong as its strongest link, not its weakest, and the resting time between sets was spent helping others to lift the weights and to become stronger.[7] Unlike other gyms in Pipeline where 'my speed might be high, and his speed might be slow', as Godwin had explained to me once, our body movements had to synchronize. While working on our bodies, we thus also strengthened our feeling of 'brotherhood' as Andrew, the former KDF soldier from this book's vignette, had called the gym members' intimate attachment to one another.

Supporting each other and spending time with one another outside of the gym further consolidated the strong social connections between the No Mercy Gym members. We invited each other for dinner or tea, ate goat head and drank bone soup in one of Pipeline's butcheries, gulped down cups of *muratina* (an alcoholic drink from central Kenya), or took post-workout porridge or medical concoctions in a place called Loliondo, named after a Tanzanian village where a local healer allegedly had performed miracles (Vähäkangas

---

7   A mentally and neurologically taxing exercise type known as a 'drop set' required the involvement of three additional people. During a bench press drop set, for instance, the lifter would start with 80 kilogrammes and finish five reps, then two people would remove five kilogrammes on each side and the person would, without placing the barbell back on the rack, lift 70 kilogrammes eight times until he had reached, for instance, 40 kilogrammes to be lifted twenty times. Throughout the exercise one person remained available for potential support. Drop sets exemplify that lifting weights in the No Mercy Gym could indeed be considered a team sport.

2015). Furthermore, the core group of the gym members assisted each other financially during emergencies and funerals, and unemployed members informed each other about jobs at construction sites where men with muscled bodies had a better chance of being employed. Interactional and institutionalized practices such as psyching one another, sharing meals, working together at a construction site, or supporting a member financially thus created and maintained the No Mercy Gym as a masculine space characterized by an atmosphere of brotherhood and braggadocio that helped men to momentarily evade the economic pressure they experienced in their marital houses.

Mental refuge and physical strength

It is difficult to identify the main factor that attracted migrant men to the No Mercy Gym. At its most prosaic, the gym, just like the investment group HoMiSiKi, helped members economically by providing another safety net in case of unforeseen costs caused by deaths or diseases. As a space for male sociality, the gym, like *jo-pap*'s base, enabled male migrants to leave their houses, where they ran the risk of becoming depressed. In an environment where men felt threatened by a discourse that pegged their usefulness to their ability to fulfil the role of the economic provider, the No Mercy Gym was a place of mental refuge. Tucked into the corner of a primary school and secluded from Pipeline's noise and the expectations of the outside world, the gym offered solace to migrant men, some of whom even came to lift weights for two hours before and two hours after work. Visiting the gym was, therefore, not only 'an aspect of the negotiation of urban free time' (Quayson 2014: 199) for unemployed male migrants but also a way in which employed men avoided spending time in their houses. As weightlifting was also mentally taxing, working out in the gym not only reduced migrant men's experience of pressure but also related somatic symptoms such as insomnia. 'When you train, you are exhausted, then you go home, and you eat and sleep, the stress is over', as a member of the No Mercy Gym summarized it.

By acknowledging Carl's authority and following his simple but strict training routine, gym members furthermore experienced and validated an alternative form of masculinity based on discipline and physical strength. Taking his advice to eat a healthy and protein-rich diet and to strictly adhere to the training timetable helped to transform members of the No Mercy Gym into stoic and humble men who appreciated hard work and consciously avoided engaging in what they considered female activities, such as rumour-mongering. Aware of circulating stereotypes that portrayed muscular men as aggressive and dumb, most members of the No Mercy Gym aspired to become what one member called 'cool gentlemen' who pursue their goals calmly and without being 'interested in a lot of stories'. In contrast to spending time in *pap,* which was a space for male wastefulness and adventures, going to the No Mercy Gym thus provided moral orientation and the opportunity to learn how to discipline oneself and others.

Like the boxing gym in southern Chicago studied by Loïc Wacquant, the No Mercy Gym was a 'sanctuary', 'a school of morality', and a 'vector of a debanalization of everyday life' (2004: 14–15). Its members relied on their own criteria of masculinity that they positioned alongside the narrative of the male breadwinner. In contrast to the migrant man's economic trajectory that was carefully observed by his intimate others, who were mostly female, his progress in the gym was predominantly evaluated by other male gym members. In the gym, men alone decided what counted as truly masculine. By lifting heavy weights and psyching each other, members of the No Mercy Gym thus consolidated an alternative narrative of what it meant to be a successful man in contemporary urban Kenya. Instead of relying on a male migrant's economic success as the prime indicator of his masculinity, gym members highlighted his physical strength, the size of his body, and his willingness to embrace and persevere through the hardships of working out in the gym. However, as the next chapter illustrates, some Kenyan men tried to redefine masculinity by taking the opposite approach. Instead of perfecting and increasing the size of their external surfaces, they searched for their true masculinity in the depth of their emotional and mental set-up.

6

Masculinity Consultants and the
Threat of Men's Expendability

> Society has changed. But female nature has fundamentally not changed.
> Female nature, just like that of men, evolved over hundreds of thousands
> of years and will not change anytime soon. If men are to live happily
> with women, they must peel back the scales that society tries to place on
> their eyes and appreciate life for what it truly is, not what it is advertised
> to be. We must open our eyes and learn from fallen men.
>
> *Masculinity consultant Jacob Aliet (2022a: 40–1)*

When I asked him about his favourite book on masculinity and manhood,
Philemon Otieno, author of biographically inspired self-help books, social
media personality, and childhood friend of Samuel and Arthur, told me to read
Brett and Kate McKay's *The Art of Manliness: Classic Skills and Manners for
the Modern Man* (2009). He had showcased the book on his WhatsApp status
on a few occasions, sometimes while surrounded by a few of his younger
male friends who considered Philemon their mentor. *The Art of Manliness*
is a collection of advice on how a man should behave in daily life and in
extraordinary circumstances. It teaches the male reader how to dress, how to
shave, and how to greet people like a man, but also how to save a drowning
person, how to make fire without a lighter, and how to take care of your
pregnant wife. The authors set the stage with a description of contemporary
gender relations:

> Discouraged from celebrating the positive aspects of manliness, society
> today focuses only on the stereotypical and negative aspects of manhood.
> […] Many people have argued that we need to reinvent what manliness
> means in the twenty-first century. Usually this means stripping manliness
> of its masculinity and replacing it with more sensitive feminine qualities.
> We argue that manliness doesn't need to be reinvented. The art of
> manliness just needs to be rediscovered. (2009: 2)

This diagnosis resembles migrant men's critique of the money-oriented
distortion of the narrative of the male breadwinner. Instead of discarding this
narrative, many male migrants attempted to reclaim its beneficial essence.

Figure 10 Self-help literature sold in a bookshop in Nairobi's central business district. Photograph by the author, 23 February 2022.

Some migrant men tried to rediscover this inner core of masculinity, their 'deep manhood' (Kimmel and Kaufman 1993: 8), by engaging with Kenyan masculinity consultants. Through workshops, self-help books, social media, and personal meetings, these masculinity consultants gave Kenyan men advice on issues related to masculinity, such as how to deal with the experience of economic pressure or how to overcome the anxiety of not performing well enough sexually.

By answering what attracted Kenyan migrant men to masculinity consultants and their advice, this chapter responds to the explosion of a market for, mostly but not exclusively US-American, self-help books such as Joseph Murphy's *The Power of Your Subconscious Mind* (1963), Robert Kiyosaki's *Rich Dad Poor Dad* (1998), Rollo Tomassi's *The Rational Male* (2013), and Jack Donovan's *The Way of Men* (2012). In an informal chat, the owner of a bookstore along Moi Avenue in Nairobi's CBD that regularly advertised books by Kenyan and Western masculinity consultants, for instance, confirmed that self-help books on masculinity were in high demand among young Kenyan men looking for guidance and male mentorship. Self-help books did not only constitute more than half of the books on offer in most Nairobian bookstores and among people selling books on the streets of the city's CBD (figure 10). They also circulated as illegal soft copies among many male and female migrants in Pipeline who littered their WhatsApp status with motivational quotes from self-help authors.

To understand the craze for self-help books, masculinity consultants, and relationship advice across Nairobi and Kenya (see Kamiri 2017), the first sections of this chapter discuss the life and worldview of Philemon Otieno, a 30-year-old male migrant from Homa Bay County to whom Samuel and Arthur introduced me in late 2019. In contrast to *jo-pap* who socialized masculinity and the gym members who focused on achieving a masculine appearance, Philemon conceptualized masculinity as an innate and God-given potential that must be nurtured through a cognitive mind-set characterized by vision, perseverance, and entrepreneurship. Nurturing one's God-given masculine core would ultimately result in economic success and thereby ease the experience of pressure.

After analyzing Philemon's religiously inspired activities and advice, the chapter hones in on two groups of Kenyan men who, influenced by Rollo Tomassi's secular and pseudo-scientific red pill movement, participated in a globally connected backlash against feminism. Using the metaphor of the blue and red pill from the 'Matrix' trilogy, followers of the red pill movement hold the opinion that the world is 'femicentric' and that men need to swallow the red pill to be 'unplugged' from the false truths of feminism (see, for instance, Aliet 2022a). So doing would allow men to reclaim their natural role as powerful and self-sustaining leaders who are needed by women. Though these two groups operated with and applied the language of the red pill movement, they did so in different ways. A small and non-hierarchically organized group of men loosely spearheaded by local self-help book authors Silas Nyanchwani (2021a, 2022) and Jacob Aliet (2022a) offered its members not only person-alized advice but also a protected platform or, as one member called it, a 'safe space' to be vulnerable. In contrast, the social media personality Amerix, a Kenyan healthcare professional who has become popular among Kenyan men over the last five years and had over one million followers on Twitter in 2022, gave the almost 100,000 members of his Telegram channel rather standardized solutions that they were not supposed to question.

By discussing these three ways in which local masculinity consultants offered solace to male Kenyans under pressure by reassuring them of men's supremacy over women, this chapter ethnographically illustrates how migrant men, against the background of the fear of their expendability, sought advice and explanations for their miserable economic and romantic situation (for an overview on Kenyan masculinity consultancy, see also Schmidt 2022a). By performing practices of wasteful masculinity in *pap* or by lifting weights in the No Mercy Gym, male migrants tried to evade women's pressure-inducing expectations in a nondiscursive way. In contrast to these nondiscursive forms of evading pressure that were often accompanied by emotional rants about specific women, or women in general, masculinity consultants provided men with an ideological critique of contemporary gender relations, which helped their male readers and male followers of their social media accounts to make sense of their relationships with women. Instead of continuing to feel pressured by female expectations, masculinity consultants taught men that women's expectations were an inevitable result of female nature that, once understood, could be turned to men's advantage. Their pseudo-scientific and religiously bolstered claims about male superiority and the female nature assured migrant men that they, despite what they felt society was propagating, were not dispensable. Men, that was the message, just had to become men again.

Visionary quantifications and the power of imagination

Say specific figures, like my net worth is $600 billion by the age of 45 years.

Philemon Otieno

Philemon had spent his childhood and youth close to a small market centre that was a short *boda-boda* ride from Chabera. His father died when Philemon was still young, and he grew up in poverty, running around in torn clothes and barely having enough food to eat. According to his narrative, his elder brother Brian one day had a vision of a British woman called Hannah who would come to Kenya to help local orphans. To reach a spiritual breakthrough, the two brothers kneeled on the bare soil every evening, directed their sight toward the United Kingdom, and prayed that Hannah would soon arrive. After an arduous time of praying, a young British woman who was keen on helping the world's poor was spotted in the area. Brian contacted the philanthropist and told her that he knew her name was Hannah and that God had sent her. The woman, whose name was Bettina but whom her father had called Hannah when she was young, interpreted the encounter as a sign of God's will, and inspired and financially assisted Brian in establishing his own church around Katito. Philemon thus did not encounter Pentecostalism in Nairobi, where he was an active member of a Pentecostal church for which he organized student and youth group meetings and services. He had instead been drawn into a charismatic form of Christianity by his brother, one of Kenya's many 'church founder-owner-leaders' (Gifford 2009: 154) who emerged in multitudes after the 'liberalization of the religious field' in the 1990s (Gez and Droz 2020: 164). Like many others, Brian had transformed his church into a successful business by disseminating a 'theological message that appeals to new followers' in order 'to attract financial investments, and redistribute them within a specific community' (Gomez-Perez and Jourde 2020: 9).

Soon after Philemon sat down at our table in The Branch, one of Nairobi's restaurants serving traditional Luo food to financially better-off customers, I realized that his plans for economic success were also influenced by globally circulating recipes of religious self-help culture.[1] Being 30 minutes late to our meeting, he apologized, ordered *dawa* (Kiswahili, 'hot lemon with ginger and honey') and some *samosa* (Kiswahili, 'fried pastry with a filling such as minced meat or potatoes'), and began telling me about his plan to visit Europe to fundraise for one of his projects in Homa Bay County. As Philemon kept teasing me with repetitive references to the lack of economic spirit of my friends Samuel and Arthur, whom he diagnosed as following a dangerous 'philosophy of poverty', I mentioned the chips business I had started with Samuel and how it had failed (see chapter 2). Philemon congratulated me and started to praise the benefits of failure. He, so the story went, had experienced the demise of no less than fourteen businesses. 'It is necessary to bounce back from failure,' he assured me, taking out a thick red notebook that contained seventeen business plans, which he called 'pipes' that he planned to 'tap into'. These investment plans built upon each other in terms of the capital required to implement them and became increasingly ambitious. His more modest business plans entailed the creation of women's groups around Chabera that would produce handmade soap bars and the sale of his own books and other merchandise that he actively advertised during church meetings (see also Bielo 2007: 316). More ambitious projects included a social media app that would take over the role of Facebook, YouTube, and WhatsApp across all of Africa and interplanetary missions to Mars, where his company would harvest rare minerals.

Describing his business ideas, Philemon tossed around extremely ambitious figures. One billion subscribers for his social media app, book sales in the hundreds of thousands, and billions of US dollars made by mining minerals on Mars. These figures had not been chosen randomly but were grounded in careful financial calculations based on detailed observations that Philemon then scaled up (see Schmidt 2017b). On one occasion when I went to meet him at a corner in Pipeline and took him to my house, he commented on the estate's high population density. If he could convince every fourth person to buy one of his books, he would sell tens of thousands of copies. He used this figure to scale up his calculations to include the whole of Nairobi, the whole of Kenya, and finally the whole of Africa, thereby jumping seamlessly

---

[1]   While the role of religion for self-help culture has been 'muted' (McGee 2005: 5) in Anglo-Saxon discourse, the reverse seems to be true for the discussion of the prosperity gospel in sub-Saharan Africa. Few scholars have talked about the craze for religious and non-religious self-help literature in Africa (McGee 2012, and Boyd 2018).

from an estate to a continent without acknowledging the problem of shifting between these levels. Such visionary quantifications were a part of a wider set of practices that causally linked mental visualization with material manifestation and relied upon what Micki McGee called 'classic American self-improvement: the power of mind over matter' (2005: 60). Quoting from chaper 13 of the Book of Genesis, 'lift up your eyes and look from the place where you are, northward and southward and eastward and westward, for all the land that you see I will give to you and to your offspring forever' (13: 14–18), Philemon concluded that 'what the eye of the mind can't see, the physical eye also cannot.'

Sitting in Philemon's living room a few weeks later with Samuel and Arthur, Philemon mentioned the '300 challenges task' he had recently introduced to his mentees. Rushing to his bedroom, he came back with two thick notebooks. One was a regular diary, the other one contained 300 goals and aims that he planned to achieve. After opening the diary, he took out and held up a cheque for five million KSh (roughly 50,000 US$) and told us that the cheque reminded him to 'work restfully' to assure that he would achieve his goal for the month of November: making a profit of five million KSh. Being impatient and curious about the '300 challenges task', Arthur asked Philemon about it, which prompted him to open the other notebook. He started to read: 'Reach happiness, build a house with eighteen bedrooms and 22 toilets, own fourteen jets, build skyscrapers all over Africa....' Before Philemon could continue to engage in self-help culture's 'pleasurable pornography of possibilities' (McGee 2005: 159), Samuel and Arthur burst into laughter and told Philemon that he was insane to think that any of these were possible, to which Philemon responded calmly that his 'intentions are like prayers. I do not believe in worrying about reaching these goals. I work restfully, and things will come.'

For economic plans, consumerist desires, and personal dreams to materialize in the future, economic actors, according to Philemon, had to define them clearly by visualizing and, if possible, quantifying them. Rather than creating pressure, carefully laying out these projects and plans helped Philemon to 'work restfully'. While Samuel and Arthur almost succumbed to the pressure caused by their own and their rural relatives' expectations, Philemon appeared to thrive when his expectations were as ambitious as possible. Believing with certainty in the power of what self-help author and pastor Chris Atemo (whose texts Philemon was well acquainted with) called 'God's gift', just like he and Brian had done until the British philanthropist had heard their prayers, Philemon's approach 'replaced an ascetic, self-disciplined work ethic with a vision of natural ease and plenitude, making way for a consumer culture bolstered by fantasies of boundless abundance' (McGee 2005: 63). Because God had already planted his gift in Philemon, questioning his ability to mine minerals on Mars was equivalent to questioning a natural fact. Just as cubs become lions – one of Philemon's favorite metaphors – he would become Africa's Elon Musk.

Focusing on the importance Philemon ascribed to the ways in which actors planned, visualized, and quantified their future success helps to illuminate what he alluded to when he equated intentions with prayers. By intending to achieve something great, Philemon, in a practice-oriented way but comparable to praying, was 'acting upon sacred beings' (Mauss 2003: 56), in this case on God's gift inside of him. According to Atemo, God's gift constituted an actor's 'capital' (2018b: 13) that ultimately remained in God's ownership. Each person was responsible for discovering theirs by engaging in a repetitive cycle of trial and error that Atemo called 'enterprise' (ibid.), which was what Philemon had alluded to when he had mentioned his fourteen failed business attempts. In as much as Philemon expected to get a response from God by praying, such as a sign or some advice, the repetitive 'embrace of the simple intention' (Scherz 2014: 133) to become successful was thus a way to call God's gift to materialize. If he were to fail again, he just needed to start afresh, finding new ways of intending to be successful.[2]

While sharing the Pentecostal idea that God wants all humans to be wealthy (Bialecki 2008, Haynes 2012, Van Dijk 2010), Philemon had created a form of prosperity gospel that freed individuals from external pressure and allowed them to 'work restfully'. In contrast to Samuel, for instance, who had the clear goal of becoming a successful lawyer, Philemon did not know how he would be successful. He just knew that he had to plan, visualize, and quantify his enterprises in detail, expect further failures, and continue to believe that one of his plans would align with the potential God had planted in him as a sacred gift. By allowing Philemon to, again and again, postpone the fulfillment of the expectation of success to a future point, when God's gift would blossom, his prosperity gospel made him and his mentees resilient to pressure.

Deep manhood

After talking about *The Art of Manliness: Classic Skills and Manners for the Modern Man* (McKay and McKay 2009) for a while, Philemon and I decided to start a reading group. In less than a day, the WhatsApp group we

[2]   Philemon's ideas not only resembled concepts from the US-American New Thought movement (see Hutchinson 2014), but also ideas I encountered while working at Maendeleo (see introduction). In recent years, topics such as the economic potential of aspirations, the need to become self-efficacious, or the power of a positive mind-set, have become important in debates among behavioural economists, actors from the development aid sector, and economic psychologists (see, for instance, Genicot and Ray 2020, Haushofer and Fehr 2014, Wuepper and Lybbert 2017).

created for that purpose included around 40 people interested in participating. Even though the online meeting had been organized at short notice and some people could not attend due to bandwidth or network problems, around a dozen people were present during the book's discussion. After a short round of introductions, one participant read aloud the first ten pages of the book, which included advice on how to find the right suit and a discussion of the benefits of different types of tie knots, such as the full Windsor and the half-Windsor. Feeling that these detailed elaborations on tie knots had little to do with the more pressing question of what it meant to be a man in contemporary Kenya, I directed the discussion back to the book's introduction by asking the participants what they thought about the authors' diagnosis that men had been feminized.

Philemon answered by elaborating on what he thought women were looking for in a man:

> A man who comes out as a leader […] somebody who comes out as calm, collected and knows what he wants in life. So, switching roles or taking over feminine roles does not really matter. You can be doing those roles, for example, I cook once in a while and when I cook, I cook well, but that doesn't strip me of the qualities of being a man […]. I think the social kind of way in which we said these are the roles of men, these are the roles of women was the wrong way to look at it.

Being a man, as another participant added, thus did not mean occupying a 'social role' or attaining specific 'surface characteristics' such as how one looked or if one prepared food. In contrast, 'real manliness' came from 'emotional maturity'. From the latter, masculine looks and practices would, as he called it, 'spring' automatically. When I asked if emotional maturity was not a quality that both men and women should strive to achieve, the participant explained that the emotional maturity of a man would be a direct result of his ability to 'take over what I can call the leadership role, because I think that is what God created man for from the inception of everything, so a woman is not supposed to overtake a man in taking what we call the leadership role, especially from what we call the family unit perspective.'

The discussion continued, with Philemon adding that 'you are not a man by how strong you are physically, but by how strong you are emotionally' and that, unfortunately, we were living in a 'society that promotes a man that is more physically, so they go for the looks, the abs, arms and everything.' However, trying to 'overcome the world' with muscles like 'boys' did not define a true man. According to Philemon, men had to 'overcome themselves' and keep on trying despite failure and external derision, to which all participants agreed. For them, masculinity was not defined by the material goods men possessed, by society's standards, or by a set of practices that men engaged in according to culturally determined gender roles. It was rather conceptualized as an attitude toward life characterized by the ability to remain 'calm' and 'collected' and by a high level of control over one's emotions and inner self. If a man controlled his emotions and worked on his talents, economic success would follow and women would automatically subordinate themselves. Masculinity, in other words, was understood as a gift from God to be rediscovered by every man deep within himself. Combining the idea of God's gift planted in humans with the belief that men were naturally calmer, more stoic, and more resistant than women, Philemon's advice seemed to boil down to the idea that men just had to be true to and nurture their male nature in order to attract economic and romantic success.[3]

Addressing the issue of economic pressure by redefining masculinity allowed self-help literature and masculinity consultancy to flourish as lucrative business models. Offering solutions to migrant men's experience of pressure thus played a significant role in Atemo's and Philemon's transformation into sought-after mentors and successful religious entrepreneurs who made money on social media and by selling books as well as merchandise, such as T-shirts or baseball caps. Yet, Philemon faced competition from other Kenyan masculinity consultants who linked their visions of how to restore patriarchy with narratives and practices adapted from the social and cultural counter-movement against feminism that has been baptized the 'manosphere', this being a largely virtual conglomeration of websites, books, blogs, and articles that advise on how to be a man in the twenty first century (Kaiser 2022, O'Neill 2018). It was in this manosphere that Philemon had once been attacked as a 'simp', short for 'sucka idolizing mediocre pussy' or 'simpleton', by followers of a radical anti-feminist movement who accused him of being too lenient and not radical enough in his attempts to 'set men free' (Atemo 2018a) by restoring their superior role.

---

[3]   In light of prevailing social trends, such as the rising numbers of single mothers and 'absent fathers' (Pala 2018), Philemon believed that it was no longer feasible for men to 'be passive in the rearing of children' and 'to leave everything to their wives while they bring home the paycheck' (Ingozi 2020: 31). In what might have been an attempt to remain attractive to female readers and followers, both Philemon and Atemo conceptualized masculinity as not only based on patriarchal leadership but also on the ability to care. In contrast to timid boys who were unable to lead and men who could only reign through violence, Philemon and Atemo advised men to mold the relation to their families after the ways in which God treated humanity. Men had to lead firmly and provide abundantly, but at the same time be lenient, caring, and forgiving.

#MasculinitySaturday: a radical anti-feminist praxeology

A time has come for men to say no to women's chaos. It is a time to take charge and refuse to be bullied into destructive surrender and unchecked capitulation to the failed feminist experiment [...]. It is time for men to rediscover the operant masculine frame needed to steer the society towards order [...]. Before it is too late.

Amerix

Mark Odhiambo, a 27-year-old migrant from Siaya County, single *ja-pap*, and unemployed university graduate, had lived in Pipeline since 2016. After graduating in physics, he struggled to find permanent employment and stayed afloat by writing essays for Chinese students. Being unsatisfied with his economic status and romantic life, he described Kenyan women as materialistic and unfaithful: 'Women are women. They are always materialistic. [...] When she needs something and there is somebody giving her a better option, she will go for it.' When asked about Amerix, who had been one of Kenya's most successful social media masculinity consultants during the time of my fieldwork, Mark got excited and claimed that the advice of Amerix had been 'educative' for him since he had first read his Twitter posts:

Amerix is talking about why shouldn't we be us? Why do you have to be dictated by a woman? Let the woman decide whatever you have to do. Be away from friends, she does not want that. Do whatever she wants? You see that? So, we were like, give us this shit. [...] From the first day, we were all into this Amerix thing. [...] there are some people who argue that Amerix is misleading the men, but then if you understand what Amerix is talking about, it is the real thing, the real situation on the ground.

Amerix, a healthcare professional hailing from western Kenya, had been giving Kenyan men controversial advice on their health, finances, and sexuality on Twitter for the last couple of years. Having branded hashtags that were widely shared by migrant men on their social media channels, such as #MasculinitySaturday or #StayTaliban, 'the man teaching men about masculinity' (Kinyanjui 2020) had become one of Kenya's most infamous social media personalities. Men not only passively absorbed his advice by following his Twitter account, but also actively engaged with his ideas in a Telegram channel that had almost 100,000 members in 2022. To understand what attracted Mark and other male migrants in Pipeline to his advice, it is helpful to give a short introduction to the red pill movement, which highly influenced Amerix's anti-feminist doctrine.[4]

---

4   Proponents of the red pill ideology avoid the term 'movement' due to the alleged scientific grounding of their advice. In his Telegram channel, Amerix, for instance,

Members of the red pill movement assume that feminism has infiltrated all areas of life, from education to the economy, over the course of the last 50 years, resulting in the replacement of the biological supremacy of men over women with a cultural supremacy of women over men. According to Jacob Aliet, author of *Unplugged: Things Our Fathers Did Not Tell Us*, joining the red pill movement 'awakens men to the reality that society is dominated by feminist values and often misandrist attitudes' (2022a: 36). The main social and political intention of the movement is to 'unplug' men from the 'matrix' of a 'femicentric' world order so that men can begin to see the reality and improve their 'game', that is the practices and tactics they rely on to become sexually, romantically, and economically successful (ibid.: passim). 'Less committed to changing the rules of the game and more concerned with discovering those rules and discussing them for the purposes of men's personal sexual advantage' (Van Valkenburg 2021: 89–90), the red pill ideology relies on evolutionary biology to argue that the behaviour of women is predetermined and therefore predictable. This predictability can be used to men's advantage if they agree to apply strategies backed up by insights from behavioural psychology. Such an integration of scientific findings makes the red pill movement's antifeminism appear 'as not radical but common, relatable, and, crucially, rational' (Jones et al. 2020: 1914). The red pill and associated movements, such as MGTOW ('men going their own way'), thereby accomplish 'lowering the barrier to entry and broadening the opportunities for recruitment' (ibid.), particularly of intelligent and educated migrants such as Mark who struggled with what they perceived as the unrealistic economic and romantic expectations of women.

Followers of the red pill ideology share some basic assumptions about female nature. They believe, for instance, that women act according to their hypergamous nature when choosing their boyfriends and husbands. In contrast to the culturally produced ideology of female romanticism, women, in other words, allegedly flock to the richest men for financial support and to those men with the best genes for reproductive purposes. This 'dual mating strategy' supposedly leads women to have sex with so-called 'alpha' males while depending financially and emotionally on 'beta' males. Furthermore, the red pill ideology assumes that women are 'solipsistic', which, in this context, refers to women's inability to consider worldviews other than their own as valid or valuable. Due to feminism's successful and total indoctrination, men allegedly no longer dare to criticize women but must constantly conform to female values, making it impossible for women to become self-critical. Lastly,

---

called the red pill movement an 'intersexual power dynamic instrument that reminds men to remain masculine. It is a compass that redirects you back to your manly path in case you veer off the track.'

proponents of the red pill movement agree that women follow Briffault's law, a hypothesis of evolutionary biology that assumes that female animals only spend time with males if they derive a benefit from it. In short, women are viewed as 'hypergamous, calculating, and uncaring' (Preston et al. 2021: 836).

Amerix's popularity with Kenyan men sprung from his ability to make use of the red pill movement's 'ideological elasticity' (Ging 2019: 644). Concepts such as female hypergamy and solipsism, for instance, resonated with migrant men's belief in women's materialistic nature and their experience of pressure caused by allegedly insatiable female desires. Moreover, Amerix transferred the technical terminology of the red pill movement to the Kenyan context. The following excerpt from his Telegram channel, for example, illustrates how he contextualized the language of the red pill movement by comparing Kenyan ethnic groups with categories of men abhorred by proponents of the red pill ideology such as 'simps', 'white knights', 'orbiters', 'incels', 'average frustrated chumps', and 'cucks'.[5] This allows him to lament about the downfall of the powerful and strong 'African man' who is masculine, non-democratic, anti-western, emotionally stoic, and physically fit:

> Radical feminism has led to the mutation of our beliefs hence giving rise to WHITE KNIGHTS (Luhyas), ORBITERS (Kambas), SIMPS (Luos), INCELS (Kalenjin), CUCKS (Kisiis), Average Frustrated Chumps (Kikuyu). […] What should men do? They should stick to their traditional beliefs in the dating market. Don't allow feminists to warp and promote the mutation of our different beliefs.[6]

For Amerix, feminism had, in other words, done more than create a femicentric world where masculine men were oppressed by women and their so-called 'effeminate' male allies. It supposedly also had, with the help of Christianity and the NGO sector, destroyed traditional African gender relations based on strict heterosexuality and marriages between strong patriarchal polygamists

---

5   These terms are widely used by followers of the red pill movement. In brief, 'Orbiter' denotes men who spend resources on women hoping that they will have sex with them in the future; 'simp' is short for 'sucka idolizing mediocre pussy' and refers to men who have embraced feminism to increase their sexual access to women; 'cuck' describes a man who accepts his spouse's hypergamous infidelity; an 'incel' or 'involuntary celibate' has lost his masculinity and can therefore no longer find sexual partners; a 'white knight' is a man who protects women despite the alleged fact that women are ruling in a femicentric world; and an 'average frustrated chump' is another term for a 'beta' male who cannot find sexual partners.

6   The characterization of *jo*-Luo as 'simps', for instance, refers to Luo men's alleged romanticism, and the description of Kalenjin as 'incels' alludes to Kalenjins' allegedly violent nature.

who dictate and submissive wives who obey. According to Amerix, this deterioration of gender roles further deprived aspiring Kenyan politicians of masculine role models. Instead of strong leaders who reject western values, such as Rwanda's Paul Kagame or Russia's Vladimir Putin, both celebrated by Amerix as true men, Kenya had embraced feminine democracy and leaders who had become mere appendages of 'effeminate' western politicians.

Although Amerix's excitement about military and totalitarian dictator-ships appealed to many young Kenyan men, the popularity of his Telegram channel largely stemmed from the easily implementable advice he offered. The practices Amerix advocated mostly touched on economic, sexual, health-related, and relationship issues. Akin to a military drill instructor, Amerix greeted his channel members every morning by reminding them to bathe using cold water and engage in physical exercise, after which he shared advice on nutritional, sexual, and economic topics. He advised men, among other things, to walk barefoot, to defecate while squatting, to use condoms, to identify single mothers and women who had abortions by looking for stretch marks on specific body parts, to perform compound weightlifting exercises, to reduce their blood pressure, to sunbathe their testicles, to practice 'autophagy' by fasting for 24 to 72 hours, to avoid ejaculation to increase testosterone levels, and to ban industrially processed foods from their diet.[7] All these different practices were part of Amerix's '4P' and '5M' doctrines that aimed at helping men to be able to 'provide', 'produce', 'precede', and 'protect'. In order to accomplish that, men needed 'money', which they could easily acquire by focusing on their 'mind, muscles, men, and material', that is by working out, socializing with other men, building a home, and 'unplugging' themselves from the 'femicentric' worldview that compelled male migrants to try to live up to the expectations of their wives and girlfriends instead of focusing on their own well-being. Men were left with the choice to either, in the words of Amerix, 'change' by embracing his anti-feminist ideology and masculinizing practices, or 'perish' if they refused to stop focusing on what women demanded of them.

While most of this practical advice aimed at changing men's behaviour in the real world, communication inside the Telegram channel was also governed by strict rules. Members were, for instance, only allowed to write in English,

---

[7]   Amerix's focus on practices that control the flow of substances in and out of the body alludes to theories about the permeability of human bodies common across Eastern Africa (see, for instance, Geissler and Prince 2010: passim, Taylor 1992). His fixation on modern sexual practices, his praise of dictatorships, and the strict distinction he made between his followers and everyone else furthermore strongly reminded me of the 'authoritarian personality' structure analyzed by Theodor W. Adorno and others (Adorno et al. 1950).

had to use perfect grammar, and were strongly discouraged from using emojis or excessive interpunctuation, such as multiple question marks, which were viewed as signs of an effeminate mind-set. Members also engaged in other 'virtual manhood acts' (Moloney and Love 2018), such as reacting to pictures showing women wearing revealing clothes by calling them out as 'sluts' or 'prostitutes'. It was also common for Amerix to post private messages that men had sent him requesting his advice. Rather than directly reacting to these messages, Amerix asked the channel members to comment on the man's problem and offer him advice. In an exemplary case, for instance, Amerix had posted a private message from a young man who was suffering from erectile dysfunction. The channel members were asked to intervene by 'list[ing] the 5 important things this soyboy should do before I tell him what to do to overcome ED'. The advice given included, among many other things, that the young man should start 'to write like a man', 'avoid unnecessary commas', 'retain his semen', 'avoid looking at naked women', 'read books', 'eat meat and eggs', 'cleanse his chaotic soul', and 'quit his dependence on parents'. Reacting to posts by Amerix in ways that proved they had understood the basics of the red pill ideology gave channel members immediate gratification. The fact that they monitored each other furthermore created an almost cult-like atmosphere of reciprocal control and communal shaming, which helped to bring forth a tight-knit virtual group where men who voiced different opinions or showed sympathy with feminism were banned and their comments deleted by their strong leader.

Highly relevant for migrant men's experience of pressure, Amerix also advised his followers not to marry or impregnate a woman before they were economically stable and repeatedly warned them not to engage in get-rich-quick schemes. By reassuring them that their economic and romantic prime time – the peak of what proponents of the red pill ideology would call their 'sexual market value' – lay in their mid- or late-thirties and that they just had to follow his daily advice and work hard, he was able to reduce young men's economic and romantic pressure. Comparable to the No Mercy Gym members' extended temporality of delayed physical success, Amerix advised men to accept that it would take time to transform from a 'beta' to an 'alpha' male. Instead of pretending to be economically successful in order to have sex with women who would only be disappointed by their lack of spending power later on, young men like the unemployed *ja-pap* Mark should focus on themselves and build strong and lasting bonds with each other. They should, as Amerix had once condensed his advice, 'follow goals, not girls'.

As one among many 'reinvigorated political patriarchs' (Mellström 2017: 1) active in the global manosphere, Amerix managed to successfully incarnate several archetypical male roles at the same time. Described as someone who

'speaks with a messianic voice from the background' by one of my male interlocutors, Amerix presented himself as a knowledgeable healthcare professional,
a fitness instructor, a fatherly figure who cared about the well-being of young
men, a defender of traditional Kenyan cultures, an anti-democrat, and a staunch
patriarch. This unique blend of masculine archetypes helped Amerix attract
men looking for a vast variety of different things, which ranged from dietary
advice to job offers that he sometimes circulated. Every follower could, in other
words and in principle, pick whatever he felt was helpful and ignore the rest.
By offering an ideological critique of feminism, however, Amerix paved the
way for potential political action as he transformed the experience of pressure
caused by the expectations of intimate others into an experience of oppression
exerted by feminism as a larger societal force. Therefore, a male migrant who
joined Amerix's channel out of curiosity or because he was looking for dietary
advice risked beoming 'radicalized' over time due to the channel's cult-like
atmosphere and the immediate gratification it offered to men who were willing
to comply with Amerix's criteria of what it means to be masculine.

His versatility made Amerix by far the most popular Kenyan masculinity
consultant who was influenced by narratives and practices from the red pill
movement. He was not, however, the only such consultant inspired by the red
pill ideology. The next section's interpretation of a men-only meeting on the
slopes of Mount Kenya shows that not all Kenyan men following the red pill
ideology had the same goals. Some of those attending the men-only meeting,
for instance, used the cover of the red pill ideology to be vulnerable and to
withdraw from the expectations of their intimate others in order to reassess
their personal relationships with women as well as the general state of gender
relations in Kenya. Though the men I met on the slopes of Mount Kenya were
financially better off than most of my interlocutors in Pipeline and did not
live in the overcrowded estate during the time of my fieldwork, meeting them
made me aware that a lot of the frustrations that I witnessed among migrant
men in Pipeline were actually shared by male Kenyans from different socio-
economic backgrounds. Discussing these men's meeting should therefore be
seen as a minor diversion helping us to better understand to what degree the
problems male migrants faced in Pipeline were shared by men nationwide.

Vulnerable men on the slopes of Mount Kenya

Nairobian girls, man, *acha tu* (Kiswahili, 'just leave it')! If some hapless
guy with disposable income and sensible behaviour shows some interest,
the girl will put her acting mask on, and can easily fool the man proper.
Nothing wrong with that, as life is a game. You play. They play. We
play each other.

Silas Nyanchwani (2021a: 104)

'What was her profession?', asked one of fifteen middle-aged Nairobian men sitting around a bonfire next to a wooden cabin on the slopes of Mount Kenya after another one had shared his frustrations and the challenges he had experienced with his ex-wife. 'She was just a scammer', he answered, and most of us broke out in laughter. Our laughter was in no way belittling; it seemed to result from the release of what Marcus, an IT professional who described himself as a former feminist who had turned to the red pill ideology because of his experiences with Kenyan women, later called 'pent-up bitterness'. One man after the other narrated similar stories: an emotionally cold girlfriend who had cheated with a colleague, a wife who had run away with the children, despite the husband's genuine attempts to provide and be a good father. In contrast to the painful topics discussed, the atmosphere was conducive to male bonding. Whisky, beer, and the absence of women paved the way for an open and honest discussion. While the first stories were narrated in an almost confessional tone, as if the men felt ashamed of opening up, soon the stories were met with laughter and self-ridicule about one's past days as a 'simp'. Sipping my too-cold beer and sharing my own romantic failures, I realized that I had become part of a communal catharsis.

The two-day retreat had been organized on a non-profit basis by three 'popular urban intellectuals' (Callaci 2017: 15): social media personality and psychologist Chomba Njoka, and the aforementioned authors Jacob Aliet and Silas Nyanchwani.[8] Some of the attendees had passed through Pipeline when starting their lives in Nairobi and a few were still struggling professionally. In comparison to most male migrants in Pipeline, however, they had well-paying and prestigious jobs. There was, for instance, an IT consultant, a journalist, a lawyer, and a psychologist. Even so, both social groups complained

---

[8]   While Jacob Aliet's *Unplugged* (2022a) is a summary of the red pill ideology interspersed with captivatingly written accounts of Kenyan men's experiences, Aliet also tries to incorporate red pill ideology and terminology into his fictional work (see, for instance, his recently published short story collection *Transference* [2022b]). Silas Nyanchwani plays around with different literary genres as well, including ethnographic descriptions, direct advice, and hyperbolic fictionalizations celebrating male sexuality and wastefulness (comparable to some Kenyan authors of the 1970s and 1980s such as Charles Mangua, David Maillu and Meja Mwangi, see Kurtz 1998, Odhiambo 2007). Nyanchwani's oeuvre – his ironic column 'The Retrosexual', which he used to publish in the weekly newspaper *The Nairobian* until Brian Guserwa took over, the novel *Sexorcised* (2020) about a man in his forties who starts dating a younger woman after his marriage collapsed, and *Man About Town* (2022), a collection of everyday observations on how gender relations unfold in Nairobi – thus constitutes an often ironic, almost kaleidoscopic collection of different perspectives, ideas, and narrative styles, trying to map out and understand what it means to be a man in contemporary urban Kenya.

about similar problems. Increasing economic pressure during the COVID-19 pandemic and an inability to meet the expectations of their girlfriends and wives were thus topics that cut across different economic classes. However, and in contrast to most *jo-pap,* such as Mark, or the gym members who, if at all, only consumed the red pill ideology through Amerix's social media outputs, the men who met on the slopes of Mount Kenya had fully adopted the narrative and language of the red pill movement. Over the two days, the men categorized women's sexual attractiveness on a scale from one to ten (O'Neill 2018: 169-70), discussed women's hypergamous nature, and shared advice on how to find out with how many men a woman had really slept. Nonetheless, as the meeting progressed, it became palpable to me that the men engaged in more than what Rachel O'Neill aptly called 'tactical fraternity among men' (ibid.: 63), whereby they tried to help each other to be sexually, romantically, and economically more successful. They also felt relieved to be able to talk about their frustrations with like-minded men.

In stark contrast to the rigid and military atmosphere of Amerix's Telegram channel, where anyone who did not embrace the red pill ideology risked being banned, some men who had attended the meeting on the slopes of Mount Kenya expressed to me that they were grateful to have found a group of men who neither judged nor ridiculed them for their past mistakes and current shortcomings. In addition to providing explanations and corresponding advice, spending time with other men had created what the former feminist Marcus called a 'family of peers' who offered each other emotional support. Satisfying the men's 'need to be heard and connect with kindred souls', as Marcus phrased it, the meeting had allowed them to discuss their frustrations and doubts about their roles as husbands, fathers, and boyfriends in a safe space. Despite their misogynistic nature, Kenyan men's anti-feminist portrayals of women thus also reflected their deep-seated anxieties. Unlike the US-American men's rights advocates observed by Jonathan Allan (2016), who only talked about their feelings to reclaim a position of power, the men who met on the slopes of Mount Kenya genuinely feared becoming expendable soon.

The threat of men's expendability

What made migrant men susceptible to the misogynistic hate of anonymous Telegram channels, the religious sermons of self-help pastors, and the clandestine atmosphere of a men's meeting on the slopes of Mount Kenya? More importantly, what does it tell us about the state of gender relations in Kenya that close to 100,000 Kenyan men felt at home in Amerix's Telegram channel, where they found solace through engaging with his anti-feminist, anti-democratic, and pseudo-scientific advice? Pondering these questions, I remembered the many instances during which my male interlocutors had expressed fears of becoming economically or sexually expendable. When Samuel, for instance, visited me in my house one day after passing the neighbour's apartment where a group of women was celebrating a birthday, he just shook his head and solemnly uttered: 'We live like animals in the jungle. Women and men separately. We only meet for mating and making babies. Maybe that's where we're heading to'. Samuel was not alone with his assessment that the future of gender relations looked bleak. One *ja-pap*, for instance, mentioned in an interview that he believed that 'most women of today prefer to be single mothers because they see that, in this life of today, as long as you can work, you are good to go. You can just get a man for leisure, it is not a must you must live with a man. [...] These our ladies, most of them, they will not live with men in the future.'

Such comments did not only entail a nostalgic longing for clear and stable gender relations. They were also imbued with fears about a future during which the 'boy child' would be forgotten (Pike 2020) and women would be able to live fulfilling lives independently of men, fears that became manifest in the stereotypes of money-minded slay queens and morally dubious single mothers. Unacknowledged male vulnerability, moreover, shone through in discussions about homosexuality and feminism. While some migrant men imagined that most women would soon embrace lesbianism and same-sex marriages, others attacked feminism when asked about it in interviews. For example, Wellington Ochieng, the moto-taxi driver we got to know better in chapter 3, called feminism a 'scam' and 'dead on arrival', while Victor Omollo, a *ja-pap* introduced in chapter 2, rejected feminism outrightly by evoking images of male strength and masculine prowess: 'How can you compare a man with a woman? If you want to compare a man and a woman, put a handcart out there, tell the man to be shirtless, and the woman, then they push the handcart. You know that this thing cannot happen'. The fear of male expendability, furthermore, became palpable in the discussion of a collection of insults shared by those men who had been at the retreat on the slopes of Mount Kenya. After analyzing the insult *makwapa ya konokono* (Kiswahili, 'armpits of a snail'), the men agreed that it was particularly powerful because it alluded to a disgusting thing that actually did not exist, thereby simultaneously evoking men's uselessness and their expendability.

Sharing one's frustrations while sipping cold beer at a bonfire, seeking pseudo-scientific explanations for the behaviour of women in the manosphere, or striving to re-establish religiously vested male authority, all these practices stemmed from the same lingering feeling that the world had turned against men, and that men would soon no longer be needed by women. Seeking validation from other men in *pap* and gyms, rejecting feminism, struggling to become economically successful providers, as well as looking for financial, sexual, and romantic advice from masculinity consultants should therefore be seen as different ways in which male migrants, without radically challenging the narrative of the male breadwinner, tried to make themselves, or at least feel, socially and romantically indispensable. Not one of the masculinity consultants who provided a variety of advice to assist men in overcoming their fear of expendability, however, had identified Kenya's political-economic system as a possible culprit for migrant men's emotionally challenging and economically often destitute situation.

Instead of criticizing or trying to change Kenya's capitalist economy and the related narrative of the male breadwinner, men directed their anger at women and focused their minds on winning what Silas Nyanchwani called the nation's 'gender wars' (2021b). Even so, the fact that many Kenyan men found the advice of masculinity consultants attractive illustrates that they were looking for a compass to orient themselves in an increasingly chaotic world. Migrant men, in other words, were longing for explanations and solutions for their experience of pressure. Blaming the unrealistic expectations of intimate others and evading pressure by lifting weights or by spending time in *pap* was no longer enough for those male migrants who were ready to fight larger societal forces to overcome their plight. Seeing and experiencing 'themselves as the beleaguered party in a zero-sum game in which every gain for women entails a loss for men' (O'Neill 2018: 147), they resorted to attacking the entire female gender, homosexuality, and feminist politics instead of criticizing Kenya's economic and political system.

CONCLUSION: PIPELINE TO NOWHERE

> Those who have money, you will find that they have a house, but the things that they have there, if you compare it with someone in the village who has a mud house, the person in the village is better-off because he has some cattle, some chicken, some sheep. If you look at the one living here in a plot, he has a TV. So, there is a big difference. […] The city people, something is lying to them.
>
> Ja-pap *Victor*

Before vacating my home in Pipeline in August 2022, I walked through the estate to identify what had changed since I had moved to the 'concrete tenement jungle' (Mwau 2019) three years earlier. Though the social, political, and economic upheavals caused by the COVID-19 pandemic were more or less a thing of the past, male migrants were now wrestling with the impacts of another crisis happening elsewhere in the world. In the wake of the war in Ukraine, prices of fuel and basic commodities such as soap, maize flour, vegetable oil, and cooking gas had shot up, putting further economic pressure on migrant men and their urban and rural families. Despite this economic crisis, which had become tangible in the sudden presence of begging street children in Pipeline around the beginning of 2022, the densification of the estate had continued to progress. Plots had been constructed, foundations had been dug, and new businesses and shops had opened around every corner. Money was available, but circulated elsewhere, being owned and exchanged by others.

In addition to these infrastructural changes, some of my key interlocutors had left Pipeline to return to their rural villages. Samuel had gone back to his ancestral home in Seme, close to the lakeside city of Kisumu, where he had started his pupillage in a law firm around July 2021. Thinking about the problems he had gone through in his dissolved marriage with Immaculate, and annoyed by the pressure and the stress of the city, he had decided to start afresh in Seme, where his father had recently settled after retiring from his job as a teacher in Chabera. When I visited him, Samuel told me that he was sure that he would never return to Nairobi. He saw his future in Kisumu, where he could speak his mother tongue Dholuo and was far away from the hustle and noise of Pipeline that he had once described as a 'sleeping giant where people are ever busy but achieve nothing'. In the village, well water was freely available every day and electricity was, ironically, also not much less reliable than in Pipeline. Maize, beans, and vegetables came directly from the fields, while milk and eggs were supplied by one's own cows and chickens. In addition, Samuel realised that many of his peers had already built their *simba* (Dholuo, 'bachelor hut') and had a better standard of living than he had had in Nairobi. It was high time to sow the seeds for a bright future in his ancestral home.

Carl, the owner of the No Mercy Gym, had separated from his wife around the same time as Samuel had left Pipeline. Disappointed with the lack of personal economic development and troubled by his marital problems, he had moved back to his rural home in Ukambani to try his luck at groundnut farming and trading. He had left the gym in the hands of Anthony and Isaac, who were struggling to keep it running, especially after some weights were stolen and their attempts to recover them had failed. They only managed to keep the gym afloat with the help of some fundraising organized by the members. Encouraged by the mental boost they received from decorating the gym with posters of bodybuilders they had found in a demolished gym in Mukuru Kwa Njenga (Ashly 2022) while strolling through the neighbourhood one evening, they began making plans to add new machines and weights. Though Carl was gone, the No Mercy Gym was still in business.

For Carl and Samuel, expectations of a better life in the city had not come to fruition. Unsurprisingly, as issues of love and finance went hand in hand in Pipeline, they had left Nairobi for romantic and economic reasons. The decision to leave Pipeline and return to one's ancestral home, however, did not always imply that a male migrant had rejected the narrative of the male breadwinner or changed his view of Nairobi as a place of economic success. Carl, for instance, regularly called Anthony and Isaac to check on the gym, and Arthur, who had also returned to Chabera at the end of 2021 due to the impossibility of finding a well-paying job in Nairobi, despite having completed his bachelor's degree, continued to raise money to pay the rent for his single room in Pipeline. Back in his village, where he lived what he described as a boring life, Arthur frequently complained about the lack of economic opportunities. Besides raising guinea fowl and occasionally overseeing his parents' shop, there was not much he could achieve in Chabera. Going back home was a result of a bleak economic situation, not a choice based upon a well-founded rejection of his migratory dreams of attaining economic success in Nairobi. Men like Arthur saw life in the village as a mere break from the mounting pressure caused by chasing money and pretending to be successful in Kenya's capital. They returned home to temporarily depressurize and recharge their energy (see Kleist 2017).

Apart from moving back to their rural homes, another solution to the pressure male migrants faced in Nairobi would have been to criticize and try to overcome Kenya's deeply unjust capitalist economic system and the related ideology of the male breadwinner. However, when I brought up the possibility of more radical economic change to some of my friends after returning from a panel discussion on 'Why does nobody speak about capitalism in Kenya?' held in a community centre in Mathare, one of Nairobi's largest informal settlements, they unanimously agreed that the organizers of the panel were unwilling to accept reality. Capitalism had come to stay, and nobody should expect to be helped by society at large. This positive acceptance of capitalism and related moral values, such as individual responsibility, coupled with a pragmatic attitude toward the emancipatory potentials of politics and democracy, might seem surprising given their bleak economic situation and the all-encompassing experience of pressure. Embracing capitalism and its values, however, is common among labour migrants worldwide who have already invested too much in pursuing their dreams to give in easily (Schielke 2020, Xiang 2021, see also Berlant 2011). For most male migrants in Pipeline, the main problem was not the economic system or traditional gender roles. Rather, it was their marginal position in the economy, a position that most migrant men still expected to soon overcome.

Yet, no male migrant I was acquainted with had upgraded to a better apartment in Pipeline, and neither had anyone moved to a more desirable neighbourhood in another part of Nairobi. Although they thus felt that they were 'languishing in abject poverty in a developed slum', as Thomas had phrased it dramatically, most of my male interlocutors carried on trying to carve out successful lives in the high-rise tenements of Pipeline. Migrating to the city had been a deep desire throughout their lives, and they were far from ready to give up on the promises of achieving material wealth and finding romantic love in Kenya's capital. The alternatives were either to return to their rural homes to recharge their energy, thereby acknowledging temporary defeat, or to remain in perpetual suspension in Pipeline, always feeling close to, yet being far away from, economic success. In such a context of perpetual suspension (Xiang 2021), objectively unrealistic goals, such as Philemon's idea to mine minerals on Mars, HoMiSiKi's plan to purchase their own *matatu*, or Godwin's goal to look like Dwayne Johnson, acquired a critical function. Relying on an extended temporality of delayed accomplishments (Guyer 2007), expecting implausible success in the far future allowed male migrants to continue believing in the certainty of their economic breakthrough. In contrast to less ambitious ideas, these plans were not easily falsifiable. Being projected far into the future, even insignificant actions could be interpreted as meaningful steps toward achieving these lofty goals. As eternal apprentices of their future economic success, most male migrants in Pipeline thus remained attached to the promises of Nairobi. One day, they kept believing, they would be wealthy, providing, and generous fathers and husbands.

Worlds without women

Rather than trying to change the system or accepting defeat by returning to the village, most male migrants in Pipeline engaged in forms of male sociality that provided refuge not only 'from the world "out there"' (Masquelier 2019: 32) but also from the pressure men experienced and the expectations they were confronted with in their urban households. Men found solace in bars, gyms, pool halls, videogame joints, betting shops, and Telegram channels where they talked to male friends, lifted weights, engaged in practices of wasteful masculinity, and looked for self-help advice from religious and non-religious masculinity consultants. Homosocial spaces and the depressurizing practices that they offered thus helped men to evade pressure, refuel their energy, and remain certain about their future success.

Men in Pipeline, and across Kenya, were not really interested in radically altering the narrative of the male breadwinner. In the case of the investment group HoMiSiKi, male migrants socialized this ideal form of masculinity. As members of HoMiSiKi, they carried on dreaming about financial success while, in the shadow of the investment group, they went out for drinks as virile, wasteful, and strong *jo-pap*. In contrast to this socialization of the ideal form of masculinity, the members of the No Mercy Gym externalized the traits of the prevailing narrative of the male breadwinner as prudent and hardworking by strengthening their bodies systematically, which they believed would help them to take over an economically and romantically more strategic position vis-à-vis other migrant men in the long run. Philemon Otieno took the opposite approach, locating true masculinity deep within each man's inner world, from where it had to be rediscovered and nurtured through an individualized ethics of vision, perseverance, and entrepreneurship. Thereby, and if necessary with the help of male mentors, such as Philemon himself, men would be able to restore the natural order of male supremacy, even if that meant withdrawing temporarily from women and focusing on themselves and their personal and economic development, as suggested by some of the Kenyan masculinity consultants inspired by the global red pill movement, such as Amerix, Jacob Aliet, and Silas Nyanchwani.

These three masculine spaces and the homosocial bonds formed within them also strongly influenced migrant men's images of women (Flood 2008). While *jo-pap* saw women as 'antelopes' (Dholuo, *mwanda*) to be hunted on the 'playing field' (Dholuo, *pap)*, participating in HoMiSiKi fuelled migrant men's hope of an economic success that would enable their wives to focus on their domestic duties. Male migrants thus upheld an inherently bifurcated image of women, who were either viewed as irresponsible slay queens or faithful and obedient wives. In the gym, equally ambiguous perceptions of women circulated. On the one hand, women were seen, especially in case men felt that they demanded too much attention, as powerful threats to their personal goals of physical transformation and economic success. On the other hand, gym members perceived women as being naturally weaker than men and thus requiring male protection. Lastly, the self-help literature and masculinity consultants I analyzed wanted to place women back into their allegedly natural position below men. By excluding women from these male spaces, where migrant men developed or (re)emphasized criteria defining what it meant to be a good man and what it meant to be a good woman, male migrants denied women the agency to participate in the conceptualization and negotiation of gender roles. What made these male spaces valuable and attractive to men, in other words, was also the absence of women and female voices.

The lies of pressured men

Focusing on heterosexual male migrants' experience of pressure triggered by their own expectations as well as those of intimate others, *Migrants and Masculinity in High-Rise Nairobi* empirically and analytically complements the scholarly output on African masculinities that increasingly has zoomed in on non-heteronormative and queer notions of what it means to be a man in Africa as well as the literature on male youth born and trying to make ends meet in sub-Saharan Africa's relentlessly growing cities. While the latter has explored how young men creatively 'hustle' through what they perceive as an uncertain present (Thieme et al. 2021), my descriptions of how educated and skilled migrant men aged between 25 and 40 tried to attenuate an almost overpowering experience of pressure paint an alternative picture of masculinity and its discontents in a twenty first-century African capital.

Male migrants in Pipeline attenuated the pressure caused by the expectations of their intimate others by creating and maintaining spaces of male sociality, such as *pap* and the No Mercy Gym, where they reassured each other of their value and masculinity. In these male refuges established in one of sub-Saharan Africa's most densely populated estates, migrant men did not attempt to alter or overcome the ideal of the male provider. Rather, socializing in these spaces enabled them to evade the pressure created by what they interpreted as a female distortion of men's provider role. In the company of other men, male migrants relaxed and regained the strength necessary to continue on what they perceived as their preordained road toward becoming economically successful men, husbands, and fathers. Migrant men thereby ignored the structural conditions of Kenya's capitalist economy that were responsible for their inability to fulfil the dominant norm of the male bread-winner. Rather than criticizing the latter, they remained intimately attached to it because they were unwilling to give up the expectation that they would soon reap the 'patriarchal dividend' (Connell 2005 [1995]: 79).

These men's intimate attachment to the notion of the male provider also points to a few crucial analytic benefits of the emic/etic term 'pressure' when conceptualized as an experience of stress caused by expectations that migrant men viewed as justified and reasonable in kind, but unreasonable in degree. Such an understanding of pressure allows us to differentiate the experience of pressure from the experience of oppression which, I suggest, tends to be caused by expectations that are perceived as neither qualitatively nor quanti-tatively justified. Masculinity consultants influenced by the red pill movement, such as Amerix, for instance, tried to turn men's experience of pressure into an experience of oppression by framing women's expectations as both quali-tatively and quantitatively unreasonable, thereby attempting to liberate men from their allegedly harmful attachments to women. Conceptualizing pressure in this way, moreover, enables us to explain why only a few migrant men sought divorce or blocked communication with their relatives in the village, even though they felt pressured by the expectations of their wives and their rural kin. The fact that women and rural relatives expected migrant men to provide was not seen as problematic as such. Most of my male interlocutors simply felt that their intimate others demanded too much.

Male migrants in Pipeline experienced pressure because they had tied their own wellbeing to the wellbeing of others, such as their urban and rural kin. They had committed themselves to the ideology of the male breadwinner as well as to Nairobi as the place where their consumerist dreams would become reality without admitting that they did not have the means or the ability to do justice to these commitments. Their experiences of pressure, in other words, enabled male migrants to remain attached to ideologies, people, and narratives that were ultimately detrimental to their well-being. If witchcraft is best understood as the dark side of intimacy, as suggested by Peter Geschiere (2003), pressure might be conceptualized as the unintended consequence of premature commitment. Victor was thus right when he suspected that something was 'lying' to male migrants expecting success in the city. Yet, he failed to realize that the pressured men of Pipeline – such as husbands who turned into 'bachelors' (*jo-pap*) when leaving the house, struggling migrants who presented themselves as successful city dwellers when visiting their rural homes, or adherents of the red pill ideology who desired to be with trustworthy women while propagating that such women do not exist – actually lied to themselves and thereby helped Kenya's capitalist economy to continue to produce and exploit their pressured bodies and minds.

It would, nevertheless, be misguided to assume that migrant men's defence of the patriarchal breadwinner narrative was forced upon them by the economic situation. Rather, and as Matthew Gutmann, one of anthropology's pioneering scholars of masculinity, has recently argued, we should not agree to 'let men off the hook' (2019: chapter 10) by placing political responsibility for changing gender relations only on the shoulders of women. If we want to make men responsible for what they are thinking and doing, however, we must first understand what they are thinking and doing. As a sympathetic but honest portrayal of male migrants' practices, dreams, expectations, and experiences of being under pressure in high-rise Nairobi, this book hopefully contributes to an empirically saturated discussion about the future of masculinities in urban Kenya. Furthermore, I hope that Kenyan men and women reading this book will be inspired and encouraged to build new narratives of what it means to be a heterosexual man in twenty first-century high-rise Nairobi that risk going beyond the capitalist image of the male breadwinner.

BIBLIOGRAPHY

Adorno, T.W., Frenkel-Brunswik, E., Levinson, D.J. and Sanford, R.N. (1950). *The authoritarian personality* (New York: Harper and Row).

Agyemang, F.S.K., Silva, E. and Aboagye Anokye, P. (2018). 'Towards sustainable urban development: the social acceptability of high-rise buildings in a Ghanaian city', *GeoJournal*, 83(6), 1317–29.

Ahlberg, B.M. (1994). 'Is there a distinct African sexuality? A critical response to Caldwell', *Africa: Journal of the International African Institute*, 64(2), 220–42.

Aliet, J. (2022a). *Unplugged. Things our fathers did not tell us* (Nairobi: Ndiko Aliet).

— (2022b). *Transference. Nothing is as it seems* (Nairobi: Ndiko Aliet).

Allan, J.A. (2016). 'Phallic affect, or why men's rights activists have feelings', *Men and Masculinities*, 19(1), 22–41.

Ambani, S. (2021). 'How Pipeline estate became the laughing stock of Nairobi', *Daily Nation*, 15 February 2021. Available at: https://nation.africa/kenya/counties/nairobi/how-pipeline-estate-became-the-laughing-stock-of-nairobi-3292108 [Accessed 24 November 2022].

— (2022). 'Children of a lesser God? Pipeline estate continues to choke under garbage', *Daily Nation*, 12 July 2022. Available at: https://nation.africa/kenya/counties/nairobi/children-of-a-lesser-god-pipeline-estate-continues-to-choke-under-garbage-3876170 [Accessed 24 November 2022].

Amman, C. and Staudacher, S. (2021). 'Masculinities in Africa beyond crisis: complexity, fluidity, and intersectionality', *Gender, Place and Culture. A Journal of Feminist Geography*, 28(6), 759–68.

Amuyunzu-Nyamongo, M. and Francis, P. (2006). 'Collapsing livelihoods and the crisis of masculinity in rural Kenya', in: I. Bannon and M.C. Correira (eds), *The other half of gender. Men's issues in development* (Washington, D.C.: The World Bank), 219–44.

Anderson, D.M. (2000). 'Master and servant in colonial Kenya, 1895–1939', *Journal of African History*, 41(3), 459–85.

Appadurai, A. (2004). 'The capacity to aspire: culture and the terms of recognition', in: V. Rao and M. Walton (eds), *Culture and public action* (Palo Alto: Stanford University Press), 59–84.

Archambault, J.S. (2017). *Youth, intimacy, and the politics of pretense in Mozambique* (Chicago: University of Chicago Press).

— (2021). 'In pursuit of fitness: bodywork, temporality and self-improvement in Mozambique', *Journal of Southern African Studies*, 47(4), 521–39.

Ashly, J. (2022). 'Kenyan police have committed murder on behalf of property developers', *Jacobin*, 13 January 2022. Available at: https://jacobinmag.

com/2022/01/nairobi-mukura-kwa-njenga-evictions-demolition-corruption [Accessed 24 November 2022].

Atemo, C.J. (2018a). *Lions uncaged. Setting men free* (Nairobi: Aura Publishers).

— (2018b). *The leprous generals* (Nairobi: Aura Publishers).

Awuor, Q.E. and Anudo, N.C. (2016). 'The portrayal of masculinity in Dholuo *ohangla* music', *Journal of Language, Technology and Entrepreneurship in Africa*, 7(2), 12–23.

Baas, M. (2020). *Muscular India: masculinity, mobility and the new middle class* (Chennai: Westland Publications Ltd).

Baral, A. (2021). '"Thanks to Corona virus": trajectories of masculinities during the Ugandan lockdown', *NORMA: International Journal for Masculinity Studies*, 16(3), 174–89.

Baym, N.K. (2015). 'Connect with your audience! The relational labor of connection', *The Communication Review*, 18(1), 14–22.

Behrend, H. (2002). '"I am like a movie star in my street": photographic self-creation in postcolonial Kenya', in: R. Werbner (ed), *Postcolonial subjectivities in Africa* (New York: Zed Books), 44–62.

Berggren, K. (2014). 'Sticky masculinity: post-structuralism, phenomenology and subjectivity in critical studies on men', *Men and Masculinities*, 17(3), 231–52.

Berlant, L. (2011). *Cruel optimism* (Durham: Duke University Press).

Berman, B.J. (1998). 'Ethnicity, patronage and the African state: the politics of uncivil nationalism', *African Affairs*, 97(388), 305–41.

Besnier, N. and Brownell, S. (2012). 'Sport, modernity, and the body', *Annual Review of Anthropology*, 41, 443–59.

Bialecki, J. (2008). 'Between stewardship and sacrifice: agency and economy in a southern California charismatic church', *Journal of the Royal Anthropological Institute*, 14(2), 372–90.

Bielo, J.S. (2007). '"The mind of Christ": financial success, born-again personhood, and the anthropology of Christianity', *Ethnos: Journal of Anthropology*, 72(3), 316–38.

Bjarnesen, J. and Utas, M. (2018). 'Introduction. Urban kinship: the micro-politics of proximity and relatedness in African cities', *Africa: The Journal of the International African Institute*, 88(S1), S1–11.

Blundo, G. and Olivier de Sardan, J.P. (eds). (2006). *Everyday corruption and the state: citizens and public officials in Africa* (London: Zed Books).

Blunt, R.W. (2020). *For money and elders. Ritual, sovereignty and the sacred in Kenya* (Chicago: University of Chicago Press).

Bolt, M. (2010). 'Camaraderie and its discontents: class consciousness, ethnicity and divergent masculinities among Zimbabwean migrant farmworkers in South Africa', *Journal of Southern African Studies*, 36(2), 377–93.

Boulton, J. (2021). *Have your yellowcake and eat it. Men, relatedness and intimacy in Swakopmund, Namibia* (Basel: Basler Afrika Bibliographien).

Bourgois, P. (2003 [1996]). *In search of respect. Selling crack in El Barrio* (Cambridge: Cambridge University Press).

Boyd, L. (2018). 'The gospel of self-help: born-again musicians and the moral problem of dependency in Uganda', *American Ethnologist: Journal of the American Ethnological Society*, 45(2), 241–52.

Bryant, R. and Knight, D.M. (2019). *The anthropology of the future* (Cambridge: Cambridge University Press).

Callaci, E. (2017). *Street archives and city life. Popular intellectuals in postcolonial Tanzania* (Durham: Duke University Press).

Carey, M. (2017). *Mistrust: an ethnographic theory* (Chicago: University of Chicago Press/Hau Books).

Carotenuto, M. (2006). '*Riwruok e teko*: cultivating identity in colonial and postcolonial Kenya', *Africa Today*, 53(2), 53–73.

— (2013). 'Grappling with the past: wrestling and performative identity in Kenya', *The International Journal of the History of Sport*, 30(16), 1889–902.

Carrier, N. (2016). *Little Mogadishu: Eastleigh, Nairobi's global Somali hub* (Oxford: Oxford University Press).

Charton-Bigot, H. and Rodrigues-Torres, D. (eds) (2010). *Nairobi today. The paradox of a fragmented city* (Dar es Salaam/Nairobi: Mkuki na Nyota Publishers/French Institute for Research in Africa).

Chome, N. (2019). 'From Islamic reform to Muslim activism: the evolution of an Islamist ideology in Kenya', *African Affairs*, 118(472), 531–52.

Cohen, D.W. and Odhiambo, E.S.A. (1989). *Siaya: the historical anthropology of an African landscape* (Oxford: James Currey).

— (1992). *Burying SM: the politics of knowledge and the sociology of power in Africa* (Portsmouth, New Hampshire: Heineman).

Cole, J. and Thomas, L.M. (eds). (2009). *Love in Africa* (Chicago: University of Chicago Press).

Cole, J. (2010). *Sex and salvation. Imagining the future in Madagascar* (Chicago: University of Chicago Press).

— (2014). 'Producing value among Malagasy marriage migrants in France: managing horizons of expectation', *Current Anthropology*, 55(S9), S85–94.

Connell, R.W. (2005 [1995]). *Masculinities* (Cambridge: Polity Press).

Cooper, F. (2003). 'Industrial man goes to Africa', in: L.A. Lindsay and S.F. Miescher (eds), *Men and masculinities in modern Africa* (Portsmouth: Heinemann), 128–37.

Cooper, M. (2019). *Family values. Between neoliberalism and the new social conservatism* (New Jersey: Zone Books).

Cornwall, A. (2002). 'Spending power: love, money, and the reconfiguration of gender relations in Ado-Odo, southwestern Nigeria', *American Ethnologist: Journal of the American Ethnological Society*, 29(4), 963–80.

Crompton, R. (1999). *Restructuring gender relations and employment: the decline of the male breadwinner* (Oxford: Oxford University Press).

Dawson, H.J. (2022). 'Living, not just surviving: the politics of refusing low-wage jobs in urban South Africa', *Economy and Society*, 51(3), 375–97.

De Boeck, F. and Plissart, M.F. (2014 [2004]). *Kinshasa. Tales of the invisible city* (Gent and Tervuren: Ludion/Royal Museum for Central Africa).

De Feyter, S. (2015). '"They are like crocodiles under water": rumour in a slum upgrading project in Nairobi, Kenya', *Journal of Eastern African Studies*, 9(2), 289–306.

Desplat, P. (2018). 'Closed circles of mistrust: envy, aspirations and urban sociality in coastal Madagascar', *Africa: The Journal of the International African Institute*, 88(S1), S117–39.

Di Nunzio, M. (2019). *The act of living: street life, marginality, and development in urban Ethiopia* (Ithaca: Cornell University Press).

Dietler, M. and Herbich, I. (2008). '"The long arm of the mother-in-law": post-marital resocialization, cultural transmission, and material style', in: B. Bowser, L. Horne and M. Stark (eds), *Cultural transmission and material culture: breaking down boundaries* (Tucson: University of Arizona Press), 223–44.

— (2009). 'Domestic space, social life, and settlement biography: theoretical reflections from the ethnography of a rural African landscape', *Arqueo Mediterrania*, 11, 11–23.

Dolan, C. and Gordon, C. (2019). 'Worker, businessman, entrepreneur? Kenya's shifting labouring subject', *Critical African Studies*, 11(3), 301–21.

Donovan, J. (2012). *The way of men* (Milwaukie: Dissonant Hum).

Donovan, K. and Park, E. (2019). 'Perpetual debt in the Silicon Savannah', *Boston Review*, 20 September 2019. Available at: https://bostonreview.net/class-inequality-global-justice/kevin-p-donovan-emma-park-perpetual-debt-silicon-savannah [Accessed 24 November 2022].

— (2022). 'Algorithmic intimacy: the data economy of predatory inclusion in Kenya', *Social Anthropology*, 30(2), 120–39.

Downey, G. (2005). *Learning capoeira. Lessons in cunning from an Afro-Brazilian art* (New York: Oxford University Press).

Durkheim, E. (1995 [1912]). *The elementary forms of religious life* (New York: Free Press).

Ehrenreich, B. (1984). *The hearts of men: American dreams and the flight from commitment* (Garden City: Anchor Press).

Elliott, H. (2022). 'Durable conversions: property, aspiration, and inequality in urban northern Kenya', *Economic Anthropology*, 9(1), 112–24.

Epstein, A.L. (1981). *Urbanization and kinship. The domestic domain on the Copperbelt of Zambia 1950–1956* (London: Academic Press).

Ese, A. and Ese, K. (2020). *The city makers of Nairobi. An African urban history* (London: Routledge).

Evans-Pritchard, E.E. (1949). 'Luo tribes and clans', *The Rhodes-Livingstone Journal*, 7, 24–40.

— (1950). 'Marriage customs of the Luo in Kenya', *Africa: The Journal of the International African Institute*, 20(2), 132–42.

Falkof, N. and van Staden, C. (eds). (2020). *Anxious Joburg. The inner lives of a global south city* (Johannesburg: Wits University Press).

Fast, D., Bukusi, D. and Moyer, E. (2020). 'The knife's edge: masculinities and precarity in east Africa', *Social Science and Medicine*, 258, 113097.

Fay, F. (2021). *Disputing discipline. Child protection, punishment, and piety in Zanzibar schools* (New Brunswick: Rutgers University Press).

Fay, F. (2022). 'Ordinary childhoods and everyday Islamic practices of protection and care in Zanzibar', *Journal of the British Academy*, 10(S2), 175–97.

Ferguson, J. (1999). *Expectations of modernity: myths and meanings of urban life on the Zambian Copperbelt* (Berkeley: University of California Press).

— (2006). *Global shadows. Africa in the neoliberal world order* (Durham: Duke University Press).

— (2013). 'Declarations of dependence: labour, personhood, and welfare in southern Africa', *Journal of the Royal Anthropological Institute*, 19(2), 223–42.

Flood, M. (2008). 'Men, sex, and homosociality. How bonds between men shape their sexual relations with women', *Men and Masculinities*, 10(3), 339–59.

Frederiksen, B.F. (2010). 'Mungiki, vernacular organization and political society in Kenya', *Development and Change*, 41(6), 1065–89.

Fuh, D. (2012). 'The prestige economy: veteran clubs and youngmen's competition in Bamenda, Cameroon', *Urban Forum*, 23(4), 501–26.

Gastrow, C. (2020a). 'DIY verticality: the politics of materiality in Luanda', *City and Society*, 32(1), 93–117.

— (2020b). 'Housing middle-classness: formality and the making of distinction in Luanda', *Africa: The Journal of the International African Institute*, 90(3), 509–28.

Geissler, P.W. and Prince, R.J. (2010). *The land is dying. Contingency, creativity, and conflict in western Kenya* (New York: Berghahn).

Genicot, G. and Ray, D. (2020). 'Aspirations and economic behaviour', *Annual Review of Economics*, 12, 715–46.

Geschiere, P. (1997). *The modernity of witchcraft: politics and the occult in postcolonial Africa* (Charlottesville, VA and London: University Press of Virginia).

— (2003). 'Witchcraft as the dark side of kinship: dilemmas of social security in new contexts', *Etnofoor*, 16(1), 43–61.

Geschiere, P. and Gugler, J. (1998). 'Introduction. The urban–rural connection: changing issues of belonging and identification', *Africa: The Journal of the International African Institute*, 68(3), 309–19.

Gez, Y.N. and Droz, Y. (2020). 'Breakthrough, blockages, and the path to self-accomplishment: the case of Pentecostal church founders in Kenya', *Africa Today*, 67(2–3), 151–74.

Gifford, P. (2009). *Christianity, politics, and public life in Kenya* (London: Hurst and Company).

Ging, D. (2019). 'Alphas, betas, and incels: theorizing the masculinities of the manosphere', *Men and Masculinities*, 22(4), 638–57.

Githinji, P. (2008). 'Sexism and (mis)representation of women in Sheng', *Journal of African Cultural Studies*, 20(1), 15–32.

Githiora, C. (2018). *Sheng. Rise of a Kenyan Swahili vernacular* (Oxford: James Currey).

Gluckman, M. (1963). 'Papers in honor of Melville J. Herskovits: gossip and scandal', *Current Anthropology*, 4(3), 307–16.

Goffman, E. (1963). *Behavior in public places: notes on the social organization of gatherings* (New York: Free Press).

Gomez-Perez, M. and Jourde, C. (2020). 'Introduction to the special issue on religious entrepreneurship', *Africa Today*, 67(2–3), 3–15.

Gondola, D.Ch. (1999). 'Dream and drama: the search for elegance among Congolese youth', *African Studies Review*, 42(1), 23–48.

Goodman, Z. (2020). '"Going vertical" in times of insecurity. Constructing proximity and distance through a Kenyan gated high-rise', *Focaal. Journal of Global and Historical Anthropology*, 86, 24–35.

Green, M. (2019). 'Scripting development through formalization: accounting for the diffusion of village savings and loans associations in Tanzania', *Journal of the Royal Anthropological Institute*, 25(1), 103–22.

Groes-Green, C. (2009). 'Hegemonic and subordinated masculinities: class, violence and sexual performance among young Mozambican men', *Nordic Journal of African Studies*, 18(4), 286–304.

— (2010). 'Orgies of the moment: Bataille's anthropology of transgression and the defiance of danger in post-socialist Mozambique', *Anthropological Theory*, 10(4), 385–407.

Guma, P.K. (2020). *Rethinking smart urbanism. City-making and the spread of digital infrastructures in Nairobi* (Utrecht: Eburon Academic Publishers).

Gutmann, M. (2019). *Are men animals? How modern masculinity sells men short* (New York: Basic Books).

— (2021). 'Masculinity', in: F. Stein, S. Lazar, M. Candea, H. Diemberger, J. Robbins, A. Sanchez and R. Stasch (eds), *The Cambridge Encyclopedia of Anthropology*. Available at: www.anthroencyclopedia.com/entry/masculinity [Accessed 24 November 2022].

Guyer, J.I. (1993). 'Wealth in people and self-realization in equatorial Africa', *Man*, 28(2), 243–65.

— (2004). *Marginal gains: monetary transactions in Atlantic Africa* (Chicago: University of Chicago Press).

— (2007). 'Prophecy and the near future: thoughts on macroeconomic, evangelical, and punctuated time', *American Ethnologist: Journal of the American Ethnological Society*, 34(3), 409–21.

Hake, A. (1977). *African metropolis. Nairobi's self-help city* (London: Palgrave Macmillan).

Haushofer, J. and Fehr, E. (2014). 'On the psychology of poverty', *Science*, 344(6186), 862–7.

Haynes, N. (2012). 'Pentecostalism and the morality of money: prosperity, inequality, and religious sociality on the Zambian Copperbelt', *Journal of the Royal Anthropological Institute*, 18(1), 123–39.

Hejtmanek, K.R. (2020). 'Fitness fanatics: exercise as answer to pending zombie apocalypse in contemporary America', *American Anthropologist*, 122(4), 864–75.

Hendriks, T. (2022). *Rainforest capitalism. Power and masculinity in a Congolese timber concession* (Durham: Duke University Press).

Herzfeld, M. (2016). *Cultural intimacy. Social poetics and the real life of states, societies, and institutions* (London: Routledge).

Hodgson, D.L. and McCurdy, S.A. (eds). (2001). *'Wicked' women and the reconfiguration of gender in Africa* (Portsmouth: Heinemann).

Honwana, A. (2012). *The time of youth: work, social change and politics in Africa* (Boulder: Lynne Rienner Publishers).

Hopkinson, L. (2022). 'Only one Mayweather: a critique of hope from the hopeful', *Journal of the Royal Anthropological Institute*, 28(3), 725–45.

Huchzermeyer, M. (2008). 'Slum upgrading in Nairobi within the housing and basic services market: a housing rights concern', *Journal of Asian and African Studies*, 43(1), 19–39.

— (2011). *Tenement cities: from 19ᵗʰ century Berlin to 21ˢᵗ century Nairobi* (Trenton: Africa World Press).

Hunter, M. (2010). *Love in the time of AIDS: inequality, gender, and rights in South Africa* (Bloomington: Indiana University Press).

— (2015). 'The political economy of concurrent partners: toward a history of sex-love-gift connections in the time of AIDS', *Review of African Political Economy*, 42(145), 362–75.

Hutchinson, D. (2014). 'New Thought's prosperity theology and its influence on American ideas of success', *Nova Religio: The Journal of Alternative and Emergent Religions*, 18(2), 28–44.

Iazzolino, G. (2023). '"Going Karura": colliding subjectivities and labour struggle in Nairobi's gig economy', *Environment and Planning A: Economy and Space*, 55(5), 1114–30.

IEBC. (2022). *Registered voters per county assembly ward for the 2022 general election* (Nairobi: IEBC). Available at: www.iebc.or.ke/docs/rov_per_caw.pdf [Accessed 24 November 2022].

Illouz, E. (2008). *Saving the modern soul. Therapy, emotions, and the culture of self-help* (Berkeley: University of California Press).

Ingozi, B. (2020). *The spirit-filled home* (Nairobi: Triumphant Faith Media).

Izugbara, C.O. and Egesa, C.P. (2020). 'Young men, poverty and aspirational masculinities in contemporary Nairobi, Kenya', *Gender, Place and Culture. A Journal of Feminist Geography*, 27(12), 1682–702.

Jackson, M. (2013). *The age of stress. Science and the search for stability* (Oxford: Oxford University Press).

Jalango, I. (2016). 'Pipeline estate is a façade of what Nairobi will be', *The Standard*, 3 April 2016. Available at: www.standardmedia.co.ke/entertainment/ lifestyle/2000197327/pipeline-estate-is-a-facade-of-what-nairobi-will-be [Accessed 24 November 2022].

James, D. (2012). 'Money-go-round: personal economies of wealth, aspiration, and indebtedness', *Africa: The Journal of the International African Institute*, 82(1), 20–40.

Jansen, S. (2015). *Yearnings in the meantime: 'normal lives' and the state in a Sarajevo apartment complex* (New York: Berghahn).

Jeffrey, C. and Dyson, J. (2013). 'Zigzag capitalism: youth entrepreneurship in the contemporary global south', *Geoforum*, 49, R1–3.

Jones, C., Trott, V. and Wright, S. (2020). 'Sluts and soyboys: MGTOW and the production of misogynistic online harassment', *New Media and Society*, 22(10), 1903–21.

Kaiser, S. (2022). *Political masculinity: how incels, fundamentalists and authoritarians mobilise for patriarchy* (Cambridge: Polity).

Kamiri, L.W. (2017). *The construction of gender in opinion articles from Kenya: a case study of magazines from the Saturday Nation and the Standard newspapers.* Master's thesis. Kenyatta University, Nairobi.

Kapferer, B. (1969). 'Norms and manipulation of relationships in a work context', in: C. Mitchell (ed), *Social networks in urban situations* (Manchester: Manchester University Press), 181–244.

Kimari, W. (2017). *'Nai-Rob-Me', 'Nai-Beg-Me', 'Nai-Shanty': historicizing space – Subjectivity connections in Nairobi from its ruins.* PhD dissertation, University of Toronto, Ontario.

— (2021). '"We will be back to the street!" Protest and the "empires" of water in Nairobi', in: S. Bekker, S. Croese and E. Pieterse (eds), *Refractions of the national, the popular and the global in African cities* (Cape Town: African Minds), 99–109.

Kimmel, M. (2019). *Angry white men. American masculinity at the end of an era* (New York: Bold Type Books).

Kimmel, M.S. and Kaufman, M. (1993). 'The new men's movement: retreat and regression with America's weekend warriors', *Feminist Issues*, 13, 3–21.

Kingori, P. (2021). 'Kenya's "fake essay" writers and the light they shine on assumptions of shadows in knowledge production', *Journal of African Cultural Studies*, 33(1), 297–304.

Kinyanjui, J. (2020). 'Eric Amunga: The man teaching men about masculinity', *Daily Nation*, 23 June 2020. Available at: https://nation.africa/kenya/life-and-style/eric-amunga-the-man-teaching-men-about-masculinity-784668 [Accessed 24 November 2022].

Kinyanjui, M.N. (2014). *Women and the informal economy in urban Africa. From the margins to the centre* (London: Zed Books).

— (2019). *African markets and the utu-buntu business model. A perspective on economic informality in Nairobi* (Cape Town: African Minds).

Kiyosaki, R.T. and Lechter, S.L. (1998). *Rich dad, poor dad: what the rich teach their kids about money that the poor and middle class do not!* (Paradise Valley: TechPress).

Klaus, K. (2020). *Political violence in Kenya: land, elections, and claim-making* (Cambridge: Cambridge University Press).

Klein, A.M. (1993). *Little big men. Bodybuilding subculture and gender construction* (Albany: State University of New York Press).

Kleinman, J. (2019). *Adventure capital. Migration and the making of an African hub in Paris* (Berkeley: University of California Press).

Kleist, N. (2017). 'Disrupted migration projects: the moral economy of involuntary return to Ghana from Libya', *Africa: The Journal of the International African Institute*, 87(2), 322–42.

Komarovsky, M. (2004 [1940]). *The unemployed man and his family. The effect of unemployment upon the status of the man in fifty-nine families* (Walnut Creek: AltaMira Press).

Koppetsch, C. and Speck, S. (2015). *Wenn der Mann kein Ernährer mehr ist. Geschlechterkonflikte in Krisenzeiten* (Berlin: Suhrkamp).

Kovač, U. (2022). *The precarity of masculinity. Football, Pentecostalism, and transnational aspirations in Cameroon* (New York: Berghahn).

Kurtz, J.R. (1998). *Urban obsessions, urban fears. The postcolonial Kenyan novel* (Trenton: Africa World Press).

Kusimba, S. (2018). '"It is easy for women to ask!" Gender and digital finance in Kenya', *Economic Anthropology*, 5(2), 247–60.

— (2021). *Reimagining money. Kenya in the digital finance revolution* (Redwood City: Stanford University Press).

Latour, B. (1986). 'Visualisation and cognition: drawing things together', in: H. Kuklick (ed), *Knowledge and society. Studies in the sociology of culture past and present*. Volume 6 (Greenwich: JAI Press), 1–40.

Lefebvre, H. (1996 [1968]). 'Right to the city', in: E. Kofman and E. Lebas (eds), *Writings on cities* (Oxford: Blackwell Publishing), 61–181.

Linder, F. (2007). 'Life as art, and seeing the promise of big bodies', *American Ethnologist: Journal of the American Ethnological Society*, 34(3), 451–72.

Lindsay, L.A. and Miescher, S.F. (eds). (2003). *Men and masculinities in modern Africa* (Portsmouth: Heinemann).

Lockwood, P. (2015). 'The solitude of the stance: the bodily autology of gym-work and boxing in an Essex town', *Suomen Anthropologi: Journal of the Finnish Anthropological Society*, 40(4), 5–28.

— (2020). 'Impatient accumulation, immediate consumption. Problems with money and hope in central Kenya', *Social Analysis*, 64(1), 44–62.

Macharia, K. (1992). 'Slum clearance and the informal economy in Nairobi', *Journal of Modern African Studies*, 30(2), 221–36.

Maina, M. and Mwau, B. (2018). 'Nairobi. The socio-political implications of informal tenement housing in Nairobi, Kenya', in: R. Rocco and J. van Balle-gooijen (eds), *The Routledge handbook on informal urbanization* (New York: Routledge), 215–25.

Mains, D. (2011). *Hope is cut. Youth, unemployment, and the future in urban Ethiopia* (Philadelphia: Temple University Press).

Masquelier, A. (2019). *Fada. Boredom and belonging in Niger* (Chicago: University of Chicago Press).

Mathews, G. (2011). *Ghetto at the center of the world. Chungking Mansions, Hong Kong* (Chicago: University of Chicago Press).

Matlon, J. (2022). *A man among other men. The crisis of black masculinity in racial capitalism* (Ithaca: Cornell University Press).

Mauss, M. (1935). 'Les techniques du corps', *Journal de Psychologie*, 32, 271–93.

— (1969 [1934]). 'Débat sur les fonctions sociales de la monnaie', in: M. Mauss, *Œuvres II: représentations collectives et diversité des civilisations* (Paris: Éditions de Minuit), 116–20.

— (2003). *On prayer* (New York: Berghahn).

Mbembe, A. (2001). *On the postcolony* (Berkeley: University of California Press).

McGee, M. (2005). *Self-help, Inc. Makeover culture in American life* (Oxford: Oxford University Press).

— (2012). 'From makeover media to remaking culture: four directions for the critical study of self-help culture', *Sociology Compass*, 6(9), 685–93.

McKay, B. and McKay, K. (2009). *The art of manliness. Classic skills and manners for the modern man* (New York: HOW Books).

McLean, K. (2021). '"Post-crisis masculinities" in Sierra Leone: revisiting masculinity theory', *Gender, Place and Culture. A Journal of Feminist Geography*, 28(6), 786–805.

Meiu, G.P. (2017). *Ethno-erotic economies. Sexuality, money, and belonging in Kenya* (Chicago: University of Chicago Press).

— (2020). 'Underlayers of citizenship: queer objects, intimate exposures, and the rescue rush in Kenya', *Cultural Anthropology*, 35(4), 575–601.

Mellström, U. (2017). 'A restoration of classic patriarchy?', *NORMA: International Journal for Masculinity Studies*, 12(1), 1–4.

Messner, M.A. (2002). *Taking the field: women, men, and sports* (Minneapolis: University of Minnesota Press).

Metcalfe, V., Pavanello, S. and Mishra, P. (2011). 'Sanctuary in the city? Urban displacement and vulnerability in Nairobi' (London: Humanitarian Policy Group (HPG Working Paper)).

Mfecane, S. (2018). 'Towards African-centred theories of masculinity', *Social Dynamics. A Journal of African Studies*, 44(2), 291–305.

Mojola, S.A. (2014). 'Providing women, kept men: doing masculinity in the wake of the African HIV/AIDS pandemic', *Signs*, 39(2), 341–63.

Mol, A. (2002). *The body multiple: ontology in medical practice* (Durham: Duke University Press).

Moloney, M.E. and Love, T.P. (2018). '#TheFappening: virtual manhood acts in (homo)social media', *Men and Masculinities*, 21(5), 603–23.

Moran, M.H. (1990). *Civilized women. Gender and prestige in southeastern Liberia* (Ithaca: Cornell University Press).

Morrison, L.B. (2007). 'The nature of decline: distinguishing myth from reality in the case of the Luo of Kenya', *Journal of Modern African Studies*, 45(1), 117–42.

Muehlebach, A. (2012). *The moral neoliberal. Welfare and citizenship in Italy* (Chicago: University of Chicago Press).

Mueller, S.D. (2008). 'The political economy of Kenya's crisis', *Journal of Eastern African Studies*, 2(2), 185–210.

Muiruri, P. (2021). 'Concern grows in Kenya after alarming rise in suicide cases. Mental ill-health and "warped" notions of masculinity among reasons mooted for rise of nearly 50 % in a year', *The Guardian*, 10 August 2021. Available at: www.theguardian.com/global-development/2021/aug/10/concern-grows-in-kenya-after-alarming-rise-in-suicide-cases [Accessed 24 November 2022].

Murphy, J. (1963). *The power of your subconscious mind* (Englewood Cliffs: Prentice-Hall).

Mutongi, K. (2017). *Matatu: a history of popular transportation in Nairobi* (Chicago: University of Chicago Press).

— (2000). '"Dear Dolly's" advice: representations of youth, courtship, and sexualities in Africa, 1960–1980', *International Journal of African Historical Studies*, 33(1), 1–23.

Mwau, B. (2019). 'The rise of Nairobi's concrete tenement jungle', International Institute for Environment and Development Guest Blog, 31 July 2019. Available at: www.iied.org/rise-nairobis-concrete-tenement-jungle [Accessed 24 November 2022].

— (2020). *Urban transformation and informal shelter. Actors, interests and change in Mathare Valley: city briefing* (London: International Institute for Environment and Development).

Nairobi Urban Study Group (1973). *Nairobi – Metropolitan growth strategy.* Two volumes (Nairobi: Nairobi City Council).

Nassenstein, N. and Storch, A. (2020). *Metasex: the discourse of intimacy and transgression* (Amsterdam: John Benjamins Publishing).

Ndegwa, B.M. (2016). *Assessing the provision of infrastructure in high density residential neighbourhoods. A case study of Embakasi Pipeline estate in Nairobi, Kenya.* Bachelor's thesis. University of Nairobi.

Ndjio, B. (2012). 'Post-colonial histories of sexuality: the political invention of a libidinal African straight', *Africa: The Journal of the International African Institute*, 82(4), 609–31.

Neumark, T. (2017). '"A good neighbor is not one that gives": detachment, ethics, and the relational self in Kenya', *Journal of the Royal Anthropological Institute*, 23(4), 748–64.

Newell, S. (2012). *The modernity bluff. Crime, consumption, and citizenship in Cote d'Ivoire* (Chicago: University of Chicago Press).

Nichter, M. (1981). 'Idioms of distress: alternatives in the expression of psychosocial distress: a case study from south India', *Culture, Medicine and Psychiatry*, 5, 379–408.

Njagi, J. (2012). 'Man kills wife and hangs himself', *Daily Nation*, 17 October 2012.

Njanja, A. (2020). 'Rickets taking toll on children in city slums', *Business Daily*, 1 December 2020. Available at: www.businessdailyafrica.com/bd/data-hub/rickets-taking-toll-on-children-in-city-slums-3211022 [Accessed 24 November 2022].

Njoya, W. (2022). 'Elections: the cruel harvest of Kenyan emotional and intellectual labor', *The Elephant*, 24 August 2022. Available at: www.theelephant.info/op-eds/2022/08/24/elections-the-cruel-harvest-of-kenyan-emotional-and-intellectual-labor/ [Accessed 24 November 2022].

Ntarangwi, M.G. (1998). 'Feminism and masculinity in an African capitalist context: the case of Kenya', *SAFERE: Southern African Feminist Review*, 3(1), 19–33.

Nyanchwani, S. (2020). *Sexorcised* (Nairobi: Gram Books).

— (2021a). *50 memos to men* (Nairobi: Gram Books).

— (2021b). 'What fuels online gender wars?', *Sisi Afrika Magazine*, 4 April 2021. Available at: www.sisiafrika.com/what-fuels-the-online-gender-wars/ [Accessed 24 November 2022].

— (2022). *Man about town* (Nairobi: Gram Books).

Obala, L.M. (2011). *The relationship between urban land conflicts and inequity: the case of Nairobi*. PhD dissertation. University of the Witwatersrand, Johannesburg.

Obala, L.M. and Mattingly, M. (2014). 'Ethnicity, corruption and violence in urban land conflict in Kenya', *Urban Studies*, 51(13), 2735–51.

Ocobock, P. (2017). *An uncertain age: the politics of manhood in Kenya* (Athens: Ohio University Press).

Odaga, A.B. (2005). *Dholuo-English Dictionary* (Kisumu: Lake Publishers and Enterprises).

Odenyo, A. and Njoroge, R. (2021). 'He could have lived anywhere but chose slum', *The Star*, 17 February 2021. Available at: www.the-star.co.ke/news/2021-02-17-mukuru-kwa-njenga-founder-to-be-buried-in-langata-cemetery-today/ [Accessed 24 November 2022].

Odhiambo, T. (2007). 'Sexual anxieties and rampant masculinities in postcolonial Kenyan literature', *Social Identities: Journal for the Study of Race, Nation and Culture*, 13(5), 651–63.

Ogot, B.A and Ogot, M. (2020). *History of Nairobi 1899–2012. From a railway camp and supply depot to a world-class African metropolis* (Kisumu: Anyange Press).

Ombati, C. and Odenyo, A. (2021). 'Musician accused of killing KDF husband "using teeth" speaks', *The Star*, 5 April 2021. Available at: www.the-star.co.ke/news/2021-04-05-musician-accused-of-killing-kdf-husband-using-teeth-speaks/ [Accessed 24 November 2022].

Omondi, D. (2022). 'Why youth face rough terrain in post-Covid world', *Financial Standard*, 2 August 2022.

Ondieki, E. (2021). 'Mukuru kwa Njenga slum founder breathes his last', *Daily Nation*, 14 February 2021. Available at: https://nation.africa/kenya/counties/nairobi/mukuru-kwa-njenga-slum-founder-breathes-his-last--3290472?view=htmlamp [Accessed 24 November 2022].

Ondieki, E.O. (2016). *Tenement housing in Nairobi: the case of Lucky Summer (Pipeline) Settlement-Embakasi*. PhD dissertation. University of Oslo, Oslo.

O'Neill, R. (2018). *Seduction. Men, masculinity, and mediated intimacy* (Cambridge: Polity Press).

Osborn, T.L., Kleinman, A. and Weisz, J.R. (2021). 'Complementing standard Western measures of depression with locally co-developed instruments: a cross-cultural study on the experience of depression among the Luo in Kenya', *Transcultural Psychiatry*, 58(4), 499–515.

Otieno, B. (2017). 'Land ministry names Nairobi estates with dangerous buildings', *Business Daily*, 31 August 2017. Available at: www.businessdailyafrica.com/news/counties/Land-ministry-names-Nairobi-estates-with-dangerous-buildings-/4003142-4078828-jx5hhf/index.html [Accessed 24 November 2022].

Ouzgane, L. and Morrell, R. (eds). (2005). *African masculinities. Men in Africa from the late nineteenth century to the present* (London: Palgrave Macmillan).

P'Bitek, O. (2008). *Song of Lawino and song of Ocol* (Nairobi: East African Educational Publishers).

Paechter, C. (2003). 'Masculinities and femininities as communities of practice', *Women's Studies International Forum*, 26(1), 69–77.

Pala, O. (2018). 'The making of a fatherless nation', *The Elephant*, 28 December 2018. Available at: www.theelephant.info/reflections/2018/12/28/the-making-of-fatherless-nation/ [Accessed 24 November 2022].

Papanek, H. (1979). 'Family status production: the "work" and "non-work" of women', *Signs*, 4(4), 775–81.

Parikh, S. (2016). *Regulating romance: youth love letters, moral anxiety, and intervention in Uganda's time of AIDS* (Nashville: Vanderbilt University Press).

Parkin, D. (1978). *The cultural definition of political response. Lineal destiny among the Luo* (London: Academic Press).

Perry, D.L. (2005). 'Wolof women, economic liberalization, and the crisis of masculinity in rural Senegal', *Ethnology*, 44(3), 207–26.

Pike, I. (2020). 'A discursive spectrum: the narrative of Kenya's "neglected" boy child', *Gender and Society*, 34(2), 284–306.

Powdermaker, H. (1962). *Copper town, changing Africa. The human situation on the Rhodesian Copperbelt* (New York: Harper and Row).

Preston, K., Halpin, M. and Maguire, F. (2021). 'The black pill: new technology and the male supremacy of involuntarily celibate men', *Men and Masculinities*, 24(5), 823–41.

Pype, K. (2007). 'Fighting boys, strong men and gorillas. Notes on the imagination of masculinities in Kinshasa', *Africa: The Journal of the International African Institute*, 77(2), 250–71.

Quayson, A. (2014). *Oxford Street, Accra. City life and the itineraries of transnationalism* (Durham: Duke University Press).

Remy, J. (1990). 'Patriarchy and fratriarchy as forms of androcracy', in: J. Hearn and D. Morgan (eds), *Men, masculinities and social theory* (London: Unwin Hyman), 43–54.

Richter, L. and Morrell, R. (eds). (2006). *Baba: men and fatherhood in South Africa* (Cape Town: HSRC Press).

Rono, J.K. (2002). 'The impact of the structural adjustment programmes on Kenyan society', *Journal of Social Development in Africa*, 17(1), 81–98.

Rose, N. and Fitzgerald, D. (2022). *The urban brain. Mental health in the vital city* (Princeton: Princeton University Press).

Ross, M. and Weisner, T.S. (1977). 'The rural-urban migrant network in Kenya: some general implications', *American Ethnologist: Journal of the American Ethnological Society*, 4(2), 359–75.

Sanders, T. (1999). 'Modernity, wealth and witchcraft in Tanzania', *Research in Economic Anthropology*, 20, 117–31.

Schellhaas, S., Schmidt, M. and Odhiambo, G.F. (2020). 'Declaring kinship – Some remarks on the indeterminate relation between commensality and kinship in western Kenya', *Sociologus. Journal for Social Anthropology*, 70(2), 143–57.

Scherz, C. (2014). *Having people, having heart. Charity, sustainable development, and problems of dependence in central Uganda* (Chicago: University of Chicago Press).

Schielke, S. (2020). *Migrant dreams: Egyptian workers in the Gulf States* (Cairo: American University in Cairo).

Schmidt, M. (2017a). '"Disordered surroundings" and socio-economic exclusion in western Kenya', *Africa: The Journal of the International African Institute*, 87(2), 278–99.

— (2017b). '"Money is life". Quantity, social freedom and combinatory practices in western Kenya', *Social Analysis*, 61(4), 66–80.

— (2019). '"Almost everybody does it…": gambling as future-making in western Kenya', *Journal of Eastern African Studies*, 13(4), 739–57.

— (2020). 'Being one while being many – social and culinary parts and wholes in western Kenya', *Food, Culture and Society*, 23(4), 472–88.

— (2022a). 'Masculinity in Kenya: the pressure to provide and perform', *The Elephant*, 18 December 2022. Available at: www.theelephant.info/culture/2022/12/18/masculinity-in-kenya-the-pressure-to-provide-and-perform/ [Accessed 24 April 2023].

— (2022b). 'The gift of free money: on the indeterminacy of unconditional cash transfers in western Kenya', *Journal of the Royal Anthropological Institute*, 28(1), 114–29.

Schwenkel, C. (2020). *Building socialism: the afterlife of East German architecture in urban Vietnam* (Durham: Duke University Press).

Sehlikoglu, S. (2021). *Working out desire. Women, sport, and self-making in Istanbul* (Syracuse: Syracuse University Press).

Sherouse, P. (2016). 'Skill and masculinity in Olympic weightlifting: training cues and cultivated craziness in Georgia', *American Ethnologist: Journal of the American Ethnological Society*, 43(1), 103–15.

Shipton, P. (2007). *The nature of entrustment. Intimacy, exchange, and the sacred in Africa* (New Haven: Yale University Press).

— (2010). *Credit between cultures. Farmers, financiers, and misunderstanding in Africa* (New Haven: Yale University Press).

Silberschmidt, M. (2001). 'Disempowerment of men in rural and urban east Africa: implications for male identity and sexual behavior', *World Development*, 29(4), 657–71.

Silver, J. (2014). 'Incremental infrastructures: material improvisation and social collaboration across post-colonial Africa', *Urban Geography*, 35(6), 788–804.

Simone, A. (2002). 'The visible and the invisible: remaking cities in Africa', in: O. Enwezor (ed), *Under siege: four African cities – Freetown, Johannesburg, Kinshasa, Lagos* (Ostfilden: Hatje-Cantz), 23–44.

— (2004). 'People as infrastructure: intersecting fragments in Johannesburg', *Public Culture*, 16(3), 407–29.

Simone, A. and Abouhani, A. (eds). (2005). *Urban Africa: changing contours of survival in the city* (Dakar: CODESRIA Books).

Simpson, W.J.R. (1915). *Report on sanitary matters in the East Africa Protectorate, Uganda, and Zanzibar* (London: Colonial Office Library).

Slaughter, J.R. (2004). 'Master plans: designing (national) allegories of urban space and metropolitan subjects for postcolonial Kenya', *Research in African Literatures*, 35(1), 30–51.

Smith, C. (2019). *Nairobi in the making: landscapes of time and urban belonging* (Oxford: James Currey).

— (2020). 'Collapse. Fake buildings and gray development in Nairobi', *Focaal: Journal of Global and Historical Anthropology*, 86(1), 11–23.

— (2023). 'City of icebergs: materiality, surface and depth in Nairobi's built environment', *Africa: The Journal of the International African Institute*, 93(1), 100–20.

Smith, C. and Woodcraft, S. (2020). 'Introduction. Tower block "failures"? High-rise anthropology', *Focaal: Journal of Global and Historical Anthropology*, 86, 1–10.

Smith, D.J. (2017). *To be a man is not a one-day job. Masculinity, money, and intimacy in Nigeria* (Chicago: University of Chicago Press).

— (2001). 'Romance, parenthood, and gender in a modern African society', *Ethnology*, 40(2), 129–51.

Smith, J.H. (2008). *Bewitching development. Witchcraft and the reinvention of development in neoliberal Kenya* (Chicago: University of Chicago Press).

Spronk, R. (2009). 'Media and the therapeutic ethos of romantic love in middle-class Nairobi', in: J. Cole and L.M. Thomas (eds), *Love in Africa* (Chicago: University of Chicago Press), 181–203.

— (2012). *Ambiguous pleasures. Sexuality and middle class self-perception in Nairobi* (New York: Berghahn).

Spronk, R. and Nyeck, S.N. (2021). 'Frontiers and pioneers in (the study of) queer experiences in Africa. Introduction', *Africa: The Journal of the International African Institute*, 91(3), 388–97.

Stasik, M. (2016). 'Real love versus real life: youth, music and utopia in Freetown, Sierra Leone', *Africa: The Journal of the International African Institute*, 86(2), 215–36.

Stephan, C., Schmidt, M. and Kioko, E.M. (2021). 'Navigating socio-economic pressures in COVID-19 urban Kenya: a relational geographies' perspective', in: P. Filion, B. Doucet and R. van Melik (eds), *Global reflections on Covid-19 and urban inequalities. Volume 4: policy and planning* (Bristol: Bristol University Press), 81–90.

Taylor, C.C. (1992). *Milk, honey, and money: changing concepts in Rwandan healing* (Washington: Smithsonian Institution Press).

Thieme, T. (2013). 'The "hustle" amongst youth entrepreneurs in Mathare's informal waste economy', *Journal of Eastern African Studies*, 7(3), 389–412.

Thieme, T., Ference, M.E. and van Stapele, N. (2021). 'Harnessing the "hustle": struggle, solidarities and narratives of work in Nairobi and beyond', *Africa: The Journal of the International African Institute*, 91(1), 1–15.

Thomas, L.M. (2003). *Politics of the womb. Women, reproduction, and the state in Kenya*. Berkeley: University of California Press.

Tomassi, R. (2013). *The rational male* (Nevada: Counterflow Media).

Trapido, J. (2021). '"Masterless men". Riots, patronage, and the politics of the surplus population in Kinshasa', *Current Anthropology*, 62(2), 198–217.

Turner, T.S. (2012). 'The social skin', *Hau: Journal of Ethnographic Theory*, 2(2), 486–504.

Vähäkangas, M. (2015). 'Babu wa Loliondo. Healing the tensions between Tanzanian worlds', *Journal of Religion in Africa*, 45(1), 3–36.

Van Dijk, R. (2010). 'Social catapulting and the spirit of entrepreneurialism: migrants, private initiative, and the Pentecostal ethics in Botswana', in: G. Hüwelmeier and K. Krause (eds), *Traveling spirits: migrants, markets and mobilities* (London: Routledge), 101–17.

Van Klinken, A. (2013). *Transforming masculinities in African Christianity. Gender controversies in times of AIDS* (London: Routledge).

— (2019). *Kenyan, Christian, queer. Religion, LGBT activism, and arts of resistance in Africa* (University Park, PA: Penn State University Press).

Van Stapele, N. (2021a). 'Providing to belong: masculinities, hustling and economic uncertainty in Nairobi "ghettos"', *Africa: The Journal of the International African Institute*, 91(1), 57–76.

— (2021b). '"When the numbers stop adding": imagining futures in perilous presents among youth in Nairobi ghettos', *The European Journal of Development Research*, 33, 130–46.

Van Valkenburgh, S.P. (2021). 'Digesting the red pill: masculinity and neoliberalism in the manosphere', *Men and Masculinities*, 24(1), 84–103.

Vigh, H. (2009). 'Motion squared. A second look at the concept of social navigation', *Anthropological Theory*, 9(4), 419–38.

Vorhölter, J. (2017). 'Homosexuality, pornography, and other "modern threats": the deployment of sexuality in recent laws and public discourses in Uganda', *Critique of Anthropology*, 37(1), 93–111.

Wacquant, L. (1995). 'Why men desire muscles', *Body and Society*, 1(1), 163–79.

— (2004). *Body and soul. Notebooks of an apprentice boxer* (New York: Oxford University Press).

Wanzala, J. (2018). 'Pipeline: where you've to get to 8th floor to catch sunlight', *The Standard,* 29 December 2018. Available at: www.standardmedia.co.ke/nairobi/article/2001307682/pipeline-nairobis-estate-that-has-a-lot-wanting [Accessed 24 November 2022].

Weisner, T.S. (1976). 'The structure of sociability: urban migration and urban-rural ties in Kenya', *Urban Anthropology,* 5(2), 199–223.

Weiss, B. (2002). 'Thug realism. Inhabiting fantasy in urban Tanzania', *Cultural Anthropology,* 17(1), 93–124.

— (2009). *Street dreams and hip hop barbershops. Global fantasy in urban Tanzania* (Bloomington: Indiana University Press).

Wenger, E. (1998). *Communities of practice: learning, meaning, and identity* (Cambridge: Cambridge University Press).

White, L. (1990). *The comforts of home. Prostitution in colonial Kenya* (Chicago: University of Chicago Press).

— (2000). *Speaking with vampires. Rumor and history in colonial Africa* (Berkeley: University of California Press).

White, L.W.T., Silberman, L. and Anderson, P.R. (1948). *Nairobi master plan for a colonial capital. A report prepared for the municipal council of Nairobi* (London: HM Stationery Office Press).

Wiegratz, J., Dessie, E., Dolan, C., Kimari, W. and Schmidt, M. (2020). 'Blog series. Pressure in the city', *Developing Economics,* 17 August 2020. Available at: https://developingeconomics.org/2020/08/17/blog-series-pressure-in-the-global-south-stress-worry-and-anxiety-in-times-of-economic-crisis/ [Accessed 24 November 2022].

Wuepper, D. and Lybbert, T.J. (2017). 'Perceived self-efficacy, poverty, and economic development', *Annual Review of Resource Economics,* 9, 383–404.

Wyrod, R. (2016). *AIDS and masculinity in the African city. Privilege, inequality, and modern manhood* (Berkeley: University of California Press).

Xiang, B. (2021). 'Suspension: seeking agency for change in the hypermobile world', *Pacific Affairs,* 94(2), 233–50.

Yose, C.N. (1999). *From shacks to houses: space usage and social change in a Western Cape shanty town.* Master's thesis. University of Cape Town.

INDEX

absence of the state   38–40
accumulating savings and credit
    association (ASCA)   97
alcohol consumption   63 n.7, 107–8,
    108 n.5
    see also sociality
Aliet, Jacob   20, 128, 130, 138, 143,
    143 n.8, 150
Amerix   20, 130, 137–44, 150
anonymity   28, 50, 70 n.1, 71, 82,
    88, 99
anti-feminism   20–1, 130, 136, 137–44
    see also feminism; misogyny;
        women
aspiration: and financial debt   53–6
    middle-class   48, 84
    Pipeline as place of   40–2, 66, 94
    rural-to-urban migration as   14–17
    self-help culture and   133–4
    see also hope; intentions; pressure
Atemo, Chris   133, 134, 136

bachelors   94, 152
    see also jo-pap
balconies   44, 70, 70 n.1
bedsitters   9, 42–3
benga music   4 n.3
betting shops   18 n.7, 54, 150
    see also gambling
bodybuilding *see* weightlifting
bravado   63–6
breadwinner narrative: about   3–7,
    81–3, 120, 146
    alleged female distortion of   8–9,
        116, 128
    reproduction of   36, 150–3
    subtle changes of   74–6

see also masculinity
bride-wealth   61, 71, 82
Briffault's law   139
brotherhood   2, 21, 122–6
    see also sociality
business ventures   53–6, 62, 81–2,
    83, 132
    see also HoMiSiKi; investment
        groups; No Mercy Gym
bypasses   25, 80

capacity to aspire   55, 56
capitalist economy   20, 21, 146, 149,
    152
    see also economic pressure
Christianity   3, 20, 131, 139
    see also religious self-help culture
civil inattention   45
collective action, lack of   46–9
collective effervescence   105
colonial history   16–17, 32, 36–7
come-we-stay marriages   70 n.1, 71
communal bathrooms   70 n.1
consumer goods   12, 43, 48, 64, 75
corruption   93, 104
COVID-19 pandemic: economic crises
    due to   5, 14, 17, 83, 147
    HoMiSiKi's collapse due
        to   107–10
    lockdown during   59–60
    masculinity and   7, 112
    pressure and   51
    social unrest due to   62
'crisis of masculinity'   7–8, 21, 79
    see also masculinity

dating   70 n.1, 72

Printed and bound by CPI Group (UK) Ltd, Croydon, CR0 4YY

09/06/2025

14685702-0005